THE

UNCONDITIONALS

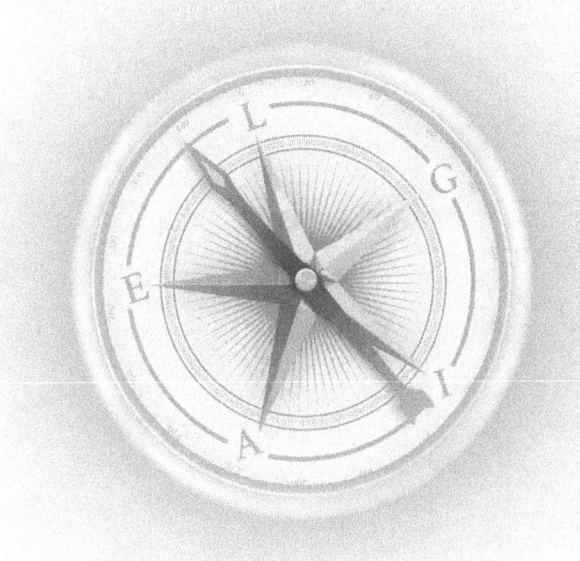

THE
UNCONDITIONALS

Five Timeless Values to Live without Limits
and Ignite Your Superpower

ANDY CROCKER

Permission to reproduce excerpts from *morningcoffeebeans.com* has been granted by Deana Landers.
Permission to reproduce excerpts from *The Gratitude Podcast* has been granted by Georgian Benta.
Permission to reproduce excerpts from *This American Life* has been granted by Frances Swanson.
Permission to reproduce excerpts from *Extreme Ownership* has been granted by Macmillan Publishers.

Editing and design by Bublish
Published by Overview Affection

ISBN: 979-8-9927897-4-4 (hardcover for retail)
ISBN: 979-8-9927897-5-1 (paperback for retail)
ISBN: 979-8-9927897-2-0 (eBook)
ISBN: 979-8-9927897-3-7 (audiobook)

For Beth, the Bug, and the Bear

Life is a test and this world a place of trial.
Always the problems or it may be the same problem
will be presented to every generation in different forms.
The problems of victory
may be even more baffling than those of defeat.
However much the conditions change,
the supreme question is how we live and grow and bloom and die,
and how far each life conforms to standards
which are not wholly related to time and space.

—Winston Churchill

Contents

PREFACE

Two things fill the mind with ever new and increasing admiration and awe,
the oftener and the more steadily we reflect on them:
the starry heavens above and the moral law within.
—Immanuel Kant

I WAS BEATEN down by both Elon Musk and Jeff Bezos . . . and survived.

It's not every day someone gets to square off against the two wealthiest people in the world, gets pummeled by both, and lives to tell the tale.

To be fair, I did ask for a challenge. I didn't realize it would mean facing Musk and Bezos. I felt like a college kid who stumbles into a Mississippi riverboat casino on a random Tuesday night and finds himself at the final table of the World Series of Poker, facing the world's two richest men. They have massive stacks of $1 million chips while I'm down to my last $1,000. You might think, "What's there to lose? Just go 'all in' and let it ride." That's exactly what I did. The outcome was predictable.

*   *   *   *   *

For a rocket scientist, landing a man on the Moon is the ultimate challenge—the holy grail. This opportunity had eluded me throughout my career. After almost fifty years since Apollo 11's historic landing, I'd resigned myself to the idea that I'd retire without having my shot.

In late 2018, NASA announced a new program to return humans to the Moon. They needed crewed lunar landers and planned to engage American industry to provide them. My company had never conducted lunar studies, let alone designed or built a crewed lander. Undeterred, I was determined to get us involved, and after some convincing, I got the company's leadership on board.

When NASA awarded the initial contracts, ours was among the eleven companies selected. Most winners were established aerospace giants, though a few were smaller, lesser-known companies like ours. I led our small team's contract work, which proved an excellent introduction to crewed lunar landers.

New presidential directives forced NASA to accelerate full lander development. In late 2019, they solicited proposals for a complete Human Landing System (HLS). Though our company had completed only one small lander study, no companies had worked on a lunar lander since the 1970s—the whole industry was starting from similar knowledge and experience levels. After internal discussions, I convinced leadership that we should bid as lead contractor.

In mid-2020, NASA announced its selections, and our team was awarded one of three HLS contracts, shocking the rest of the industry, as many hadn't even heard of our company. The other winners were SpaceX, run by Elon Musk, and Blue Origin, run by Jeff Bezos. We found ourselves competing with companies led by the world's two wealthiest people. The first contract phase was a significant award, and our team made huge strides. I was thrilled with the team we'd put together and immensely proud of our accomplishments, but the real prize was the full HLS development contract. It required another massive proposal effort, limited to the three current contractors. This time, we felt like we were competing against Musk and Bezos themselves.

NASA planned to announce the HLS development winners in May 2021. I sat in a large executive conference room with company leadership, awaiting the call. That morning, I wore a T-shirt showing our HLS design and listened to motivational music, trying to prepare mentally for either outcome. But no matter how much you brace yourself, bad news still stings when you've poured your heart into a project. We lost. So did Bezos's Blue Origin team. Musk's SpaceX had included a $3 billion company investment that our team could never match. We were devastated.

Despite the setback, our team remained determined. NASA offered a midsize contract to refine designs and mature lander technologies. We proposed and won again. Within a year, NASA released another solicitation for full HLS development. We debated internally for months. This time, our only competition was Blue Origin, but we'd still be competing against a team backed by a multi-hundred-billionaire. Ultimately, we decided to go all in again.

> We set our sights on the moon to elevate ourselves.
> —Kate Purmal, Lisa Goldman, Anne Janzer[1]

On announcement day, I repeated the ritual: motivational music, gathering in the executive conference room, awaiting NASA's call, trying to clear my mind . . . with the same result. We lost again. Bezos's Blue Origin had included a multi-billion-dollar investment, and once again, we couldn't approach their bid price.

The loss and the project's end were crushing, even though I'd known it was possible. I'd devoted five years to it, hoping to spend the rest of my career getting humans back to the Moon again and again. Instead, our work ended abruptly, the team disbanded, and I moved to a different project.

It marked a turning point for me. HLS had been the most rewarding endeavor of my career, and I knew I'd never top it—at least not in terms of the project's purpose. I had to step back and consider: if I can't pursue the grandest purpose, what are the other aspects of endeavors that motivate me? What are the different aspects of any endeavor for anyone? Also, beyond our careers, what parts of life are most important? What should I care about? What matters most?

* * * * *

Throughout my life, I often thought about the most important personal values and how to apply them to make the most of my life. Like most people, though, these reflections were usually fleeting, lacking the depth and consistency to bring about meaningful change.

When my wife and I had our first child, I felt inspired. I began to make notes on the lessons I wanted to pass on to my children. Among these, I dedicated the most time to personal values, considering how my kids could grow into their best selves. Yet this burst of thought lasted only about six months. Then I turned fifty. While the milestone didn't trigger depression or a mid-life crisis, it carried a certain gravity. The following year, my team lost our last HLS competition, and I switched projects. Finally, the night after the first day of the school year, I asked my kids about their new classes. My son said, "I'm a senior!" The reality hit me.

Suddenly, the combination of completing a fiftieth trip around the Sun, questioning my next career move, and realizing my kids had nearly grown up coalesced into a personal commitment. I decided to finish what I'd started. I didn't know what my random notes, favorite quotes, and notions about what matters most would turn into, but I undertook to find out.

* * * * *

> Building character and quality of life is a function of aligning
> our beliefs and behaviors with universal principles.
> These principles are impersonal, external, factual,
> objective, and self-evident.
> They operate regardless of our awareness of them
> or our obedience or disobedience to them.
> —Stephen R. Covey[2]

I'm drawn to success stories, biographies of influential figures, and original, profound ideas. I love clever quotes that capture the essence of deep concepts. I naturally seek to understand how things work, though I lean more toward conceptualization than hands-on engineering. My personality type is balanced idealist, meaning that while maintaining high standards, I remain open to different perspectives. I value order and appreciate methodical approaches. I enjoy seeing the big picture and dissecting ideas to understand underlying principles. In summary, the search for meaning is in my bones. It's integral to who I am. I love piecing together seemingly disparate ideas into a coherent whole. These dispositions shaped this book's structure and content.

On one hand, writing a book about foundational values isn't a claim to have mastered any of them—I haven't. I'm no more qualified to give life advice than others. I have as many faults as anyone. I spend time on things that don't matter, focus on things I can't control, sometimes feel smaller than I am, and other times inflate my importance. I think about tasks before people, missing opportunities for friendship. I'm likely unaware of many other shortcomings.

On the other hand, I'm as human as everyone else. I've been on the planet for half a century, and I've been fortunate enough to visit many parts of it. I've had access to broad knowledge and an appreciation for real wisdom. Through dedicated research, personal observations, and firsthand lessons learned (usually the hard way), I've selected values that I believe most influence a person's well-being and fulfillment. These values are timeless, unaffected by changing circumstances. While I'd like to think the values are universal, I recognize that culture, environment, upbringing, and socioeconomic status influence how individuals and communities perceive them. I hope to demonstrate that they're enduring, fundamental character strengths, distinct from short-lived trends or generational worldviews.

To my children: if you can embody all the values in this book, you'll be among the best people in the world. If you usually strive for most of them, you'll be a better person than I. But no matter what you do, your mom and I will always be proud of you and love you unconditionally.

Andy Crocker (a.k.a. Dad)
December 31, 2024

> If a man is fortunate he will, before he dies, gather up as much as he can
> of his civilized heritage and transmit it to his children.
> And to his final breath he will be grateful for this inexhaustible legacy,
> knowing that it is our nourishing mother and our lasting life.
> —Will Durant

INTRODUCTION

Wisdom is having things right in your life and knowing why.
—William Stafford

WE'RE ENDLESSLY BOMBARDED with messages on how to matter—how to appear more attractive, accomplish more in less time, earn more money, or ascend to the C-suite. Nothing's wrong with looking good, earning money, or succeeding at work. However, those things don't matter on their own. Without a proper foundation, they don't add value to our lives or the world. Nothing's inherently wrong, either, with commercials telling us how to look good or books teaching us how to gain influence or succeed at work. Some convey worthwhile messages that can benefit us in the short run, but few have lasting impact, and most miss the point altogether. They focus on making us better friends, parents, employees, or leaders yet often overlook what truly matters—how to be a better person.

We aren't trained for most of our life roles—friend, student, parent, and employee. As we grow up, we watch people around us in these roles, and we might get advice from parents or friends. Typically, we step into these roles clueless and learn as we go. If we're conscientious or fortunate enough to receive training, we might learn the basics of our roles and techniques for improving performance. However, nearly all training overlooks that every life skill must be built on the same foundation. If that foundation is shaky, any knowledge and abilities built on top of it will also be unstable. Everything rests on what matters most—who we are.

Ideally, we should all start with the foundation. The right way to build a stable structure is from the ground up. At a young age, we should be taught the fundamental values of life, those that have stood the test of time, to firmly ground us in what matters. But most of us don't get the chance. We aren't surrounded by people who've built strong foundations, and we're not mature enough to learn it on our own. So we piece together our foundation by observing those around us and building on it as we go through life. When we realize—often later in life—that our foundation is weaker than it needs to be, we may wonder if it's too late. Fortunately, it's never too late. We can always strengthen who we are by embracing and reinforcing the ideals that help us become the best version of ourselves.

*   *   *   *   *

Many self-improvement, business, and philosophy books portray the present as uniquely troubled, suggesting their insights are vital remedies for dire times. Authors often claim unprecedented challenges demand novel solutions. They seem to derive satisfaction from the belief that we live in the worst of times, asserting that no previous generation has confronted the breadth and depth of problems we face today. They intend to create a sense of unity and urgency around their proposed solutions.

Most authors' claims are accepted because they're based on cognitive biases for which we're all prone to fall. Recency bias leads us to give greater importance to recent events than past ones. Availability bias, coupled with our limited memory capacity, causes us to recall new information more readily than old. Finally, egocentricity bias—the most human of all predispositions—compels us to believe that our experiences matter more than anything else. Combined, these biases create a false sense of the unpleasant present in our minds, often paired with another illogical idea: the current generation represents the pinnacle of human achievement. Sociologist Jib Fowles coined the term *chronocentrism* in 1974 to describe the belief that one's own time is paramount, suggesting that every era has led to the present, reinforcing the notion that our time might be the last. (Perhaps we can forgive this final fallacy since, after all, this era is *our* last.)

Authors exploit these biases and our life experiences to argue that innovative solutions are necessary for the exceptional trials of our complex modern world. We can't help but buy their books. Often, their ideas are fleeting fads. Occasionally, one endures because it's clever, catchy, or genuinely effective.

However, few acknowledge the truth: our trials aren't tougher; they're just different. Our time isn't more important; it's just new. The modern world isn't the peak of human development; it's merely the most recent, soon followed by the next.

Nothing is inherently special about now. It's only special to us because we're living it.

* * * * *

Writing this book wasn't straightforward. I didn't develop a plan, follow that plan, and six months later—voilà—have the book I imagined. However, looking at it now, I realize the winding path led me to a better place. I suppose it usually works that way.

Had I been asked at the start to describe my vision for the book as a dream home, I would've depicted something like a cozy driftwood hut sitting on a tranquil beach—makeshift and situated on sand but with a beautiful view of the sunset over the outgoing tide. Now, from the vantage point of completion, I see that I constructed a brick-and-mortar house atop a hill—not a towering mountain, but a rise high enough to see where I've been and point out to others the paths to take and to avoid.

Instead of opening this book, imagine you've just inherited my mental dream home. You'll want assurance that it's sturdy, built on firm ground, and can withstand the elements. This section introduces you to that house, from soil to ceiling. I describe the land it rests on, its foundation, structure, walls, and roof to give you confidence that you can sit inside and look out the expansive windows, taking in the landscape from my intended perspective. Use the graphic below to help visualize the concepts in the next few paragraphs.

The book is based on **premises** (which I'll call the land under the house) and centered on fundamental **principles** (the house's foundation). Everything else depends on the premises and the principles, so this section explains them first. The rest of the book is constructed to explain **what the principles are** and **why they matter** (the structure). However, knowing the what and why of these principles isn't enough to avoid the mistakes we naturally make (bare structure can't protect from the weather), so I explain **where we go wrong** most often. I then offer solutions (the walls)—not my own but **answers from timeless wisdom**—that are affixed to the what and why and anchored to the principles. Finally, I illustrate **how to live the principles**—i.e., turn wisdom into action (the roof)—to pursue personal success, well-being, and fulfillment.

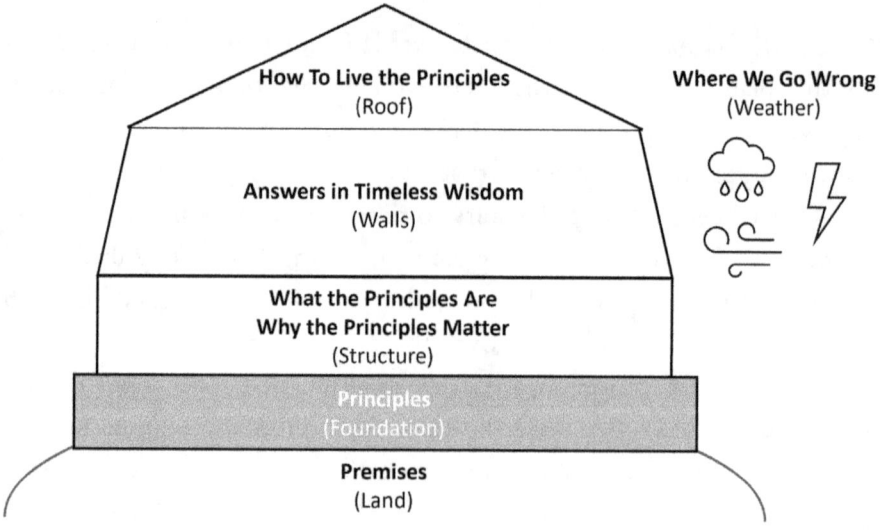

The elements of my mental dream home
(or how this book is structured)—built from the ground up

Premises are statements that form the basis on which arguments are developed and conclusions are drawn. In the following paragraphs, I present four premises born of the truths expounded above—the permanence of human problems and the criticality of fundamental values in overcoming those problems. These premises form the land on which my mental house is built. They're the assumptions on which the rest of the book is established. The premises compelled the conception and direction of this book. The premises aren't the house itself, but the house rests on and depends on the stability of the premises. The premises aren't the book's what, why, or how—they don't explain fundamental principles or how to incorporate them—but they explain why I decided to write about such principles.

The first premise of this book:

Today is more like the past than it is different, so solutions from the past still work today. The things that create success, well-being, and fulfillment are the same as in the past.

When we accept this, we shift our perspective. We understand the world goes through cycles revolving around the same core questions. Today's problems are fundamentally like those of previous generations, so the solutions we seek have been discovered before.

Throughout history, many have sought the right paths to success. Most have asked the wrong questions, assuming their times called for new answers. However, the wisest understood that the most important issues are eternal. They collected wisdom from their predecessors, added to it as they could, and provided solutions for posterity. We shouldn't view our generation as the culmination of history but as an opportunity for accumulation, to gather the wisdom of the ages. We don't have to reinvent the wheel. What matters now has always mattered.

> Clear back to ancient times,
> thoughtful people have made lists of useful principles.
> —Stephen R. Covey

The second premise:

We can find solutions to today's (and yesterday's) problems in timeless wisdom. Living by foundational, knowable principles leads to success, creates well-being, and fulfills us.

Great thinkers throughout history have pondered what's essential, good, and right. But what qualifies someone as a great thinker?

- **Originality:** Introducing new ideas and challenging conventional wisdom.
- **Depth of Thought:** Thoroughly understanding the subject and exploring complex issues.
- **Communication Skills:** Expressing ideas clearly and persuasively.
- **Recognition:** Widely acknowledged for their contributions.
- **Impact:** Having significant, lasting effects on their fields and society.
- **Legacy:** Inspiring and shaping the thoughts of future generations.

Great thinkers have provided answers to abiding questions. By incorporating their solutions, we can achieve success, live well, and find fulfillment. I call these solutions "timeless wisdom." I've chosen great thinkers based on the above qualifications and what they thought, said, wrote, and did concerning success, well-being, and fulfillment. They found answers to everlasting questions in our core values—how we should think, act, interact, and what to strive for.

Many of us believe we have it all figured out by adulthood. Some of us assume our parents provided the foundation we need to live a good life and that any gaps can be filled along the way. Unfortunately, despite their best intentions, many parents didn't have all the answers, or, as children, we may not have been mature enough to grasp the lessons they tried to impart. Others think we learned everything we need to know in school, but formal education isn't designed to teach the fundamental building blocks of human existence.

The good news is that the values that matter most aren't secrets. They've just been diluted, scattered across history, and lost amid the noise. We're often too distracted or busy to recognize that we're missing what's most important. So most of us never discover these values that can help us become our best selves.

The third premise:

Conditionality allows externalities to determine how we feel, behave, and act, pushing us away from foundational principles and from success, well-being, and fulfillment.

The following chapters explain conditionality in detail. But, in short, conditionality is dependency on external factors. It means we allow people, things, and events outside ourselves to drive our feelings, behaviors, and actions. For example, if our love for someone depends on what they've done for us, it's conditional love.

One problem with conditionality is that we give up control of our decision-making. We aren't in control if things outside us govern how we feel, behave, or act. So conditionality isn't in control. It takes direction (consciously or not) from outside or others. It's reactive. Because it's out of control and reactive, conditionality is weak.

Another issue is that lack of control prevents us from holding to our principles. Their changelessness makes them foundational; they're always true, regardless of circumstances. However, when we let external factors control our feelings, behaviors, and actions, we violate the changeless nature of those principles, so we can't follow them. Conditionality pushes us away from our foundational principles.

For instance, we believe that love is a core value. "Love one another" is a principle most of us accept. However, when we use a person's race, religion, or nationality as a factor in our feelings for them, we love conditionally. Conditional love is unstable. If there's something about a person's religion that we vehemently disagree with, conditional love can't handle the pressure, and our feelings toward that person change from love to something else. Whatever that something else is, it's not a fundamental principle that can guide us toward personal well-being.

> Since we are the product of our own history, we see current prophecy within the context of past wisdom. We listen to as wide a range of contemporary thought as we can attend to. Then we choose those we elect to heed as prophets—both old and new—and meld their advice with our own leadings. This we test in real-life experiences to establish our own position.
>
> —Robert K. Greenleaf[1]

The fourth premise:

To be our best, we must take control of our feelings, behaviors, and actions. We conquer conditionality by holding to our foundational principles unconditionally.

How do we overcome conditionality? Conditionality separates us from the principles that timeless wisdom teaches are critical to fulfillment. So, to seek personal well-being and fulfillment and work toward becoming our best, we must take control of our lives. We must move as far from conditionality as possible. The opposite of conditional is *unconditional*.

Unconditional means without conditions. It means changeless—independent of external factors. When we hold to our principles unconditionally, we don't let circumstances affect our feelings, behaviors, or actions. We're in control—proactive and powerful. Neither objects nor outcomes determine our choices. We don't make decisions based on who anyone else is or what they have done or might do. We make decisions based on foundational principles.

*   *   *   *   *

I've titled this book *The Unconditionals* because the values I advocate are the most fundamental elements of being human. They define us and shape all we do. The Unconditionals are the values upon which personal well-being and fulfillment most depend. They distinguish successful and fulfilled people from unsuccessful, unfulfilled ones.

There's no situation where The Unconditionals don't apply. They're unlimited, boundless. They're absolute, universally valid, and independent of external factors. They're complete, encompassing everything and leaving nothing out. They're unquestionable. They're pure, free from faults or defects. Unconditional means nonnegotiable.

The Unconditionals aren't targets or stretch goals; they're ideals. Like driving toward the horizon, we know we can't reach them; pursuing them is about the journey, not the destination.

Ideals are like stars; you will not succeed in touching them with your hands,
but like the seafaring man on the desert of waters,
you choose them as your guides, and following them, you reach your destiny.
—Carl Schurz

If following The Unconditionals is the best way to achieve well-being and fulfillment, why don't we? Conditionality is easier. It comes naturally—our instincts trigger conditional thoughts and behaviors. Also, it's the way of the world. So striving for unconditionality can feel like battling the world and ourselves simultaneously. Yet, it's worth the struggle.

When we understand the impact that unconditionality can have in our lives, a light inside us turns on. But we should want more than a light hidden inside—and we can have it. When we go beyond understanding and work to embody The Unconditionals in our thoughts, words, and actions, it becomes a characteristic that sets us apart. When we make unconditionality our aim, that light inside becomes lightning that flashes and illuminates everything around us by releasing the power of our principles. It opens new possibilities in how we live, giving us advantages over others and our former selves. When we strive for unconditionality by consistently pursuing The Unconditionals, it transforms us, and we can reach heights we'd never dreamed of.

Those benefits—distinguishing from the crowd, offering a unique advantage, and causing a transformation—are the definitions of a superpower. Unconditional is a superpower, and we can have it if we're willing to work for it. That's why I chose the subtitle *Five Timeless Values to Live Without Limits and Ignite Your Superpower.*

Nothing so marks a man as imaginative expressions.
A figurative statement arrests attention
and is remembered and repeated.
—Ralph Waldo Emerson

I understand those with deep spiritual beliefs might say there's more, and I agree. Connection with the divine and the promise of life after death are heavenly pursuits. Nothing in this book suggests those aren't primary principles. Frankly, eternity is (at least) a step beyond my objectives for this book. The Unconditionals are fundamental but not final. This book isn't meant to boil the ocean or fancied as holy water. At best, I hope it's refreshing and stimulating. Perhaps I'll tackle the meaning of this life—and the next—in another book. (Kidding.)

How the Book Is Organized

In our ongoing metaphor, the house is built on a foundation of core values. This book is based on The Unconditionals, arranged into chapters focused on five foundational principles:

- Chapter 1—Unconditional Love
- Chapter 2—Unconditional Gratitude
- Chapter 3—Unconditional Integrity
- Chapter 4—Unconditional Accountability
- Chapter 5—Unconditional Endeavor

These values shape who we are and how we think, engage with the world, connect with others, and act. I've ordered them based on how they define, sustain, and harmonize our lives. Each is crucial for living our best life. While independent, they complement each other and are most effective when practiced together.

The Unconditionals are centered on love. Love is the most basic and vital human value, emotion, and experience. It must be felt and given unconditionally—limitless and unchanging. As we embrace The Unconditionals, everything we do and are comes from Unconditional Love.

I've also ordered them by four core life areas: inside, outside, connection, and action. Unconditional Love comes first because it's critical in all aspects of life—internally, externally, for connection, and for action. Love undergirds them all. The first core area—inside—looks within ourselves, our inner thoughts and feelings. Gratitude comes from inside. The second area—outside—looks at ourselves from the outside—our public self, image, and how we portray ourselves. Integrity is how we represent ourselves. Connection—the third area—is about interacting with the world. Accountability is critical to that connection. The fourth area is about doing things—action is tangible and physical, about what we do. Endeavor turns action into achievement and growth.

> Science is organized knowledge. Wisdom is organized life.
> —Herbert Spencer

How the Chapters Are Organized

As a structure in a real house is framed on its foundation, in our metaphorical house, we build on the five foundational values with an understanding of what they are and why they matter. We recognize that structure alone can't protect us from weather (i.e., knowing the values' how and why isn't enough to keep us from going wrong), so we erect walls for protection (we seek answers in timeless wisdom). Then, we install a roof over our heads (learn how to live those principles in our life roles). Each chapter of the book is organized into consistent major headings:

- **What It Is:** Clarifies what each value is (and isn't). Sets the context for the chapter.
- **Why It Matters**: Explains why each value is essential.
- **Where We Go Wrong:** Addresses ways and reasons we fail to follow or live by each value.
- **Answers in Timeless Wisdom:** Provides insights from great thinkers about each value.
- **How to Live It:** Advises on applying each value to various aspects of our lives, including personal, relational, as a parent, at work, and as a leader.

Quotes from sources relevant to The Unconditionals are incorporated throughout all chapters, not just the "Answers in Timeless Wisdom" sections. Historical examples, personal anecdotes, and stories illustrate key points, reinforce the timeless nature of the core values, and serve as guideposts as we pursue those values. However, most of us want more direct application. The "How to Live It" sections offer guidance on integrating The Unconditionals into our lives.

* * * * *

When I started this book, I didn't know where it would lead. After months of study, writing, and crafting, I realized the five foundational principles must be unconditional, and a light went on inside me. But it took much longer, diving deeper and allowing the differences between conditional and unconditional to sink in, for me to grasp their meaning. When I did, the light became lightning. I finally saw the full power of the principles. Most importantly, I recognized that, in this book, I could fast-track the process for others. By revealing The Unconditionals and demonstrating how to pursue them, I could help others activate a superpower hidden within themselves. I sincerely believe The Unconditionals are the five foremost values for personal well-being and fulfillment. I've poured my heart into this book to convey their importance and potential impact. My greatest wish is that the book will benefit at least one person who will pass on a similar message to another.

Summary

We're constantly confronted with shallow notions of success—wealth and status—that imply our happiness depends on external factors. However, we all eventually discover that true fulfillment comes from our core values.

By cultivating the values that matter most—and pursuing them unconditionally, undeterred by circumstance—we can live meaningful lives. The path isn't easy. It leads away from the conventional ways of the world and our instincts. It requires controlling our thoughts, words, and actions. Gradually, we can close the gap between who we are and who we aspire to be. As we think, speak, and act with intention and build habits aligned with our values, we experience a transformation.

I challenge you to begin with an open mind to discover and embody The Unconditionals. When you embrace your core values and strive to be your best self by living those values without conditions, you unlock the power to make a difference—for yourself, those you love, and those whose lives you touch.

I challenge you to

Make Unconditional Your Superpower.

My fondest hope for you is that you find yourself on the pages of this book. Not the self you think you are and not the self you fear you might be, but rather the selfless self whose face you had before you were born.

—Michael Neill,

foreword to Clare Dimond's *Home: The Return to What You Already Are*

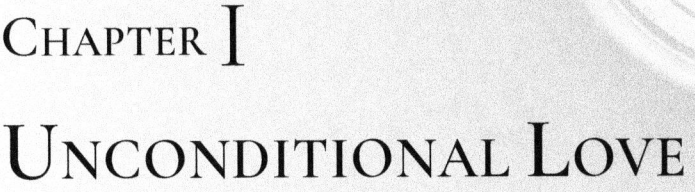

Chapter I

Unconditional Love

I love you because I love you,
because it would be impossible not to love you.
I love you without question, without calculation,
without reason good or bad, faithfully,
with all my heart and soul, and every faculty.
—Juliette Drouet

What It Is

I WALKED NEXT to my wife, Beth, as she was wheeled toward the operating room (OR). When we arrived, I was told to wait outside and get dressed while she was prepped. Those few minutes felt strange, waiting alone in a sterile hallway while doctors did who knows what to my wife. I felt like I should think deeply to prepare for what was ahead. Instead, my most profound thought was, *How the heck do you get these stretchy paper booties over your shoes?* I put on the surgical booties, gown, mask, and gloves and waited. Nurses passed by, saying, "Just a few more minutes," which made waiting harder. Finally, the doctor called, and I ran to the OR door.

The scene was a blur. I remember only vague images. Doctors and nurses in green uniforms scurried like an army unit preparing for battle. The walls were lined with instruments. Beth's bed was surrounded by devices and poles with dripping drugs. Before I could look around, I was told, not asked, to sit on a stool next to Beth's head. A green sheet over her neck extended three feet to her right and left and into the air, leaning toward me like a camping tarp. So I could see only Beth's head, the anesthesiologist behind, and his monitors. The sheet is standard for C-sections to avoid fathers passing out or getting sick.

Beth looked good. She was calm (thanks to heavy sedation). We talked as much as circumstances allowed. She was worried that she didn't have her glasses. She had taken them off during the sweating and screaming in the labor and delivery room. How she had the lucidity to realize she might not see the baby clearly, I'll never know.

Then everything happened quickly. The doctors said something about an incision. I heard utensils clinking and flesh being manipulated, but the sounds seemed far away, like elevator music. After sitting for only a few moments, I was asked if I wanted to watch them pull the baby out. They had to ask me twice—the anesthesiologist was the one to finally get my attention. Fuzzy-headed, I stood and looked toward Beth's midsection.

As soon as my eyes focused and I saw the doctors' hands inside my wife, they began to pull our baby out.

As long as I live, even if I lose my senses or mind, I will never forget seeing our first child, our son, for the first time. But as intense as the memory is, I can't describe it well. I was overwhelmed. As he took his first breath, I lost mine. In a wave of emotion, air rushed out of me, tears filled my eyes, and my hands unconsciously covered my mouth. I couldn't speak; I only cried. When I could breathe again, the air carried something else: new love. At first sight, I fell for him powerfully and deeply. That feeling has only grown, but it was real from the moment he entered our lives.

Beth told me later my reaction worried her, having never seen anything like it from me. From her view of my quivering chin, it must have been hard to distinguish joy from panic. With a tight throat, I whispered, "He's beautiful." That was all I could say.

As quickly as he was pulled out and checked, the nurses were ready to take him to the nursery. I hated leaving Beth alone without the son she had carried for nine months, but we had no choice. After he was brought to her for a quick kiss, he and I left. I pushed his bassinet down the hall, watching him the whole way. My head spun with exhilaration, relief from old worries, and realization of new ones, but I beamed. I couldn't help saying over and over, "I'm your daddy," while tears streamed down my face. The words meant nothing to him; I was saying them more to myself. It was just sinking in.

*　　*　　*　　*　　*

Nineteen years have passed. I've long forgotten what it was like to be childless. Aside from the times Beth and I shared as a couple, I don't want to remember. I'm not the same person. Our son's first breath started new lives for us too. Our childbirth experience was good training for parenthood. No matter how much we planned, and despite any natural abilities or advantages we might have had, there was no way to prepare fully. Things happen. We do our best to react with wisdom, compassion, and the support of those close to us.

Another change that's hard to prepare for as new parents is the overwhelming feeling of love. We know beforehand we will love the child but can't fathom the depth or fullness. It's like trying to describe water to someone who has never been wet before they jump into the ocean.

Marital love is close—deep, wide, and beyond explanation. It's wonderful to choose someone and have them choose you from among all the people in the world and decide to spend your life together. But it's a choice you or your partner could have not made. Sometimes people even unmake those choices.

Having a biological child is more profound: We don't just make a choice; we make a person. It's our most important responsibility and amazing capability as humans. When the child arrives, we immediately feel the weight of responsibility, but—hopefully—we also feel buoyed by indescribable love for our creation. Upon seeing the child, made of us, that love explodes, ignited by new life. (Though not an adoptive parent, I imagine the feelings of adopting a child are similar: a mix of duty and concern, overwhelmed by love for the new family member.)

Just as I clearly remember our first child's birth, I recall my amazement at our second's. The experience was just as mind-blowing, but what I remember most is realizing a truth neither explainable nor understandable until the child arrived. Leading to the birth, I was worried because I couldn't imagine loving another person as deeply and freely as I loved our first. I was sure I'd either have to give up some of my love for the first or have insufficient love for the second. Of course, as all multichild parents discover, I needn't have worried. As Robert Brault beautifully said, "A parent's love is whole, no matter how many times divided."

As parents, we would do anything for our children. We would sacrifice our lives for them if necessary. We would and do give them everything we can because we love them.

A parent's special love for a child is the closest earthly example of Unconditional Love. We don't love them because they ask, earn it, or necessarily deserve it. We forgive their mistakes. It doesn't matter if they love us back. We love them because we can't not love them.

Many argue that parental love, especially maternal love, is unconditional. As I'll explain, it's not. Many also believe such pure love is only possible between parents and children. Again, not true. Still, because so many of us experience it and the feelings involved, parental love is instructive for comparison and discussion.

> To love somebody is not just a strong feeling—
> it is a decision, it is a judgment, it is a promise.
> If love were only a feeling, there would be no basis
> for the promise to love each other forever.
> —Erich Fromm

First, let's discuss what love is, or the various types we experience. Understanding these types and associated feelings helps us comprehend what is and isn't Unconditional Love. Also, Unconditional Love can seem like an abstract concept, so it helps to ground ourselves by reviewing these types and relating them to our lives.

The Types of Love

In 1960, British writer C. S. Lewis published *The Four Loves*, which identifies types of love and explores their natures. Although many have developed other philosophies of love, Lewis's four types represent generally accepted notions, are relatable, and are easy to understand.

The first type that comes to mind for most of us is romantic love (from the Greek *eros*). It's the feeling of being in love or loving another person. It's the type most celebrated because it burns the hottest. Lewis calls it the most enthusiastic human pleasure, but he says its intensity can be good and bad. It can justify selfishness, he says. In the modern world, romantic love is often pursued to the point of worship.[1] We've all experienced romantic love's pleasure, intensity, and ups and downs. We also agree it's very different from parental love.

The second type is social love, or friendship (from the Greek *philia*). This love between friends can be as close as siblings in strength and duration. It exists between people who share values, backgrounds, or interests. Lewis says it's the "least biological, organic, instinctive, gregarious . . .

[and] natural of loves." Friendship isn't necessary for life. We choose and share it freely. Lewis laments modern society has muted it, saying, "To the Ancients, Friendship seemed the happiest and most fully human of all loves, the crown of life and the school of virtue. The modern world, in comparison, ignores it."[2] We all recognize friendship love and know we're fortunate when we can share it. We also know it's different from romantic love. Our hearts and minds react differently, even if we can't explain it.

The third love is affection (from the Greek *storge*), which Lewis calls the empathy bond. It's shared between family or those as close as family, bonded more by chance than choice. The archetype is parents' affection for their children. Lewis says it's the most emotive love, built on natural fondness from familiarity. It's given freely, usually unrelated to worthiness, and offered unearned. It can form the foundation for strong, lasting happiness. However, Lewis points out that affection's strength makes it susceptible to corruption by taking it for granted, not reciprocating, stooping to jealousy, or smothering. Despite its power, it can wither.[3] Therefore, affection falls short as a goal. Parents may find it hard to imagine their love corrupted, but we all know of cases where bad behavior has destroyed it. It may not happen to us, but we must acknowledge affection love is imperfect.

> Love is not affectionate feeling,
> but a steady wish for the loved person's ultimate good
> as far as it can be obtained.
> —C. S. Lewis

The final type is Unconditional Love (from the Greek *agape*). Lewis calls it charity, but we shouldn't confuse it with philanthropy. He clarifies it as "God love"—the love God has for people.[4] Lewis wrote from a Christian perspective, but the concept of *agape* love as an ideal, regardless of circumstances, isn't unique to Christianity. As perfect love, it's not something we can expect to achieve, but it's the proper goal and basis for our lives.

Unconditional Love is both feeling and practice. It's affection without limitations. It doesn't change, wither, or break. It can't be earned or awarded. There are no standards to meet. It's offered without question, judgment, or expectation. It accepts people as they are, no strings attached. It doesn't require reciprocation.

Unconditional Love comes from pure desire for the subject's well-being—nothing more. It's always available. It overcomes frustration, anger, and disappointment. It forgives mistakes every time. It ignores what anyone thinks.

This book supports Lewis's views, particularly that Unconditional Love is ideal and unreachable. Friendships aren't unconditional, no matter how long and deep. Spousal love, although encompassing most aspects of romantic, friendship, and affection, isn't unconditional. Parental love, as close as we can get, isn't unconditional, either,[5] because it can question, doubt, and have times of weakness. No matter how strong our love for our children, maintaining perfect unconditionality is almost impossible if they repeatedly make mistakes or reject our love.

Unconditionality

Unconditionality goes beyond how we feel about and act toward certain people. Unconditional means impartial, ubiquitous, and timeless. It applies to everyone, everywhere, always. We can't claim to pursue Unconditional Love if we withhold love for any reason, including unfamiliarity or distaste for someone's beliefs. Pursuing Unconditional Love doesn't mean we agree with or want to be with everyone, but we genuinely wish for all people's well-being and give respect, kindness, and compassion—love's key elements—without conditions.

We love our partners, friends, and relatives, but we love them with Lewis's first three types of love, and that's not enough—those loves are limited. If we rely on only those emotions, our love breaks down. We must overcome limitations by loving them unconditionally, despite their weaknesses or ours.

Unconditional Love requires loving all people for no reason except *they're human*. We may not know them, or they may seem different, but because they exist, we should love them. To borrow from René Descartes's immortal first principle—cogito, ergo sum (I think, therefore I am)—the first principle of The Unconditionals is "They are, therefore I love them."

Most of us can accept the humanity of everyday acquaintances. We see them, pass them, bump into them, or casually interact with them. Even without meaningful relationships, we acknowledge they have lives, thoughts, and feelings like we do. Knowing nothing about them, we must love them unconditionally because they're human.

Here's where it gets tough. There are billions of people in the world we've never met and will never meet. They're no more real to us than names of countries on a globe, pictures in a book, characters in a story, or numbers in a table. We lack human connection, but unconditionality still applies. We need only know they exist to extend the same rationale as to family, friends, and acquaintances. They're human, so we try to love them unconditionally.

Unconditionality can't stop at friends and family, nor should it only be directed outward. We must grant *ourselves* unconditional self-love, complete and doubtless. Self-love isn't narcissism but acknowledgment of our worth. We can't earn it with money, recognition, influence, or affection. We love ourselves simply because we're alive. And we must love ourselves to love others fully. Healthy self-love is essential for genuine connections with others.

> You can't really love someone else
> unless you really love yourself first.
> —Fred Rogers, "Mister Rogers"

When we accept that we should love others simply because they're human, we must flip that around: we exist, so others should love us simply because we're human. A corollary to the first principle is "I am, therefore I am loved." This can be more powerful, but more difficult to accept, than the first principle. Some of us don't feel loved or worthy of love, so we can't unconditionally love ourselves or others.

Believers in a loving God can take refuge in a faith that God loves them unconditionally. God loves us not because we're worthy but because we live or have lived. If the omnipotent Creator loves us, others can and do love us. If God and others love us, we can't justify not loving ourselves. Nonbelievers may not lean on faith but have parents, siblings, or friends who love them as unconditionally as humans can. Sometimes we don't feel it, but there's no denying that love exists. Accepting we're loved opens a world of possibilities, releasing us to love others and live without self-judgment. We're free to become who we're meant to be.

Why It Matters

UNCONDITIONAL LOVE COMES first in this book because it's the foundation on which all values are built. As mentioned in the Introduction, Unconditional Love is first because it matters everywhere and always—inside, outside, for connection, and for action. Unconditional Love is the fundamental force of the universe.

Basing our virtues on ideals that can't be reached may seem foolish, as if we're setting ourselves up for failure. Yet the goal isn't to reach the ideals but to aim for them—the pursuit is the point. When we aspire for Unconditional Love, we can experience romantic, friendship, and affection love along the way. Humans can never be perfect, but if we keep the ideal in sight, we'll accomplish more than we ever thought possible.

> Love is not primarily a relationship to a specific person;
> it is an attitude, an orientation of character
> which determines the relatedness of a person to the world as a whole,
> not toward one "object" of love.
> —Erich Fromm

Many great thinkers throughout history have emphasized the importance of pursuing Unconditional Love. Saint Thomas Aquinas, an Italian-Dominican friar, philosopher, and theologian, regarded love as the greatest of all virtues. He wrote that the love of God (both from God and to God) is the guiding principle for human actions and relationships, meaning Unconditional Love should be our primary objective throughout life.

"So," you might say, "a medieval saint says I should love others unconditionally, but so what?" The reason it matters is that we're made to love and be loved. It's vital to our existence and well-being. Following is proof.

First, love boosts emotional health. It makes us feel wanted and accepted. It makes us feel human. These benefits come to both givers and receivers of love. Love produces positive emotions such as happiness, joy, and contentment and provides emotional resilience. Knowing we're loved helps us cope with stress, grief, and adversity.

Studies have shown that love has various mental and physical benefits, including lower stress levels, improved heart health, and longer life expectancy. Some research has focused specifically on Unconditional Love. A 2009 study examined brain regions stimulated by Unconditional Love. The results suggest that feeling Unconditional Love activates some of the same areas of the brain's reward system as romantic love.[6] In 2010, a study showed that children who feel loved unconditionally by their parents/caregivers tend to be more resilient in adulthood and experience fewer mental health symptoms than those who do not.[7] Furthermore, findings from a 2013 study support the idea that showing Unconditional Love to children enhances their lifelong health and well-being, protecting them against the effects of trauma or abuse.[8]

Unconditional Love provides a sense of security in both childhood and adulthood. Knowing someone loves us no matter what builds independence, self-worth, and confidence. If we know someone will love us even if we make mistakes, we feel comfortable making our own decisions and learning from them. To paraphrase Fred Rogers of *Mister Rogers' Neighborhood*, the world needs a sense of worth, which we can achieve only when we believe we're worthwhile and unconditionally love ourselves and each other.

Unconditional Love builds meaningful connections. It strengthens relationships, promotes cooperation, and encourages understanding. In friendships, it can survive conflicts, drifting apart, and divergent life goals. In romantic relationships, it remains strong when facing challenges like serious health problems or changes in appearance or personality. Unconditional Love inspires altruism, meaning we help others without expecting anything in return. When we love unconditionally, we're generous purely for the benefit of others. We also forgive mistakes and continue to accept our loved ones, even if their choices upset us.[9]

> When we love a person, we accept him or her exactly as is:
> the lovely with the unlovely, the strong with the fearful,
> the true mixed in with the facade, and of course,
> the only way we can do it is by accepting ourselves that way.
> —Fred Rogers, "Mister Rogers"

Unconditional Love is a catalyst for growth and self-improvement. We often try to be better people for the sake of our loved ones and our relationships. Unconditional Love gives us satisfaction and is essential for creating a just, caring, and peaceful society.

What It Isn't

Striving for Unconditional Love doesn't mean accepting unhealthy relationships. There's a big difference between loving someone and accepting harmful behaviors. Conflicts are normal in relationships, and pursuing Unconditional Love doesn't mean avoiding them or overlooking problems. But it also doesn't mean ignoring relationship issues, neglecting our own needs, or tolerating abuse. While Unconditional Love can involve sacrifice, it doesn't require giving up everything we need for ourselves. Unconditional Love creates a sense of security that must include mental, emotional, and physical safety. It doesn't mean staying in unhealthy or unsafe situations. We must prioritize our well-being, or we can't love others fully. We can step back from a relationship that constantly drains us and still have compassion for the other person. It's also possible to leave a relationship out of Unconditional Love for that person and ourselves.[10]

✳　✳　✳　✳　✳

In summary, Unconditional Love contributes to our emotional, mental, and physical well-being, strengthens social bonds, supports personal growth, and promotes a sense of purpose. It plays a crucial role in human relationships and the overall well-being of individuals and society. It's the foundation for good people, good communities, and a good world.

Even when we know all the good things Unconditional Love offers, we still stumble. Natural tendencies and societal forces pull us in other directions. The next section explains these influences. Once we understand where we go wrong, we can find remedies—the two sections that follow provide solutions found in timeless wisdom and explain how to incorporate those solutions into our lives.

Where We Go Wrong

DESPITE ITS BENEFITS, the world often sees Unconditional Love as naive. Maintaining romantic love with our spouses until death do us part is tough, and many fail. Feeling affection for our children and close family when they wrong us is also hard, and many fail at that too. Keeping up with friends and investing in meaningful relationships is challenging, and we also fail here. So why should we try to love anyone unconditionally, let alone everyone?

> The beginning of love is the will to let those we love be perfectly themselves,
> the resolution not to twist them to fit our own image.
> If in loving them we do not love what they are,
> but only their potential likeness to ourselves, then we do not love them:
> we only love the reflection of ourselves we find in them.
> —Thomas Merton[11]

Most of us think, *I'm doing all right. I love the people I'm supposed to love . . . most of the time.* We may view love as a spectrum, with love at one end and hate at the other. This makes it easier to justify our behavior. Sure, we might not aim for Unconditional Love, but we feel okay as long as we're on the loving side of the spectrum. As long as we avoid being hateful most of the time, we think, *I'm good enough, right?*

The problem is that sticking with love is hard. It's like the love spectrum is on a slope, with love at the top. Constantly striving to love feels like an uphill climb, or, more accurately, it's like trying to climb a slippery slide that's just been waxed. Slippery slopes are dangerous. One misstep, and down we go. The love spectrum is like that: if we're not careful, we can slide from love to disinterest to dislike . . . all the way to hate.

It's easy to find examples of love quickly sliding toward hate. Without looking hard, I found this story on social media site Reddit (the username was deleted, so there's no attribution):

I remember a moment with my ex. I know I loved him. But we got into an argument about something that happened with our child. . . . He called me a monster and terrible human being . . . I hated him with such hatred, I didn't want to see him. I didn't want to speak to him. I wanted to hurt him. . . . He was so angry at me. I was angry at him. I've never wanted someone to hurt as much as I wanted him to hurt in that moment. . . . I have never been filled with so much hate as I was that night. . . . I never trusted him again as my partner after that day. . . . I never trusted him with my feelings again.[12]

We've all seen love slide toward disinterest or dislike, and most have experienced it firsthand. We claim to have good reasons for our change in feelings: incompatible values, betrayal, neglect. In extreme cases, our feelings may slide so far away from love that we experience hate.

The Trouble with Hate

Rebecca Saxe describes hate as a mix of "malice, repugnance, and a willingness to harm." It's a toxic emotion that fixates on a person's nature, motives, and traits.[13] Hate targets many groups: differing religions, countries, races, political parties, and neighbors. Whenever people worship, live, look, think, or speak differently—if they're unlike us in any way—someone probably hates them.

Hate is pervasive. We can recognize it in countless instances of extreme violence and atrocities throughout history and around the world:

- For over 350 years, Catholic monarchs persecuted and executed thousands of Jews and Muslims to root out heresy during the Spanish Inquisition.
- The Holocaust, orchestrated by Nazi Germany during World War II, resulted in the systematic genocide of six million Jews and millions of others deemed undesirable.
- During the 1950s and 1960s American civil rights movement, racism and segregation led to significant violence, such as the 16th Street

Baptist Church bombing in Birmingham, Alabama, and the killings of leaders Medgar Evers and Dr. Martin Luther King Jr.

Unfortunately, none of the advancements of modern society have been able to eradicate hate, and the atrocities it causes have remained depressingly consistent over time:

- Since 2003, the Sudanese government–backed Arab militia has targeted non-Arab groups in Darfur, committing mass genocide and creating a refugee crisis.
- A gunman with hatred for Jews attacked the Tree of Life synagogue in Pittsburgh, Pennsylvania, in 2018, killing eleven worshippers and injuring several others.
- In 2019, extreme anti-Muslim hatred drove a white supremacist to kill fifty-one people and injure dozens more in shootings at two mosques in Christchurch, New Zealand, broadcasting the massacre live on social media.

Why Do We Hate?

Hate is a primal emotion, always lurking beneath the surface, but it doesn't come out automatically. It's a learned response. It usually grows from fear, insecurity, or mistrust of the unknown. When we face something or someone we don't understand, we feel uneasy, which can lead to fear and then to hate. Hate can also stem from low self-worth, lack of self-compassion, or attempts to fill an emotional void. Society may create hate to justify violence, like in war.

Humans instinctively form groups, often split those groups into us—the in-group—and them—the out-group, and develop love for us and suspicion of them. If encouraged, this suspicion can turn into aggression. Behavioral researcher Patrick Wanis explains that aggression can lead to hate. It's a quick reaction to perceived threats based on survival instinct, not logic. He says, "Hatred is driven by two key emotions of love and aggression: one, love for the in-group—the group that is favored; and two, aggression for the out-group—the group that has been deemed as being different, dangerous, and a threat to the in-group."[14]

Hate is pernicious. It can develop from nearly nothing. One of the most alarming experiments on in-group/out-group bias happened not in a lab but in an elementary school classroom. It was devised by Iowa third-grade teacher Jane Elliott in 1968, the day after Dr. Martin Luther King Jr.'s assassination. She divided her class into groups based only on eye color. First, she made the blue-eyed children superior and the brown-eyed children targets of discrimination. Within minutes, the blue-eyed children ridiculed their brown-eyed peers, calling them stupid and excluding them during recess. Then, Ms. Elliott reversed the roles, giving the brown-eyed children dominance. Immediately, they adopted the same harsh behaviors, punishing their blue-eyed classmates. This experiment, shown in the PBS Frontline documentary *A Class Divided*, demonstrates how quickly and dramatically even seven-year-olds can be influenced by group dynamics.[15] More succinctly, it shows the slippery slope between love and hate and how light a push is needed to cause us to slide toward the latter.

Hate can also come from fear of bad traits within ourselves. It's a subconscious defense mechanism, a misguided attempt to eliminate our undesirable characteristics. Freud calls it projection. Psychologist Brad Reedy says, "We developed this method to survive because any 'badness' in us put us at risk of being rejected and alone." We repress things others tell us are unlovable or morally wrong, and we develop hate toward those who show them. "We think that is how one gets rid of undesirable traits, but this method only keeps repression going, leading to many mental health issues."[16] Although we act like it's due to a lack of acceptance of another's traits, projection indicates a lack of self-acceptance due to traits we dislike in ourselves.

Similarly, a lack of self-compassion fuels hatred. If we feel insecure, we project it onto others. We attack them to defend against threats to our self-esteem. Dr. Reedy says, "If we find part of ourselves unacceptable, we tend to attack others to defend against the threat. If we're okay with ourselves, we see others' behaviors as 'about them' and can respond with compassion. If I kept hate in my heart for [another], I would have to hate myself as well. It's only when we learn to hold ourselves with compassion that we may be able to show it toward others."[17]

Hatred can fill a void. It creates a sense of belonging and camaraderie, though harmful. It distracts from deeper issues like helplessness, inadequacy, or shame. Psychologist Bernard Golden, author of *Overcoming Destructive Anger: Strategies That Work*, points out that hate can offer a break from inner suffering: "Acts of hate are attempts to distract oneself from feelings such as helplessness, powerlessness, injustice, inadequacy, and shame. . . . The individual consumed by hate may believe that the only way to regain some sense of power over his or her pain is to preemptively strike out at others."[18]

There are many examples of hate manifesting as attempts to regain a sense of power:

- Nazism blamed Jews for Germany's economic hardships. They used propaganda to unite the population against a common enemy and distract from internal failures.
- Those who feel disenfranchised may seek a sense of identity by joining extremist groups that target perceived enemies. For example, white supremacist movements in the US attract individuals who feel threatened by social and demographic changes.
- Young people in marginalized communities join gangs to escape feelings of helplessness. Gangs provide a sense of belonging but create violence against rival groups to assert dominance and distract from their socioeconomic struggles.

Societal factors also escalate hate. Our culture glorifies competition, promoting the us-versus-them mentality. Silvia Dutchevici, president and founder of the Critical Therapy Center, says our emphasis on competition can foster hate: "We're taught to hate the enemy—meaning anyone different than us."[19] The vitriol associated with competition can become comical.

This whole concept of the team—"Your team," "My team," . . . "That's our team." Really? Is it our team? Who are these guys? Where are they from? They're not from around here. They're just paid to wear those clothes. The uniform is the only constant in sports. The guys are moving around, different teams . . . teams are moving from different towns. We're really just rooting for our clothes to defeat the clothes of the team from the other city. That's what sports is. We're rooting for laundry, and nothing else. I always find it weird how upset we get when a guy leaves our team and then plays against our team: "Different shirt! I hate this guy! I can't believe he's wearing that shirt!" In the meantime, everyone we see every day is wearing a different shirt. We don't get upset with them, for some reason.

—Jerry Seinfeld[20]

Seinfeld's comic bit should make us pause and wonder: What if we could look at every controversial circumstance from the perspective of an audience member watching a stage performance? In the heat of the moment, when we're engaged in an us-versus-them situation, if we could step back and look at ourselves objectively, would we feel the same disgust? Or would we laugh at our silliness? (It would certainly help if we could have a guy with a New York accent and just the right amount of snark in his tone as our narrator.)

Hate is irrational at its core. It comes from ancient animalistic instincts and forms in the reflexive part of our brain, the limbic system. That system acts and reacts unconsciously, so we don't initially decide to hate someone. We're not aware of those first sensations of discomfort. Something in our subconscious—a trigger—causes us to interpret that discomfort as a sense of dislike or disgust. Although that trigger is reflexive, it's not inborn. As noted above, it's learned, typically from either lessons or experiences that connect fear or unease with that trigger.

What determines if that spark of hate turns into burning hatred? When we accept the irrational trigger as truth. We allow it to expand from the quick-acting, unthinking part of our brain (the limbic system) to the slow-acting, thinking part (the cerebral cortex). We hold on to hate and let it grow. We begin to believe there's logic associated with it. We create lies to convince ourselves that hate comes from a place of reason. We fan the spark into a flame.

This expansion into our thinking brain can happen consciously or unconsciously, most often the latter. For example, with hate based on race or religion, deep-seated bias is like dry kindling to any spark of discomfort. The same applies to hatred traceable to past injustices. In these cases, there's a built-in, justified reason that, unless we willfully interrupt it, automates the transition from our unthinking brain to our thinking one.

Sometimes we consciously add fuel to the fire. We intentionally create connections between reason and revulsion; we manufacture hate on purpose. Research has shown that dehumanization—seeing others as inferior, uncivilized, or less than human—shuts down our capacity for love. It reduces us to machines, exempt from moral rules. Dehumanization is used in warfare to create feelings of hate. People who commit hate crimes often justify their actions by dehumanizing their victims.[21] They accept the hate they or others have constructed so that they believe their actions are honorable. The hate overwhelms their sense of right and wrong.

Social media creates the perfect conditions for hate to develop. It enables anonymity, which removes inhibitions and accountability while amplifying negativity. Those who feel inadequate may resort to online hate speech and trolling to assert dominance and mask insecurities. Social media algorithms are designed to show users content that aligns with their interests, creating echo chambers where we're exposed only to opinions that reinforce our views and increase polarization. Controversial content tends to get more attention, encouraging provocative behavior. Social media's impersonal nature can then lead from dehumanization and desensitization to hateful behavior. Online hate is also associated with isolation. A report from the organization Ditch the Label found that online hate speech increased by 38 percent in the United States and the United Kingdom during lockdowns in the first months of the COVID-19 pandemic.[22] Of course, not all social media spreads hate. It's also used to promote positive causes, connect with friends and family, and share valuable information. Still, social media seems to have made the slope from love to hate more slippery.

Hate is just as injurious to the hater as it is to the hated.
Like an unchecked cancer,
hate corrodes the personality and eats away its vital unity.
—Martin Luther King Jr.

The Connection between Love and Hate

Researchers have discovered unique patterns of activity for hate in the brain's cerebral cortex. Interestingly, these areas closely correspond to the ones activated in studies of love, suggesting a strong link between the two emotions and providing a physical explanation for how easily we may slide from one to the other. A primary difference is whether these corresponding parts of the brain are active or inactive when each emotion is felt. When feeling love, these parts are inactive; when feeling hate, they're active. Prior research had associated these areas with judgment and calculation. So, when feeling love, we're less critical of others; when feeling hate, we feel judgmental and may calculate moves to harm another. The researchers suggest these differences in brain patterns may be related to a shift from external considerations to an internal focus associated with anxiety. The fact that brain areas and patterns associated with love and hate are tightly connected may account for the close linkage between the two in our lives.[23]

This neural connection between love and hate makes sense when we recognize that feelings of hate and our typical feelings of love are conditional. Usually, when we feel love toward someone, the emotion is dependent on the object—we love them *because of who they are*. Conversely, when we feel hate, the emotion comes from an irrationally adverse reaction—though we may lie to ourselves that it's rational—to something *about the person*. In both cases, the feelings are dependent. They're conditional.

With this in mind, picturing love and hate as opposite ends of a spectrum seems like an effective analogy. The two are connected in the brain, and we know from experience how easy it is to slip from the former to the latter. What's critical to recognize, though, is that this is the *Spectrum of Conditional Love*. One extreme is conditional love, and the other is hate.

All of the emotions on this spectrum are contingent on the perceived characteristics of the objects.

Our brains are wired for conditional love and hate, so we can't avoid experiencing the full spectrum of these emotions as humans. But these emotions don't encompass who we really are. They may initially spark within our innate, quick-acting, irrational brains, but they only become full emotions when we allow them into our rational brains. The Spectrum of Conditional Love is natural, but it's learned. We're taught directly and by example that love and hate depend on how we perceive others—who *they* are.

> I have . . . decided to stick with love,
> for I know that love is ultimately the only answer to mankind's problems. . . .
> I have seen too much hate. . . .
> and I say to myself that hate is too great a burden to bear.
> —Martin Luther King Jr.[24]

Answers in Timeless Wisdom

LOVE HAS MORE pages written and songs sung about it than any other human value. We share endless ideas about love, but they're almost always conditional. We hear about romantic, friendship, and parental love, and we talk about loving our pets or possessions. We frame love in dependent terms: we love someone *because* . . . or we're loved *because* . . . That leaves us wondering, *What happens if those conditions change?*

The Spectrum of Conditional Love consists of contingent emotions, from love to hate, based on how we perceive others. When we love this way, not only is our love constrained, but we're constrained, handcuffed by the dependencies we've created.

The solution is Unconditional Love. It's not dependent or determined by the objects of our love. There's nothing they can do to earn or squander it. Unconditional Love isn't about who *they* are. It's about who *we* are. It insulates us from the Spectrum of Conditional Love. It unburdens us from keeping track of why we love someone (or don't) or spending mental and emotional energy caring about the conditions or limitations of our love.

Because conditional love is what we're used to—maybe all we've ever seen—we might believe it's the only kind of love we can feel or understand. But conditional love isn't absolute. It's a decision rooted in irrational thoughts and cultivated by a lifetime of learning, and it can be unlearned. We can overcome conditional thinking through conscious choice, which we must do repeatedly in our mature, rational brain. We can choose to love unconditionally. With Unconditional Love, we're unchained from contingencies so we don't have to feel dislike or hate. We're not immune to betrayal or disappointment, but we can love, no matter what happens.

The triggers in our limbic system—prejudices, biases, insecurities, or irrational fears—are unique to each of us, shaped by what we've been taught and our environment. Some may be so ingrained that they're impossible to eradicate, but we can learn to recognize them. The first step is awareness. Physical signals often precede consciousness of triggers. We may feel our heart rate increase, muscles tense, or breathing change. Over time, we can identify our triggers. An awareness technique introduced by Michele McDonald in the 1980s is the RAIN method:

- **R**ecognize the trigger
- **A**llow the experience without trying to change it
- **I**nvestigate with curiosity and self-compassion
- **N**onidentification (remember that we're not our thoughts or reactions)[25]

The second step is learning to manage our reactions—creating "a space between stimulus and response."[26] Mindfulness practices can help us learn to make this space. When we feel triggered, taking a conscious breath can provide critical space between the trigger and our reaction. When we notice them—when we become ill at ease or feel pangs of disgust—we must act to smother those sparks before they grow into flames. We must use our thinking brain to realize that hate is evil and irrational, then quench rather than feed it by choosing Unconditional Love.

Hatred that already burns within us, that's grown into our thinking brain, takes more effort to put out. We must actively and thoroughly douse it with Unconditional Love. First, we work to recognize the hate in ourselves—this may require help from others. Then, we drench it with the knowledge that hate is conditional, sparked by some irrational trigger and then allowed or encouraged to grow based on certain characteristics of the hated object. The hate isn't part of us. It depends on us continuing to fuel it with validation. Finally, we decide that who we are isn't conditional, so neither will we love conditionally. We only keep hate from smoldering and potentially reigniting by constantly striving for Unconditional Love. Unconditional Love requires intentional, rational thought and compassionate action. It's a decision—a decision to claim the power over hate and conditionality. That power is Unconditional Love.

* * * * *

In the following pages, I share words from great thinkers who taught, preached, and wrote with passion and depth about Unconditional Love. Many come from bygone times, but their ideas still apply. Today's big questions are the same as yesterday's. Ancient theologians, philosophers, and ethicists were their days' self-help gurus, and their wisdom is timeless. What matters now has always mattered. The solutions come from our core values, which define us.

About twenty-four-hundred years ago, Aristotle explored the nature of love in his monumental work *Nicomachean Ethics*. In it, he declares that Unconditional Love is the foundation of all human virtues. He says we must love others for who they are, not for anything they do. He also stresses that our love must be selfless, not dependent on what we want from others. If we can love in this way, we can live in harmony.[27]

> Love is the cause of unity in all things.
> —Aristotle

Around four hundred years after Aristotle, Paul the Apostle delivered the divine truth that Unconditional Love is the starting point of all that matters and everything we can hope to be:

> If I speak in the tongues of men or of angels, but do not have love,
> I am only a resounding gong or a clanging cymbal.
> If I have the gift of prophecy and can fathom all mysteries and all knowledge,
> and if I have a faith that can move mountains, but do not have love,
> I am nothing.
> If I give all I possess to the poor
> and give over my body to hardship that I may boast, but do not have love,
> I gain nothing.
> —1 Corinthians 13:1–3 (New International Version)

Within the last century, Reinhold Niebuhr, an American theologian and ethicist, discussed the conflict between love and human sinfulness in *The Nature and Destiny of Man*. He recognizes that for love to overcome sin, it must be more than just an emotion. He describes love as a moral principle of acceptance, wisdom, and courage:

- Acceptance is the knowledge that humans are fallible.
- Wisdom is the understanding that Unconditional Love can't be earned.
- Courage is the willingness to give Unconditional Love despite all our failings.

This is a perfect description of Unconditional Love. It recognizes limitations and imperfections but loves anyway.[28]

In his celebrated book *The Art of Loving*, German-American psychologist, sociologist, and philosopher Erich Fromm investigates the true meaning of love and its importance for personal growth and well-being. Although he doesn't identify it as such, he describes Unconditional Love. He argues it isn't just a feeling but requires effort and practice (a conscious choice) and involves respect and care (action). He believes self-love, recognizing our worth and aiming for personal fulfillment, is essential for genuine relationships to flourish—we must love ourselves first. He says love is dynamic and needs continuous attention—we can easily revert to conditional love unless we actively choose unconditionality. Fromm envisions a society based on Unconditional Love. In such a society, he says, we'd focus on cooperation instead of competition and kindness instead of greed.[29]

> If I truly love one person I love all persons, I love the world, I love life.
> If I can say to somebody else, "I love you," I must be able to say,
> "I love in you everybody, I love through you the world,
> I love in you also myself."
>
> —Erich Fromm

Elements of Unconditional Love

History's greatest thinkers repeatedly affirm the significance of Unconditional Love. They proclaim it's the nucleus of our character, with all other values building upon it. They attest it can overcome our weaknesses. To fully understand and live it, we must know its constituent parts: respect, kindness, and compassion.

Respect

Respect is at the heart of human morality and Unconditional Love. It's a fundamental principle that demands we treat all individuals with dignity, regardless of background, position, or beliefs. It means being tolerant of differences and considerate of others' feelings and rights. It means using language that uplifts rather than denigrates. It requires refraining from insults, threats, or violence. Respect compels one to deal with disagreements peacefully, seeking understanding and resolution rather than conflict.[30]

Saint Thomas Aquinas teaches the importance of respect. He believes every person, created in God's image, possesses inherent value and deserves respect. Similarly, eighteenth-century philosopher Immanuel Kant says respect demands treating people as unique treasures, not tools to achieve our goals. In Buddhism, the principle of nonviolence, or ahimsa, is a bedrock ethical value requiring deep respect for and commitment to avoid harming any living being. Confucianism's *ren* (humaneness) tells us to treat others with respect, nurture bonds, and contribute to society's well-being.[31]

Like Unconditional Love, unconditional respect is independent of who others are or what they've done. It can't be earned. We must freely give it to everyone, generously and consistently.

*   *   *   *   *

Mister Rogers' Neighborhood was an influential American children's television series from 1968 to 2001, created and hosted by Fred Rogers. It covered a broad range of topics, including social issues other children's shows avoided.[32]

Dr. François S. Clemmons met Rogers while pursuing graduate music studies at Carnegie Mellon. After hearing him sing spirituals at Third Presbyterian Church on Good Friday in 1968, Rogers was moved to ask Clemmons to be on the show. "Fred came to me and said, 'I have this idea:

You could be a police officer,'" recalled Clemmons, who was surprised by the offer. "I grew up in the ghetto. I did not have a positive opinion of police officers," he said. As a Black man, he wondered why a white man would ask him to play a role Black people feared. He initially turned it down, but Rogers encouraged him: "Franc, people are going to look up to you for singing that way and going around the neighborhood, being a part of the community. That is going to change a lot of people's opinions about policemen." Clemmons agreed.[33]

When Clemmons joined the cast, he became the first African American with a recurring role in a children's TV series. Through 1993, he was featured in ninety-eight episodes. He wasn't just the friendly neighborhood police officer. He became a Grammy-winning singer, performing in over seventy musical and opera roles and founding the Harlem Spiritual Ensemble. Still, he remained faithful to Rogers and the show. "For me, [Rogers] fulfilled the role of mentor, fan, and surrogate father," he said. After Clemmons moved to New York for his opera career, he flew back to film episodes of the show. He shared Rogers's devotion to enriching children's lives.[34]

> We are all one family in the world. Building a community that empowers everyone to attain their full potential through each of us respecting each other's dignity, rights, and responsibilities makes the world a better place to live.
>
> —Pope John Paul II

From his twenty-five years on the show, there was one scene Clemmons (and many others) remembered with fondness and appreciation. When he started on the show, racial tensions were high. Despite the Civil Rights Act of 1964, Black citizens were still not treated as equal members in much of American society. In particular, public recreation remained widely segregated. Like buses and lunch counters, public swimming pools were often places of protest and backlash.[35,36]

In this environment, Rogers performed a simple but profound act in episode 1065, which aired on May 9, 1969. The cast acted as if it was a hot day in the neighborhood. When Mister Rogers encountered Officer

Clemmons, he invited the policeman to join him and cool his feet in a plastic children's wading pool. Clemmons initially declined, saying he didn't have a towel, but Rogers said Clemmons could share his. So while many community pools across the country prevented Blacks from sharing the water with whites, Mister Rogers and Officer Clemmons sat side by side, removed their shoes and socks, rolled up their pant legs, and placed their feet in the same pool. They talked and laughed together. When Clemmons had to go, he used Rogers's towel to dry his feet, and then Rogers used the same towel to dry his own. Their casual intimacy dramatically diverged from the insidious racism that enveloped the nation. Later in life, Clemmons recalled, "It was a definite call to social action on Fred's part. That was his way of speaking about race relations in America." He demonstrated Unconditional Love in the form of personal respect.[37,38]

In Clemmons's last appearance in 1993, they recreated the pool scene from twenty-four years earlier. Clemmons sang "Many Ways to Say I Love You." On this occasion, however, Clemmons didn't just use Rogers's towel. Rogers took the towel and dried Clemmons's feet, a gesture of deep respect, humility, and equality. It was another call for love and unity. Clemmons recounted how Rogers made him feel accepted and valued despite the societal challenges he faced every day. He also said he'd never forget how Rogers wrapped Clemmons's last show. As always, Rogers hung his sweater and said, "You make every day a special day just by being you, and I like you just the way you are." But this time, he looked right at Clemmons. After they wrapped, Clemmons asked him, "Fred, were you talking to me?" Rogers replied, "Yes, I have been talking to you for years, but you heard me today."[39,40,41,42]

Throughout his life, Fred Rogers personified striving for Unconditional Love. His interactions with François Clemmons exemplified unconditional respect, against the norms of his day, as an essential element of Unconditional Love.

* * * * *

Unconditional respect honors the inherent dignity of every person, regardless of their actions or beliefs. By extending this respect to all, even those with whom we disagree, we maintain our values and model a key aspect of Unconditional Love. We sow seeds for greater collaboration, understanding, and positive change in our relationships and communities.

Kindness

Kindness is helping someone or being generous without expecting anything in return. It comes from a genuine desire to meet the needs or ease the suffering of others. Kindness transcends cultural boundaries. It reaches across differences, breaks down barriers, builds bridges, and creates goodwill. It's the rope that binds society together, transforming transactional encounters into positive connections that can lead to lifelong friendships. Acts of kindness improve the lives of others and make our own lives better. Both the giver and receiver feel the warmth that comes from adding positivity to someone's day.

Kindness is central to all religious traditions. The Bible's Golden Rule declares the importance of treating others with the same kindness one wishes to receive: "Do to others as you would have them do to you."[43]

In the Qur'an, the holy book of Islam, Muslims are told to act with kindness toward all as a religious duty and a path to spiritual growth. In Hadith, a record of the words of the founder of Islam, the Prophet Muhammad says, "Accustom yourselves to do good if people do good and not to do wrong (even) if they do evil." This is a rephrasing of the Golden Rule. Prophet Muhammad also says, "Kindness is a mark of faith, and whoever is not kind has no faith."[44]

Buddhism greatly emphasizes kindness. The concept of *mettā*, or loving-kindness, lies at the heart of Buddhist teachings. It involves cultivating boundless love and goodwill toward loved ones, enemies, and strangers. This practice aims to expand our capacity for compassion and foster a harmonious society. Buddhism also highlights self-kindness. Recognizing our own suffering and treating ourselves with kindness is essential on the path to enlightenment.[45]

> My religion is very simple. My religion is kindness.
> —Tenzin Gyatso, the 14th Dalai Lama

Lao Tzu, the Chinese philosopher and founder of Taoism, teaches that kindness is a fundamental virtue. He believes that treating others with kindness creates a more harmonious and interconnected world. Lao Tzu's teachings emphasize acting without self-interest, giving without conditions, and seeing without preference.[46]

> Kindness in words creates confidence.
> Kindness in thinking creates profoundness.
> Kindness in giving creates love.
>
> —Lao Tzu

* * * * *

A young man named Mark was walking home from school one day when he noticed that a boy ahead of him had tripped and dropped all the books he was carrying, along with two sweaters, a baseball bat, a glove, and a small recorder.

Mark knelt and helped the boy pick up the scattered articles. Since they were going the same way, he helped the boy carry part of the burden. As they walked, he discovered the boy's name was Bill, that he loved video games, baseball, and history, and that he was having lots of trouble with his other subjects.

They arrived at Bill's home first, and Mark was invited in for a Coke and to watch some television. The afternoon passed pleasantly with a few laughs and some shared small talk; then Mark went home.

They continued to see each other around school, had lunch together once in a while, then both graduated from junior high school. They ended up in the same high school where they had brief contacts over the years. Finally, the long-awaited senior year came, and three weeks before graduation, Bill asked Mark if they could talk.

Bill reminded Mark of the day years ago when they had first met. "Did you ever wonder why I was carrying so many things home that day?" asked Bill. "You see, I cleaned out my locker because I didn't want to leave a mess for anyone else. I had stored some of my mother's sleeping pills and was going home to commit suicide."

Bill told Mark that he realized he didn't want to die after spending time together talking and laughing. "I would have missed that time with you and many other good times in my life that followed. Mark, I am trying to say that you did a lot more when you picked up those books that day. You saved my life."[47]

* * * * *

Simple acts of kindness can yield overwhelming results.

Like unconditional respect, giving unconditional kindness to others doesn't depend on whether or not they deserve it. None of us deserves it. It's freely given as an essential element of Unconditional Love. We constantly encounter opportunities to practice unconditional kindness. The smallest acts count—a spontaneous compliment, door held open, or wave for someone to go ahead in line. When we intentionally incorporate kindness into our interactions, our capacity for love expands, enriching our life and the lives of those around us.

> There are three ways to ultimate success:
> The first way is to be kind.
> The second way is to be kind.
> The third way is to be kind.
> —Fred Rogers, "Mister Rogers"

Compassion

Compassion is a vital part of striving for Unconditional Love. The word *compassion*, derived from Latin, means "to suffer together with," reminding us that all people suffer, and one of our human responsibilities is to share and try to relieve some of that suffering. Psychological researchers have identified three main components of compassion: noticing, feeling, and responding. Noticing is recognizing another's pain. Feeling is an emotional reaction to adopting the person's perspective. Responding is desiring to ease the person's pain and often acting on that desire. Compassion goes beyond wishing the best for others or feeling their emotions; it's wanting to alleviate their suffering and doing something about it.

In his autobiography *Confessions*, fourth-century Christian theologian Saint Augustine examines the nature of Unconditional Love. He describes a love with immeasurable capacity.

> What does love look like? It has the hands to help others.
> It has the feet to hasten to the poor and needy.
> It has eyes to see misery and want.
> It has the ears to hear the sighs and sorrows of men.
> That is what love looks like.
>
> —Saint Augustine

Saint Augustine's description alludes to noticing, feeling, and responding, so we know he's speaking of compassion. The Prophet Muhammad also encourages compassion, extolling it as a mark of strong faith and urging believers to demonstrate it in their actions.

> He is not a believer whose stomach is filled
> while the neighbor to his side goes hungry.
> —Prophet Muhammad, Hadith

The inevitability of human suffering is a fundamental tenet of Buddhism. Just as essential is our response: compassion is the combination of spontaneous emotion and conscious decision that leads to the selfless intention to free others from suffering.[48] Buddhism teaches that because everyone experiences suffering, we should have compassion toward all. Thích Nhất Hạnh, a prominent Vietnamese Buddhist monk, urges us to translate compassion into action, saying, "Compassion is a verb." Tenzin Gyatso, the current Dalai Lama (spiritual leader of the Gelug school of Tibetan Buddhism), is renowned for his teachings on compassion. He defines it as "an openness to the suffering of others with a commitment to relieve it."[49] He says compassion is necessary for humanity's survival.

> If you want others to be happy, practice compassion.
> If you want to be happy, practice compassion.
> —Tenzin Gyatso, the 14th Dalai Lama[50]

Practicing compassion can be emotionally demanding, especially when confronted with the overwhelming suffering in our world. We must balance our compassion for others with self-compassion. Taking care of our emotional well-being isn't selfish but necessary to be able to help others. We must prioritize moments of rest and renewal, knowing that our capacity for compassion grows stronger with self-care.

Like the other elements of Unconditional Love, unconditional compassion isn't contingent on the character or conduct of others. We're moved to act, whether sister or stranger, without hesitation or limitation. When we notice someone in pain, feel with them, and respond with care and tangible support, we embody Unconditional Love. Through consistent compassion, we strengthen our shared humanity, contribute to a more caring community, and experience expanded personal fulfillment.

*　*　*　*　*

In December 1938, a young British stockbroker named Nicholas Winton planned to travel to Switzerland for a ski vacation. However, a friend asked him to visit Czechoslovakia instead. Winton's friend arranged for him to visit refugee camps filled with Jews and political opponents of the Nazi party. People across Europe had been alarmed by violence against Jewish communities in Germany and Austria during the Kristallnacht riots the month before. Kristallnacht, or the Night of Broken Glass, was a pogrom against Jews carried out by Nazis when shards of broken glass littered the streets from the destruction of more than two-hundred-fifty synagogues and seven thousand businesses, and thirty thousand Jewish men were arrested and incarcerated in concentration camps. Everyone suspected the Germans would soon invade and occupy Czechoslovakia and the rest of Europe.[51]

At the camps, Winton saw the desperation of families seeking to flee the country, or at least get their children out, before the Nazis invaded. He sympathized with them—he wanted them to escape and live in peace. More than that, he had empathy for the plight of the children—he felt deep emotion, almost sharing the families' burden. Further, he had compassion—he decided to act to try to reduce their suffering. He learned of efforts by agencies in Britain to rescue German and Austrian Jewish children called Kindertransport. He summoned volunteers who, in cooperation with the British Committee for Refugees from Czechoslovakia, organized a similar rescue operation for children from Czechoslovakia.[52]

Winton and the others worked tirelessly to arrange safe passage for the children. They negotiated with governments, found British foster homes, and secured travel documents. Winton raised money for the children's transport and a financial guarantee demanded by the British government for each child's eventual return home. By day, Winton worked at the stock exchange, but he devoted his afternoons and evenings to the rescue efforts.[53]

The first transport left Prague by plane for London on March 14, 1939, one day before the Germans occupied Czechoslovakia. After the Germans established a protectorate in Bohemia and Moravia, Winton's group organized seven more transports. They left Prague by rail, traveled across Germany to the Atlantic coast, continued by ship across the English Channel to Britain, and finished by train to London. The last trainload of children left Prague on August 2, 1939. Rescue activities ceased when Germany invaded Poland, and Britain declared war on Germany in early September 1939. In all, the Czechoslovakian Kindertransport saved 669 children.[54]

Winton's group's efforts required significant personal sacrifice. They took time off work, spent their own money, and faced numerous bureaucratic obstacles in addition to constantly risking discovery by the German army. Despite these challenges, they were determined to save as many children as possible. Their selfless actions demonstrated profound courage and compassion—Unconditional Love in action.[55,56,57]

> Not all of us can do great things.
> But we can do small things with great love.
> —Mary Teresa Bojaxhiu, "Mother Teresa"

*   *   *   *   *

Perhaps no one ever spoke with more passion or immediacy than Dr. Martin Luther King Jr. He envisioned a harmonious "beloved community" where mutual respect, understanding, and cooperation thrive. Even from the front lines of the civil rights battle, he believed we should dedicate ourselves to shaping a world where love triumphs over the forces of hate. In his Nobel Prize acceptance speech in 1964, Dr. King said, "I believe that unarmed truth and unconditional love will have the final word."[58]

At a 1966 Convocation at Illinois Wesleyan University, Dr. King said, "*Agape* is understanding, creative, redemptive goodwill for all men. It is an overflowing love which seeks nothing in return. Theologians would say that it's the love of God operating in the human heart."[59]

King's blueprint for a just and compassionate world is that Unconditional Love isn't confined to heaven but is an earthly objective in our daily lives. We accept our differences because we love unconditionally.

Unconditional Love unfetters us from the Spectrum of Conditional Love. It releases us from evaluating everyone's behavior in every situation to decide how or what to feel about them. It liberates us from the pain, drama, and uncertainty of conditionality. We can be free and fearless, knowing that respect, kindness, and compassion don't depend on external factors. We can rest in the constancy of Unconditional Love.

How to Live It

UNCONDITIONAL LOVE DOESN'T come naturally. We have to train ourselves to make love our first thought rather than mistrust or fear. When we do, we're freed from conditionality. We stop dissecting people's actions to decide how we feel about them. We're at peace because Unconditional Love depends only on who we are—nothing else.

*　*　*　*　*

In 1996, Bud Welch's life was shattered when his daughter Julie, only twenty-three years old, was killed in the Oklahoma City bombing. Timothy McVeigh was convicted of domestic terrorism for the attack that claimed 168 lives, including Julie's. Consumed by grief and anger, Welch initially supported McVeigh's execution, believing it would bring closure. However, as time passed, he realized that hate was eating away at him, the same feelings that had driven McVeigh to commit his heinous act. Welch made the difficult decision to reach out to McVeigh's father with compassion instead of mistrust and disgust.[60]

When they met, Welch saw in Bill McVeigh another father who was suffering. He realized Bill was as much a victim of his son's actions as anyone else. Instead of anger, Welch offered empathy and friendship, a decision that profoundly impacted both men. For Welch, connecting with Bill helped him navigate his grief and inspired him to advocate against the death penalty, arguing that it perpetuates a cycle of violence without providing real healing. For Bill, Welch's forgiveness and friendship offered a lifeline during deep personal turmoil, helping him cope with guilt and shame over his son's actions.[61] This unlikely friendship demonstrates how choosing love over hate, even in the face of unimaginable loss, can lead to personal growth and positive change.

Love is the only force capable of transforming an enemy into a friend.
—Martin Luther King Jr.

* * * * *

This section explains how to strive for Unconditional Love personally, in relationships, as parents, and in professional environments. By interacting with respect, kindness, and compassion in our roles as friends, colleagues, and parents, we can build stronger, more meaningful connections. Integrating love into every aspect of our lives fosters thriving, supportive environments where everyone feels seen, appreciated, and empowered.

Personal

Loving ourselves is vital to mental and emotional well-being. One study found that long periods without self-love can shrink part of the brain that controls movement, memory, and emotions, leading to problems with motor and cognitive function.[62] Too many of us undervalue our unique qualities. Self-love encompasses self-compassion, self-acceptance, self-care, and self-confidence, all keys to a fulfilling life.

Practicing self-compassion is crucial. When we face challenges or make mistakes, self-compassion means acknowledging our feelings, letting go of regrets, and reminding ourselves that we don't need to be perfect to be loved. It's essential to challenge negative thoughts with positive self-affirmations. When that isn't enough, we should seek support from friends, family, or a therapist to remind us of our worth.[63]

Positive affirmations promote self-acceptance. They remind us of our value and boost self-esteem. Practicing gratitude improves our self-image. Thinking about what we're thankful for helps us appreciate what we have and who we are. Mindfulness, being present in the moment, improves self-awareness and self-acceptance.[64] When we respect ourselves, others respect us.

Our entire life . . . consists ultimately in accepting ourselves as we are.
—Jean Anouilh

Self-care involves caring for our physical, emotional, and mental health through exercise, therapy, meditation, hobbies, reading, relaxing, a balanced diet, and adequate sleep. Setting healthy boundaries in relationships and commitments is also crucial—saying no without guilt is essential for personal well-being.[65]

Embracing opportunities for learning, growth, and self-improvement boosts self-confidence. Setting achievable goals nurtures our belief in our abilities, and celebrating small and large achievements reinforces that confidence.[66]

Self-love is courageous. Our culture, which ties personal value to external metrics like appearance, social status, and productivity, causes comparative thinking. We connect self-worth to achievements or others' approval. Social media and constant connectivity make it easier than ever to compare ourselves to others. Breaking free from this mindset requires courage, conscious effort, and practice. Accepting our perceived flaws and mistakes is most challenging. We hold on to current imperfections or past failures as evidence that we don't deserve acceptance or love.

Unconditional Love means we can give ourselves a break. It means flaws and failures don't matter—we're all inherently valuable and deserving of love, especially self-love. If we're used to devaluing ourselves, self-love can feel awkward. We may not know where to start. We can start by finding one thing we appreciate about ourselves each day. We acknowledge there will always be areas to improve—it's true of everyone—but we recognize incremental progress and delight in it. Over time, we'll cultivate a strong, stable sense of self-love.

*   *   *   *   *

I developed self-confidence at an early age. Likely the result of being the firstborn of a firstborn—the first child and grandchild on my father's side—in a doting, supportive family, I remember feeling like I could do most things I set my mind to. (I recognize it isn't bestowed on everyone, and I didn't do anything to earn it, so I've always appreciated this early self-confidence as the gift it surely is.) However, as a teenager, I became painfully aware that self-confidence is not the same as self-acceptance or self-love. Just because I was confident in my abilities to learn and achieve goals didn't mean I had a strong, positive self-image or saw worth in myself for who I was. Like many, I've had my share of struggles with self-image. As an adult, I've even experienced periods of genuine depression when self-love seemed very far from possible. It's only been during middle age—and due, in no small part, to writing this book—that I've grasped that the inherent worth of all people includes myself (self-acceptance) and understood that self-acceptance is a necessary part of self-love. Of course, this knowledge won't preclude future self-worth struggles, but at least I'll have a solid basis for recovery.

Relational

Unconditional Love makes it easier for us to deal with other people. When our love is conditional and we encounter strangers or people with differences from us, we naturally slide down the spectrum because we don't know what they can give us to justify our love. When we love unconditionally, we don't have to think about it; we love them simply because they're human, regardless of their beliefs or characteristics or whether they can do anything for us.

> The greatest compliment that was ever paid me
> was when one asked me what I thought, and attended to my answer.
> —Henry David Thoreau

Unconditional Love engages respect, kindness, and compassion in our relationships. Relationships built on Unconditional Love share power. Neither person gets everything they want, but both are equally rewarded. One of the most sincere signs of respect is listening to what others say. Active listening deepens our connections and understanding. We communicate openly and without defensiveness, with both people expressing their feelings while considering the other's viewpoint. We look past minor arguments and focus on the bigger picture, avoiding actions that could harm or undermine others. Respect means encouraging and supporting each other's growth. Kindness requires patience and forgiveness when others make mistakes. We must recognize that disagreements and blunders are part of all relationships. We show kindness through care and support, but we must remember that Unconditional Love expects nothing in return. We encourage and uplift each other. Compassion helps us understand each other's feelings and circumstances without judgment. We offer support during difficult times, genuinely trying to meet each other's needs without keeping score.[67]

Striving for Unconditional Love in our relationships can be a learning process. We'll likely experience frustration and misunderstandings, but growth often involves discomfort. We must be patient with ourselves and our loved ones, learn from problems, and appreciate progress. When we try to give respect, kindness, and compassion unconditionally, we become the best friend, partner, spouse, and teammate we can be.

As a Parent

I started this chapter with a story about parental love because it's the closest I've experienced to Unconditional Love and the closest any of us will experience in our lifetimes. Before becoming parents, we can't fully grasp it; once we do, we can't forget it. The problem is that although we may never forget the feeling, we forget that Unconditional Love is both feeling and function. It requires both emotion and exertion. It can't stay in our hearts, or it withers and dies there. We must share it frequently and freely.

Our love for our children must be unbroken and unqualified. It shouldn't hinge on their actions or achievements. We can't fully explain this Unconditional Love to our children. They can only grasp it if they become parents themselves. Our task is to live it, to embody it.

We show love to our children by creating an environment where they feel cherished and secure. We prove love is an action by our behaviors toward, for, and around them. We convey it through physical affection like hugs, kisses, and cuddles, through touch that is always respectful, kind, and compassionate, even in discipline. Most importantly, we tell them that we love them—often. Our words should be positive and affirming, making it clear that we love them as they are.

* * * * *

I'm lucky to have a spouse who enhances my efforts—and, when I fall short, overcomes my failures—to create a home environment where our children feel cherished, valued, and secure. Due mainly to my wife's loving nature (and my best intentions), our kids know they can always be open, vulnerable, and comfortable—they can be themselves—at home. Every evening, they recount the day's events to Beth. If they're happy, she joyously shares their happiness. If they're angry, she listens without judgment. They know they'll receive corrective feedback if needed, yet they also know they're loved unconditionally, so they can share their faults without losing our love. That unwavering confidence in our love is the greatest gift we can give them.

* * * * *

Love doesn't have a pattern, but it does have a purpose. Its aim isn't to change those we love but to give them what they need to flourish. Its object isn't to dictate our loved ones' destinies but to support them as they shape their own. We don't show them the way but help them find their path, even if it differs from the one we'd choose for them.

Love is the highest form of communication. It's the best way to develop our children's humanity. Teaching love should be a cornerstone of our kids' early education, and everything else should build on it. We teach love through quality time, actively engaging in our children's lives. They feel loved when we prioritize spending time with them. In their early years, when we're with them constantly, it's not just about the quantity of time but the quality. Beyond the routines of feeding and diaper changes, it's crucial to play for its own sake. (This applies to the rest of their lives too.) Time gets more fragmented as they grow, but we can still carve out meaningful moments. Activities like reading together—whether life lessons or pure enjoyment, at bedtime or in a park—are invaluable. Singing together, even if just in the car, and establishing family traditions—tied to holidays or everyday moments like family dinners—strengthen our bonds. Laughter, shared as often as possible, is another powerful expression of love.

> To the world, you may be one person,
> but to one person, you may be the world.
> —Theodor Seuss Geisel, "Dr. Seuss"

We should also cry together, to demonstrate that feeling and expressing emotions is healthy and to create a safe environment where feelings are openly shared and accepted. We should discuss positive and negative emotions, helping our children understand their significance and finding resolutions where possible. Sharing our feelings builds trust and connection while showing empathy for their concerns teaches them to consider others' perspectives. We must apologize when we make mistakes—and we will—often. We must forgive when they make mistakes—and they will—often. While nothing they do can make us stop loving them, they must learn that asking for and offering forgiveness is rooted in love. Finally, we model love by extending it to others. We show our children what love looks like through our relationships with partners, family, and friends, offering them a broader understanding of love's many forms.

Trying to parent with Unconditional Love but knowing we'll fall short can be dispiriting. We fear our faults will screw our children up. No parent is perfect, and it's not about perfection but presence. We all have days when we're stretched thin and don't meet our own expectations. When we make mistakes, we apologize and use them as opportunities to model humility and growth. What matters most is consistent effort to create a loving environment. Our children will remember the accepting, supportive environment we provide. Our aim should be to instill in them the belief that by striving for Unconditional Love, they can reach their highest potential.

*   *   *   *   *

During Nicolae Ceaușescu's leadership of Romania from the mid-1960s to the late 1980s, the totalitarian regime encouraged high birth rates without providing economic support, resulting in many children being abandoned in orphanages. The government neglected and mismanaged these orphanages, leading to decades of chronic underfunding, corruption, malnutrition, and a lack of medical care. The worst damage was psychological, as the children were denied basic human contact, even when they cried. Once removed from the orphanages, the children were often severely emotionally underdeveloped. Many struggled after adoption, experiencing various neurological, learning, and adaptive problems.[68] Their brains had been altered. They couldn't trust other humans. They didn't comprehend love.

> Until he was seven, Daniel Solomon slept sitting up. . . . [He] didn't have another option. He lived in a crib in an orphanage in Romania with another child. . . . Heidi Solomon got a magazine in the mail from the adoption agency . . . "I don't really know how . . . but I remember telling my husband, 'I think this is our son.'" . . .
>
> [Heidi said,] "His birthday is in March, and . . . [Daniel] said, 'They don't have March in Romania, because I never had a birthday before.'" . . . Daniel had never confronted the idea that he had . . . actual parents, people who could have, had they elected to, provided a birthday at some point before his eighth year of life. This whole concept deeply disturbed him, and even though Heidi did her best to explain the difference between biological and adoptive families, it seems that Daniel didn't get it, because he walked away from that conversation fundamentally confused about his relationship to Heidi and Rick. "I started thinking that they were my biological parents," [Daniel said]. "And I was really mad at them that they put me there for seven and a half years. . . . I guess that's when all hell broke loose." . . .
>
> Daniel conceived a powerful hatred of his parents, a deep anger that he couldn't shake even after the difference between biological and adoptive parents had been explained again and again and his actual relationship to Heidi and Rick became clear. . . . His tantrums

became tornados of rage: seven-, eight-hour marathons where he would throw literally anything he could get his hands on. . . .

"There was a time where I remember my dad had to hire this person to come to our house because my mom didn't feel safe with me in the house," [Daniel says]. . . . But Heidi wouldn't give up on Daniel. Changing her son became a kind of singular focus, an idea that obscured all other considerations. "One time, a case manager sat down and said, 'This is what's I think's gonna happen: Daniel's gonna hurt you, you're gonna be in the hospital, he'll be in juvenile detention, and your husband's gonna leave you.'" . . . One day after school, when Heidi was busy making a snack for Daniel in the kitchen, he grabbed a knife from the counter and held it to Heidi's throat. . . . [The narrator asks,] "How do you love somebody who is homicidal?" "*Because he was my son!*" [Heidi exclaims]" . . .

When Heidi heard about a doctor in Virginia who appeared to have had some success with a highly intensive program . . . , she leapt at the opportunity. . . . At first, Daniel hated the treatment, and . . . his behavior actually deteriorated. But then something happened. "I think it was around the third week that . . . something changed." Daniel says he actually came to understand, maybe for the first time, that his mother loved him. . . .

After eight weeks, Daniel was cured of his violent behavior. It was gone, done. No more tantrums, no more throwing, no more threats. . . . The rabbi at their synagogue called Heidi to tell her that Daniel had won . . . the valedictorian of the confirmation class. . . . One element of the award is that the winner gets to make a speech. . . . Daniel told Heidi and Rick that he wanted them to think of his speech as a gift. . . . [Daniel said,] "I'd like to thank two people: my mom and dad. The reason I'm here today, and the kind of person I am today, is because of you. . . . You guys are both amazing. I love you very much." It was, Heidi says, without doubt, the most spectacular moment of her life.[69]

The story of the Solomons is a powerful example of the transformative nature of Unconditional Love. By embodying the essence of Unconditional Love as adoptive parents, Heidi and Rick helped Daniel overcome profound emotional scars and learn how to love.

At Work

"Love at work" sounds inappropriate, but Unconditional Love is essential in the workplace. Fundamentally, business is about people. When people thrive, a business thrives. People need to feel needed. At work, that's conveyed as appreciation and respect, which are most readily accepted when given unconditionally. Our colleagues want to feel that they matter beyond their job performance. They matter for who they are.

Although passionate love at the office is a no-no, we can demonstrate Unconditional Love by knowing and caring for our coworkers through good times and bad. We all deserve jobs that fulfill us mentally and emotionally.

Respect begins with showing interest in colleagues as people. We give them our full attention. When speaking to them, we put down the phone or stop typing and make eye contact. Patient listening is among the least practiced but most appreciated ways to love our coworkers. Listening that acknowledges issues and emotions conveys respect and builds trust.[70] Respect also means treating everyone with dignity, regardless of background or beliefs. We recognize associates' work and thank them for their contributions. We build trust, security, and belonging by respecting boundaries. Precise, polite communication helps maintain harmony by preventing misunderstandings and addressing conflicts calmly and professionally.

> The deepest hunger of the human soul
> is to be recognized, valued, appreciated, and understood.
> —Stephen R. Covey

We show kindness by helping colleagues without expecting anything in return. Small yet impactful actions, like speaking encouragement, sharing resources, or bringing in a treat, foster a supportive environment. We also demonstrate kindness by noticing when a coworker struggles with personal or professional challenges and offering help without waiting to be asked. Kindness includes flexibility to accommodate personal needs, like adjusting deadlines or work arrangements, to support a colleague's work-life balance. For kindness to be unconditional, we forgive team-mates when they've wronged us and continue to care for them.[71]

*　*　*　*　*

After my team lost the last HLS contract opportunity with NASA, I was despondent. I knew the coming weeks would be tough—finishing contract requirements amid the gloom of our defeat, watching many out-standing colleagues depart, and finding new projects for remaining team members, including myself. I didn't look forward to going to work. One of those days, I received a call from a senior team member who had been CEO of a major aerospace company but had come out of semiretirement to join our team. He said, "I hoped we'd win because of your leadership and hard work on this project . . . We all wanted to win for different reasons, but one reason I wanted to win was so you'd be rewarded for your leadership effort. I want to thank you for that." His call didn't fix the problem. We still lost, and it still hurt. Yet, despite being hurt by the loss himself, the love he showed by thinking of me and calling to share a kind word significantly impacted my mood. I realized that the respect, kindness, and compassion our team shared was more important than the contract.

*　*　*　*　*

While sympathy (thinking kind thoughts) and empathy (sharing emotions) are important, compassion combines thoughts, feelings, and actions. Compassion at work means understanding our coworkers' pains and trying to help relieve them. It means offering emotional support during tough times and following up afterward.[72]

> Love is an active power in man; a power which breaks through the walls
> which separate man from his fellow men, which unites him with others;
> love makes him overcome the sense of isolation and separateness,
> yet it permits him to be himself, to retain his integrity.
> In love, the paradox occurs that two beings become one and yet remain two.
> —Erich Fromm

We must avoid making assumptions or judgments and try to see from others' points of view. When we find others struggling, we must go beyond feeling *for* them (sympathy) and feeling *with* them (empathy); we must ask how we can help. This doesn't mean we have to fix their problems—in most cases, we won't be able. Instead, we seek to alleviate their pain in large or small ways.[73] That's compassion at work . . . at work.

In summary, we all can cultivate compassionate cultures at work. We can show interest, pay attention, and use facial and body language, thoughts, and words to demonstrate care. If a person or situation challenges our ability to be compassionate, it's essential to show love anyway. As some say, fake it till you make it. The good news is that research shows when we express emotions, even if they aren't initially genuine, we eventually begin to feel them. Emotions are contagious—when we transmit compassion, it will be received and multiplied, creating a compassionate culture.[74]

Fostering an environment of Unconditional Love at work can be challenging. It's easy to be in work mode or mentally separate our professional from personal lives. Yet, we need love as much in the workplace as anywhere. For many, the most comfortable place to start is respect—extend respect that's untethered to conditions. Every colleague in every situation deserves unconditional respect. Then advance to unconditional kindness, then compassion. Each tiny act of respect, kindness, and compassion amplifies our professional growth and personal fulfillment, inspires others to be their best, and over time, can accumulate to transform the culture.

As a Leader

Leading isn't about telling others what to do. That approach typically fails. Influential leadership requires connection, commitment, and compassion. As leaders, we show that job performance isn't the only thing that matters. We recognize our colleagues are imperfect, just like us. We understand they have lives outside of work and sometimes encounter issues that interfere with their jobs. We can show Unconditional Love for those we lead without sacrificing business goals. Leadership with love seeks to deliver safety, care, trust, and loyalty. It fosters an environment conducive to thriving. Teammates who feel loved are happy and connected with our vision, values, and messages. In short, Unconditional Love is the key to successful leadership.[75]

In addition to the ways we love relationally and as coworkers, there are several important ways to exhibit Unconditional Love as leaders:

- **Ask:** Inquire how others are doing.
- **Listen:** Give attention with genuine concern, promoting collaboration and innovation.
- **Communicate:** Foster a safe environment for open communication.
- **Know:** Find out who they are and care about them.
- **Regard:** Recognize all as unique individuals and accept them as they are.
- **Appreciate:** Privately—and sometimes publicly—acknowledge others' efforts.
- **Encourage:** Find out what's important to them. Look for ways to help them achieve their goals and offer kind words when they encounter challenges.
- **Support:** Having done the things above, we'll know when they're stressed or troubled; help generously and appropriately.
- **Train:** Insist on excellence, but make expectations clear and instruct when necessary. Give frequent, constructive, and caring feedback. Realize that shortfalls happen; steer them toward success; don't condemn.
- **Be flexible:** Create firm boundaries but be sensitive to others' needs.
- **Celebrate:** Share successes. Reward accomplishments. Recognize important events in the lives of team members.[76]

Every member contributes to team culture, but it starts with the leader. Leaders have the most influence because they typically make and enforce the rules. We can create compassionate cultures by including *care* or *love* in our organizations' value statements and ensuring that team policies reflect and nurture compassionate cultures. We must acknowledge that others watch us for examples of desired behavior.[77]

> When people respect you as a person, they admire you.
> When they respect you as a friend, they love you.
> When they respect you as a leader, they follow you.
> —John C. Maxwell

For leaders, clear communication is paramount to respect. We must be honest, consistent, and open, sharing successes and challenges. We respect others by listening and considering their input. It's essential that we recognize team members' contributions by acknowledging their efforts publicly, when possible, and demonstrate trust in their judgment and abilities by delegating tasks that align with their strengths and offer meaningful authority. We encourage their growth and avoid micromanagement. We provide timely, supportive feedback to help them improve without undermining their confidence. To respect the team, we respect their time by being punctual and ensuring our meetings are focused and efficient.

Conditionality often seems to be part of team culture. If someone isn't cutting it or makes many mistakes, we typically can't keep them around and just love them. We have to act in the best interests of the person and the team, which may mean letting the person go. Unconditional Love dictates that leaders are as generous, forgiving, and understanding as possible. It doesn't mean we retain underperforming members to the team's long-term detriment, but we consider their feelings and do all we can to help them find places where they can thrive. Leaders show kindness through approachability, creating an environment where teammates feel comfortable sharing their thoughts and concerns. We must use positive, encouraging language and, in all cases, refrain from insults, anger, or threats. As kind leaders, we prioritize the well-being of our team, supporting their need for a healthy balance between their professional and personal lives. We check in on their families and their mental health. In every way we can, we aim to meet the needs of our team members and create a work environment where everyone feels cared for.

As compassionate leaders, we actively seek our team's well-being beyond their productivity. It's our responsibility to know our team's morale and emotions as much as possible. Leading with compassion means wanting to minimize their difficulties—not only thinking about it but doing whatever we can. We consider the impacts of our decisions on our team, putting ourselves in their shoes to grasp how changes might affect them personally and professionally. We recognize that all members will occasionally experience challenges, and we rally the team to offer support during those times. As individuals, we listen to understand and offer help or, if necessary, we simply listen. When conflicts arise, we address them with thorough consideration. We focus on finding root causes and resolving issues fairly. By taking these steps, we can demonstrate our commitment to compassionate leadership.

Leading with love can feel counterintuitive in a results-driven world, but it's a leader's responsibility to foster a respectful, kind, compassionate environment. We must model the mindset and behaviors we want in our teams. It may require breaking old patterns and starting anew. The key is striving for the ideal every day. We can start with one new practice, such as actively listening or recognizing someone's effort. If we slip into micromanagement or criticism, we acknowledge our mistake and gently redirect ourselves. Each interaction is an opportunity to strive for Unconditional Love. Gradually, our actions will inspire and empower our teams to do their best individually and collaboratively and achieve their highest potential.

> Caring about the individual works
> because it's a paradigm focused on people, not things;
> it's focused on relationships, not schedules;
> it's focused on effectiveness, not efficiency;
> it's focused on personal leadership, not resource management.
> —Stephen R. Covey

Chapter Summary

Unconditional Love is the foundation of a life lived well. By loving others simply because they're human, without expectation or judgment, we free ourselves from transactional, conditional love that can quickly change to hate. Unconditional Love empowers us to release resentment, overcome fear, and affirm the inherent worth in every person.

Pursuing Unconditional Love can transform us, but it requires commitment and courage. It calls us to extend unquestioning respect, kindness, and compassion to others. No matter who they are, where they're from, what they look or sound like, or even what they think of us, we love them. We must also respect, be kind, and have compassion for ourselves, as self-love is the wellspring from which our capacity to love others flows.

When we work to embody Unconditional Love in our thoughts, words, and actions, it sets us apart. It creates new possibilities for how we live, giving us advantages over others and our former selves. When we strive for Unconditional Love, it opens us to the other Unconditionals and pushes us toward our best selves. Unconditional Love is a superpower that can be ours if we're willing to work for it.

Encouragement and Questions for the Reader

You may feel overwhelmed by the pressure to exemplify Unconditional Love. You may be so used to conditionality that you struggle to improve. Personal growth isn't an end but an eternal expedition. You can't reach the ideal—no one can—but you get better as you pursue it. Improvement is always incremental. Every decision to love yourself, not for what you've done or will do but who you are, builds you up. Every choice to love others, not for what they've done or can offer but because they're human, contributes to a respectful, kind, compassionate world. Choosing Unconditional Love is the most important decision you can make.

The following are questions to ask yourself. As you seek to cultivate greater love, use them to help you choose one area where you can strive for unconditionality.

- When you encounter someone with opposing views, do you extend them basic human kindness? What would it look like to treat them with Unconditional Love?
- Do you accept and love yourself unconditionally or place limits on your self-love based on external expectations or perceived flaws? What can you do to develop self-compassion?
- In your relationships, do you offer respect, kindness, and compassion freely, or is your love based on others' actions? What steps can you take to love more unconditionally?
- As a parent, do you give your children affection and support regardless of their achievements or mistakes? How can you model Unconditional Love in your words and deeds each day?
- Do you genuinely care about your work colleagues as human beings, or do you value them based on their productivity or what they can do for you? What can you do each day to contribute to an unconditionally compassionate workplace culture?
- In positions of leadership, do you treat all team members with equal respect and understanding or play favorites? How can you lead with more kindness and compassion?
- What's one daily practice you can start today in pursuit of Unconditional Love as a lifelong commitment and source of profound fulfillment?

CHAPTER II

UNCONDITIONAL GRATITUDE

It is not joy that makes us grateful, it is gratitude that makes us joyful.
—David Steindl-Rast

What It Is

GRATITUDE IS VERSATILE. Like love, it's an emotion and an action. It's something we feel and show to others. We receive it, and we give it away. We experience it alone, and we share it.

Gratitude is a mix of contentment and thankfulness. It's a happy appreciation for people, experiences, nature, achievements, and personal qualities.

Top researchers on gratitude have defined it as a two-step process: 1) "recognizing that one has obtained a positive outcome," and 2) "recognizing that there is an external source for this positive outcome."[1] However, this definition misses other important factors. People also feel gratitude toward God, fate, or nature, which are external but less tangible. Most importantly, deep, lasting gratitude can exist independently without a clear cause.

Typically, we experience gratitude because of something pleasant that's happened or something we've received. That's conditional gratitude. Unconditional Gratitude is also positive, but it's not necessarily in response to anything specific. It's independent and absolute, with no assumptions or expectations. It's a way of being.

Gratitude involves recognizing and acknowledging kindness, support, and positive experiences received from others and appreciation for other good things. In the Bible Belt, where I'm from, we often refer to a good thing that happens as a blessing. A blessing is a gift, benefit, or favorable circumstance that improves our situation or well-being. A simple example of a blessing is good health.

> Gratitude is an antidote to negative emotions,
> a neutralizer of envy, hostility, worry, and irritation.
> It is savoring; it is not taking things for granted; it is present-oriented.
> —Sonja Lyubomirsky

What makes Unconditional Gratitude a fundamental value is that it directs our focus to the positive aspects of our lives. It doesn't dwell on what's wrong; it appreciates what's right. It changes our perspective from glass half empty, beyond glass half full, to an overflowing cup. We can release hollow desires, bitterness, and resentment. It turns strangers into friends and acquaintances into family. It nourishes our souls.

Unconditional Gratitude is particularly powerful when applied indiscriminately—for big events and small, for what we have and don't have, for people in our lives and those who aren't. We live in the moment but appreciate our full lives—past, present, and future. Unconditional Gratitude is experiencing life as a blessing.

Chapter 1 introduces the first principle of The Unconditionals and its corollary: "I am, therefore I am loved." It means love isn't contingent on anything except being alive. Similarly, Unconditional Gratitude depends on nothing; we're grateful simply for being alive. So the second principle is "I am, therefore I have gratitude."

Like Unconditional Love, this is easier said than done. We tend to label people, things, events, and ourselves as good or bad, usually based on how they affect our current desires. Unconditional Gratitude asks us to avoid labels and appreciate everything as it was, is, and will be. This doesn't mean giving up goals, ignoring challenges, or not trying to prevent bad things from happening. It means seeing whatever happens as part of life and accepting both good and bad as chances for learning and growth.[2]

* * * * *

In March 2011, my mother died unexpectedly, and the circumstances were hard to understand. My family grieved and asked why a lot because of the suddenness and lack of closure. The abrupt void felt like only sorrow could fill it. Neither then nor since has my family understood why. I believe there's no rationale. What enabled me, and all of us, to escape grief's grip was gratitude. I'm grateful for the thirty-eight-plus years I had a loving birth mother. I appreciate our many wonderful times together. I can feel gratitude for some of what has come from her death—getting closer to family, learning to express emotions more fully, and understanding others' grief like never before. I've come to realize that gratitude is when memories are kept in our hearts instead of our heads.

* * * * *

Gratitude is not only the greatest of virtues but the parent of all others.
—Marcus Tullius Cicero

I put Unconditional Gratitude in this part of the book for several reasons. First, cultivating Unconditional Gratitude can profoundly impact our mental, emotional, and physical well-being. Of all the values, it offers the most direct path to happiness. It creates contentment with what we have (reduces materialism), who we are (increases self-esteem), and who we're with (improves relationships), all leading to greater well-being.

Second, Unconditional Gratitude fits well with the book's overall structure. After all-encompassing Unconditional Love, the remaining four Unconditionals are associated with the four core life areas of inside, outside, connection, and action. Gratitude is both a feeling (inside our heads) and a way to interact with the world (outside). It involves relating to others (connection) and requires action to reach its fullest potential. Gratitude is woven through all the core areas of our lives, but it starts and lives inside us.

Third, Unconditional Gratitude is closely connected to Unconditional Love. Gratitude and love are meaningful, powerful, and positive. When combined and unconditional—unrestricted, universal, and complete—they can't be overcome. Unconditional Gratitude for what we have opens our hearts to create space for Unconditional Love. Likewise, Unconditional Love for ourselves and others clears our minds and allows us to give thanks unconditionally.

Where Does Gratitude Come From?

Studies have shown that gratitude is in our brains and DNA. In fact, less sophisticated animals—many mammals, birds, and fish—show behaviors scientists link to gratitude. (Most pet owners have experienced puppy face-licks or kitten leg-rubs after doing something nice for them, which seems like gratitude.) Researchers think gratitude developed—in all animals—from a need to turn strangers into allies who can help us survive. In humans, neuroscientists have found brain areas that light up when we feel and express gratitude, and geneticists have discovered genes that might help us experience it. However, gratitude is still learned in our environment. The point is that gratitude's roots run deep within us.[3]

> There are two kinds of gratitude:
> The sudden kind we feel for what we take;
> the larger kind we feel for what we give.
> —Edwin Arlington Robinson

Elements of Unconditional Gratitude

Thankfulness is the most obvious element of gratitude. It involves noticing and appreciating good things. Saying thanks is simple but essential. Whether felt or expressed, thankfulness is positive and invokes happiness. Having an attitude of gratitude works because thinking about gratitude makes us feel good. Being grateful for what we have naturally brings more positive experiences.

Thankfulness isn't sugarcoating negatives but choosing to focus on positives. We count our blessings instead of our burdens. Thankfulness often leads to wanting to give back. When we're grateful, we notice kindness and generosity from others and want to return it or pass it on. It's easy to forget that we receive much more than we give, but our lives can only become rich with gratitude.

Contentment is another element. With gratitude, we focus on what we have instead of what we don't. We worry less about wants. This makes us think less about material possessions and external validation. We value experiences and relationships more.

Unconditional Gratitude goes further. It's deeper and independent of anything we have or don't have, making it less prone to fading away or degenerating into ingratitude.

Unconditional Gratitude lives in the present. When we practice it, we appreciate what we have now instead of dwelling on past regrets or future worries. We enjoy pleasant moments—a beautiful sunset, a delicious meal, or a heartwarming conversation—fully. It's linked to mindfulness, requiring being present and aware of life's good things. Practicing mindfulness can help us feel and show more gratitude.[4] When we're quiet and present, we notice that small, serene moments give the rest of our busy lives special meaning. Unconditional Gratitude also involves a full life cycle outlook. It lets us appreciate goodness now while seeing the lasting value of positive thoughts, relationships, and experiences. It helps us make sense of our past, gives us peace today, and supports a hopeful vision for tomorrow.

Instead of focusing on what we want but don't have, Unconditional Gratitude centers us on being satisfied with having and being just as we are. It combines optimism, thankfulness, contentment, presence, and perspective into an unbeatable personal trait. When practiced well, it fills our thoughts and shines through our behaviors.

Why It Matters

If you concentrate on finding whatever is good in every situation,
you will discover that your life will suddenly be filled with gratitude,
a feeling that nurtures the soul.
—Rabbi Harold Kushner

JOHN'S LIFE WAS a disaster. He was broke, overweight, on his second divorce, and living in an awful apartment without air conditioning. He was an employer, but he couldn't afford to pay his staff because his clients weren't paying their bills on time—or at all. On New Year's Day, while hiking in the hills around his home, John had an epiphany. He set a goal to write one thank-you note each day for the next year, a total of 365. He wanted to find a reason to be thankful every day. As he started this practice, he realized there were things under his nose to be grateful for that he hadn't noticed.[5]

John Kralik has written, and received, thousands of thank-you notes. In his book *A Simple Act of Gratitude*, he says writing thank-you notes taught him to focus on the good things in life. Having this focus produces positive emotions, but he says writing the notes—and being grateful—is simply the right thing to do. We tend to notice the bad things that happen daily, but what if we focus on one good thing? Kralik thought he had nothing to be thankful for, but he sought and found those things, and expressing gratitude for them changed his outlook and life.[6]

*   *   *   *   *

Cultivating Unconditional Gratitude has many benefits. It boosts mental health by increasing positivity and reducing anxiety. When we feel grateful, our brains release dopamine and serotonin, both of which regulate moods and emotions, helping us feel happy, content, and less stressed.[7] A study conducted at the University of California, Davis, found that people who cultivated gratitude had 23 percent lower bloodstream cortisol (stress hormone) levels, resulting in better mood and more energy.[8] Gratitude has also been shown to alleviate depression symptoms.[9]

It improves our emotional health. Grateful people feel supported socially.[10] Counting blessings improves self-esteem[11,12] A 2003 study discovered that when people counted their blessings by writing positive things, they felt better about their lives and were more optimistic and likely to help others than those who wrote about daily hassles or ordinary events.[13]

Gratitude also improves physical health. Remember the limbic system—the reflexive, irrational part of our brain that acts without thinking? It's also responsible for regulating bodily functions (and we're all glad they're regulated without thinking about them). A series of 2009 magnetic resonance imaging (MRI) studies showed that feelings of gratitude activate the limbic system to reduce blood pressure, improve immune function, balance metabolism and hunger, and help other natural processes work more smoothly.[14] Heart failure patients with greater gratitude reported better sleep quality, less fatigue, and lower cellular inflammation.[15] Chronic pain patients with higher gratitude experienced lower depression and anxiety and better sleep.[16] Increased gratitude led to fewer depression symptoms in patients with chronic arthritis or inflammatory bowel disease.[17] As gratitude calms the mind, it helps the body heal.

Gratitude provides resilience during challenging times by offering perspective and helping us focus on what's going well. It reframes negative experiences, highlights positives, and can help find meaning in adversity, offering hope.[18]

> Countless studies have shown that consistently grateful people
> are more energetic, emotionally intelligent, forgiving,
> and less likely to be depressed, anxious, or lonely.
> —Shawn Achor[19]

*   *   *   *   *

When my mother died suddenly, two recurring thoughts devastated me. First was the realization that my young children—ages four and less than one at the time—wouldn't experience the extraordinary Unconditional Love of their grandmother. Second was that she wouldn't be there to give it. Gratitude freed me from the grief. I'm thankful to be able to share happy memories of her with my children and grateful for her example of Unconditional Love, which helps me strive to love my children the same way every day.

*　*　*　*　*

By focusing on what we have instead of what we don't, gratitude makes us less prone to materialism. It shifts our motivation away from possessions and status and emphasizes the merit of nonmaterial aspects of life. One study found that participants induced to feel more gratitude had increased life satisfaction and lower materialism.[20] They didn't need to acquire new things to feel satisfied. When we feel gratitude, we're less envious and more generous. We share our time and resources and contribute to a sense of community.[21]

Gratitude encourages personal reflection and supports learning from experience. It's a valuable tool for personal growth and self-improvement. A grateful mindset enhances motivation and goal achievement and provides a sense of purpose.[22]

Gratitude helps us be present and notice the positives around and within us, improving self-awareness and enabling mindfulness. When we're comfortably self-aware, we can focus less on ourselves and more on others. Gratitude is a catalyst for empathy and compassion. It increases emotional intelligence and helps us understand and manage our and others' emotions.

As gratitude fosters positive feelings and enhances emotional intelligence, it improves our relationships. It's been described as a social glue that fortifies relationships by encouraging us to acknowledge and appreciate others' efforts, creating gratitude in them. Gratitude increases trust, cooperation, and intimacy.[23] A study of couples found that individuals who expressed appreciation for their partners felt more favorable toward them and more comfortable expressing relationship concerns.[24]

Expressing gratitude increases positive relational behaviors, like helping others, and induces feelings of warmth, humility, and connectedness.[25]

Gratitude also has a significant impact in the workplace. Research shows gratitude contributes to greater employee satisfaction and performance. A study of teachers and finance professionals found a culture of gratitude significantly improved job satisfaction.[26] Another study involving call center employees revealed that those who exhibited higher levels of gratitude were more motivated to achieve top performance than others.[27] Moreover, gratitude promotes prosocial behavior at work, leading to more helpful and respectful interactions. One study discovered that employees who were more grateful felt a greater sense of responsibility toward colleagues and societal issues.[28] Another found that employee gratitude levels predicted organizational citizenship behaviors, such as assisting others with work problems.[29] Cultivating a grateful work culture can lead to more motivated, helpful, and high-performing employees.

Leaders who say thank you motivate their teams to work harder. In one study, researchers randomly divided university fundraisers into two groups. One group made phone calls to solicit donations like they always had. The second group received a pep talk from the director of giving, who expressed gratitude for their efforts. Those who heard her message made 50 percent more calls than those who didn't.[30] In another study, workers who believed their organization supported their needs reported higher gratitude, leading them to perform helpful behaviors more frequently.[31] Another study reported that 81 percent of working adults say they'd work harder if their bosses were more grateful for their work.[32] In another, 96 percent of men and 94 percent of women said bosses expressing gratitude are more likely to succeed.[33] In summary, team members who feel appreciated perform better, and appreciative leaders are more successful.

Gratitude is a powerful agent of optimism. It sparks a fire in us that shines a light on all that is good. It accentuates the positives, which boosts happiness and contributes to well-being and life satisfaction.[34] That fire of optimism also warms our hearts. Many studies have directly linked gratitude with well-being and life satisfaction.[35]

Despite all its benefits, we often let negativity overwhelm gratitude. The next section explains how; by understanding where we go wrong, we can choose a better path. The two sections that follow show how Unconditional Gratitude helps us grow, remind us that recognizing and appreciating the good brings joy, and profoundly enrich the quality of our lives and the lives of those around us.

Where We Go Wrong

SAYING THANK YOU is simple, yet we often forget or become engrossed in our thoughts. When busy or distracted, we might not recognize others' kindness, so we miss the opportunity to express gratitude. Sometimes, if we notice the kindness, we assume the person already knows we're thankful, so we don't say it out loud. (Hint: Say it anyway. Don't assume they know.) Other times, we know we should say thanks but don't due to discomfort with emotion. We might harbor negative feelings, like pride or resentment, which stop us from expressing thanks. We might not feel grateful because we think the person should do these things for us. We might belong to cultures or groups where saying thank you isn't as common.[36]

Some may think forcing gratitude makes it fake. Southern hospitality—the commonly held notion that people from the Southern United States are polite, warm, and welcoming—exemplifies this. Some believe Southerners are taught good manners, so saying thank you is natural and sincere. Others think the politeness is fake and hides true feelings. Like most stereotypes, there are examples to support both views. Having lived in the South most of my life, I think Southern hospitality is mostly genuine, though people can use politeness as a mask. Saying thank you often doesn't mean it's insincere, but we should remain mindful of its meaning.

> The doctrine I should always have liked to teach. . . .
> is the idea of taking things with gratitude, and not taking things for granted.
> —G. K. Chesterton

In chapter 1, I introduced the Spectrum of Conditional Love, explaining how we can slide from love to hate when our love is conditional. Similarly, we can imagine a *Spectrum of Conditional Gratitude*, with gratitude at one end and ingratitude at the other. Ingratitude is unappreciation, a failure to acknowledge or value assistance or kindness received from others. It's displeasure about what we think we don't have instead of thankfulness for what we do have. At its worst, such as when we feel we've been treated unfairly, ingratitude can emerge as resentment or indignation. We can slide toward ingratitude when our gratitude is conditional due to several common pitfalls. One is entitlement, which is an expectation of benefits or special treatment without putting in the effort to earn them. While entitlement can manifest as ungratefulness, its root cause is often unaccountability, covered in detail in chapter 4. Two other major gratitude pitfalls are worry and complaint.

The Trouble with Worry

Worry involves thoughts about potential problems and how things might go wrong. It's associated with a lack of control over future events and anticipation of adverse outcomes. Worry can cause feelings ranging from slight unease to paralyzing fear. It's internally focused; we may share it, but worry tends to be introspective.

Worry is normal. It can be helpful when it leads to proactive planning or spurs action, like taking care of ourselves or others and supporting worthwhile causes. When we fixate on minor inconveniences, we lose perspective, distort our view of life, and overshadow real issues. Worry is harmful when it festers in our minds, and excessive worry can become incapacitating.

> Don't worry. Never worry. If it is something you can fix, fix it.
> If it is something impossible to fix, all your worrying won't help.
> —Mary Hemingway[37]

When people worry too much about trivial issues, we say they're experiencing first-world problems, meaning their issues are minor, blown out of proportion, and disconnected from real struggles of the world. The phrase suggests such problems only exist in developed, industrialized countries because they take modern conveniences and high living standards for granted. Unfortunately, most of our daily worries for those who live in developed countries fall into this category. Concerns about our appearance, things we want but don't have, and how we compare to others can dominate our thoughts, leaving little room for more important issues.

Worrying about first-world problems is harmful for other reasons. Stress and anxiety can become disproportionate to the significance of our worries, making us emotionally numb. It can be harder to understand or relate to the struggles of those facing poverty, illness, or conflict. Our empathy can crumble under the weight of our self-absorption. This can lead to apathy and inaction toward important issues as we focus our energy on trivial matters.[38] Constantly dwelling on trivialities can lead to emotional problems like depression. These fixations often involve social comparisons, continually measuring our lives against others' and seeking external validation that hurts our self-esteem and leaves us unsatisfied. First-world problems can also obscure opportunities for personal growth.[39]

Worry is conditional. It imagines that life will worsen *if* our worries come to pass (and, if things remain unchanged, life is better *because* the worries weren't realized). On the Spectrum of Conditional Gratitude, worry falls below gratitude—how far below depends on the extent of the worry—and is well down the spectrum toward ingratitude. Once we're captured by constant worry, it doesn't take much for us to slip into ungratefulness or resentment.

*   *   *   *   *

I often sing the first few words of the melody to Weird Al Yankovic's song "First World Problems" to my kids as an unsubtle hint that I think whatever worry they've just expressed is trivial. (It doesn't work in the moment, but I hold out hope the lyrics will stick in their brains and affect their thinking as adults.) Some of the worries I commonly try to sing away stem from personal comparisons. Like most teens, my kids frequently view carefully curated highlights of others' lives on social media, and like most, they're susceptible to comparing those glamour shots to their own realities, causing them to worry about their looks, style, or status. Such comparisons aren't only unfair; they're also unhealthy, and they can lead to anxiety and worse.

In fairness, I must admit that I can be as guilty as my children. My comparisons aren't about appearance, brand prestige, or social standing, but they're just as unfair and unhealthy. I'm prone to career comparisons. I unconsciously assess job titles, salaries, and accomplishments of former classmates and colleagues, and I feel jealous when I read about peers' promotions. I allow these comparisons to undercut objectivity and prevent me from properly appreciating the wonderful things about my career and life. I usually keep myself from going too far down the rabbit hole, but I'm well aware that adults are just as susceptible as children to harmful anxiety caused by needless worry.

The Trouble with Complaint

Complaint involves expressing dissatisfaction with something. It voices grievances, often directed at others or a situation. It seeks validation or change by expressing displeasure and is usually accompanied by feelings ranging from irritation to anger.

While worry and complaint both express dissatisfaction, critical differences exist. Worry is future-oriented, while complaint focuses on the present (and sometimes the past). Worry tends to be introspective, while complaint is directed outward and defined by expression. Just as worry can lead to constructive action, complaint sometimes provokes useful change. However, like worry, complaint can become chronic and excessive.

We think complaining helps us. Dr. Robin Kowalski, professor of psychology at Clemson University, says, "Many complaints involve attempts to elicit particular interpersonal reactions from others, such as sympathy or approval. For example, people may complain about their health, not because they feel sick but because the sick role allows them to achieve secondary gains such as sympathy from others or the avoidance of aversive events." Kowalski's research shows that "symptoms increase with symptom reporting."[40] The more we complain, the more problems we find. Complaining doesn't reduce our burdens; it increases them.

Some consider complaining healthy—a cathartic, emotional release that's good for the psyche. However, Dr. Brad Bushman, professor of communications and psychology at Ohio State University, researched catharsis theory and found that instead of helping, expressing displeasure harms the self and others. He says, "Our research clearly shows that venting angry feelings increases aggressive inclinations; it does not decrease them."[41]

> Man invented language to satisfy his deep need to complain.
> —Lily Tomlin

A counterargument might be that verbally venting frustration is more constructive than physically acting on it. To be clear: complaint isn't venting frustration; it's inherently negative. When we feel like victims of injustice or unfair circumstances, we respond to negativity with negativity. In his article "The Science of Happiness: Why Complaining Is Literally Killing You," Steven Parton hits the nail on the head: "Negativity . . . causes stress . . . [leading to] elevated cortisol levels [that] interfere with learning and memory, lower immune function and bone density, increase weight gain, blood pressure, cholesterol . . . and lower life expectancy."[42]

Humans have a built-in negativity bias. Similar to its impacts on feelings of hate, our limbic system is wired to be more attuned to negative stimuli than positive ones.[43] This causes us to focus more on negative news. We're also susceptible to confirmation bias, which drives us to seek evidence confirming our current views and avoid or discount opposing information. We're wired to notice negatives and hold tightly to our truths. Complaint comes naturally.

* * * * *

In 2006, Will Bowen, a pastor at Christ Church Unity in Kansas City, Missouri, observed something concerning in his congregation. Everyone complained. He heard grumbling about the weather, groaning about work, griping about other members, and grousing about minor inconveniences like traffic or slow internet. Complaints were so prevalent that they created an atmosphere of negativity that hindered the congregants' engagement and enjoyment. Worst of all, Bowen was as guilty as any of frequent complaints.[44]

Frustrated with himself and distressed about the environment, Bowen raised the issue with the church assembly. He pointed out that complaining is counterproductive. Most complaints are about trivial matters, things we can't control, or issues we won't do anything about, and in those cases, complaining only increases pessimism and cynicism.[45]

Instead of just complaining about the complaints, Bowen proposed a simple but innovative exercise: He distributed purple bracelets to all parishioners and instructed them to switch the bracelet from one wrist to the other whenever they caught themselves complaining, criticizing, or gossiping. The objective was to help participants become more aware of their complaints and gradually reduce them. He challenged them all, including himself, to go twenty-one consecutive days without complaining.[46]

> Happiness comes when we stop complaining about the troubles we have
> and offer thanks for all the troubles we don't have.
> —Thomas S. Monson

Initially, many people, including Bowen, struggled. Complaints had become so entrenched that going a day without switching the bracelet was difficult. Eventually, they began to notice changes. They caught themselves before complaining or criticizing. Negative talk decreased. They focused less on problems and more on solutions.[47]

The most potent payoff Bowen and his congregation realized was that as grumbling subsided, gratitude grew. By focusing less on what was wrong, they noticed—and appreciated—more about what was right. Relationships improved, stress levels declined, and happiness increased for individuals and the church.[48]

Bowen was profoundly impacted. His outlook and interactions radically changed. His successes inspired him to write *A Complaint Free World: How to Stop Complaining and Start Enjoying the Life You Always Wanted*. The book gained international attention and sparked a global movement. As of the Kindle version's publication date, more than fifteen million people across 106 countries had taken the purple bracelet challenge, sharing their experiences and successes. Bowen also founded the organization A

Complaint Free World and works worldwide to help individuals and organizations become happier, more productive, and more grateful.[49]

*   *   *   *   *

Complaint is a first-world epidemic. It seems that when our lives become easier, we don't complain less; we complain more. Hedonic adaptation causes positive feelings about things we perceive as good to diminish over time. When the newness fades, so can the goodness; what was previously a pleasant surprise becomes expected. Gratitude shifts to complaint. To paraphrase Bowen: We live in the safest, healthiest, and most prosperous time in human history. Yet, what do we do? We complain![50] It's a slippery slope from gratitude to ingratitude.

Bowen provides examples where, outside the first world, complaints aren't as prevalent. In parts of Africa, it's considered rude to complain because it's seen as an attempt to unload your burden onto someone else. In many African cultures, they don't say I'm sorry when someone encounters a problem. Instead, they say *pole* (pronounced "po-lee"), which in Swahili means something like "I understand what you're going through, but I trust you'll be able to get through it." They're empathetic and encouraging, not negative. Bowen mentions that *complain* translates to "hug your ego" in Chinese, but I think he's slightly misinterpreting the translation. In Mandarin, the word *complain* uses two symbols meaning "embrace" and "resentment." It suggests the Chinese view complaint as holding on to bitterness—clinging to ingratitude.[51]

Like worry, complaint falls far below gratitude on the Spectrum of Conditional Gratitude. Because it's outwardly negative with the potential to infect others, complaint is closer to the bottom. It's not just in Mandarin that complaint is like embracing resentment.

> Everyone remembers the remark of the old man at the point of death:
>> that his life had been full of troubles
>> most of which had never happened.
>> —Winston Churchill

Even those of us who aren't regular complainers often lack gratitude. We believe we'll be grateful when we finish school, land our dream job, earn enough money, retire, and so on.[52] This approach makes gratitude contingent.

When gratitude is contingent, it falls on the spectrum of conditionality, where it's easy to slip into worry and complaint. Worrying about first-world problems makes our gratitude dependent on events out of our control. Complaining about things we don't like makes gratitude dependent on specific changes. If we aren't grateful for what we have, how can we justify wanting something more or different? Ingratitude stems from the irrational belief that gratefulness depends on things going our way. Ingratitude is irrational because it's conditional.

Conditional gratitude seems natural, but it's learned. Our brains have learned over millions of years to notice negatives reflexively, and we've been taught to believe gratitude is contingent. Although ingrained, these reactions aren't part of us. They're bad habits. To overcome them, we must learn to ignore illogical intuition, leave behind lifelong learning, and embrace Unconditional Gratitude.

Answers in Timeless Wisdom

UNCONDITIONAL GRATITUDE IS the solution. It isn't driven by objects or outcomes. It can't be bought or earned. It doesn't depend on what we have or who's right or wrong. It unyokes us from the Spectrum of Conditional Gratitude and protects us from the slippery slope to ingratitude. Unconditional Gratitude shows us the dearness of life. If we're alive, we have a reason to be grateful unconditionally.

Practicing Unconditional Gratitude is more than saying thank you occasionally. It's a way of thinking and living. It's exchanging worry for preparation and complaint for appreciation. It's facing challenges with confidence in what we have instead of fearing what we lack. It's letting go of what's out of our control and being thankful for both easy and hard times. It means our gratitude doesn't depend on our circumstances; it only depends on accepting life's blessings.

* * * * *

Early in this chapter, I shared my experience with my mother's sudden death. Gratitude for her life defeating grief over her death is the clearest proof I can offer of Unconditional's power over conditional. I couldn't have emotionally moved on without choosing to focus on appreciation despite my anguish. I didn't disregard my despair; I decided my gratitude doesn't depend on the situation, no matter how disturbing. I don't always choose unconditionality first—grief still strikes—but only through unconditionality can I get back to gratitude.

* * * * *

Unconditional Gratitude is a universal thread woven through spiritual and philosophical thought. Most religious traditions emphasize gratitude as a means to be our best selves or connect with God. The Bible contains many verses underscoring the importance of Unconditional Gratitude.

One verse advises, "Give thanks in all circumstances; for this is God's will for you in Christ Jesus,"[53] reminding us to remain thankful regardless of the situation. Another verse encourages us to be "always giving thanks to God the Father for everything, in the name of our Lord Jesus Christ,"[54] implying that our gratitude should never waver. Gratitude is an act of faith, not contingent upon external conditions. The Psalms include expressions of gratitude, such as "Give thanks to the Lord, for he is good; his love endures forever,"[55] and "This is the day the Lord has made; let us rejoice and be glad in it."[56] These verses remind us that every day is a gift. Another verse proclaims, "Every good and perfect gift is from above, coming down from the Father of the heavenly lights, who does not change like shifting shadows,"[57] stressing that God is constant, so gratitude should be constant and unconditional.

> Do everything without complaining.
> —Philippians 2:14 (New Living Translation)

Gratitude (*shukr*) is a cornerstone of Islamic faith. Muslims are encouraged to express gratitude for Allah's blessings. The phrase *Alhamdulillah* (meaning "All praise is due to Allah"), often repeated daily, serves as a constant reminder to be thankful. The five daily prayers provide opportunities to thank Allah for His guidance and blessings. Charity, or *sadaqah*, is a way to show gratitude by sharing blessings with others. Islam teaches that gratitude should be shown in good and hard times, rooted in faith rather than circumstance.[58]

Buddhists associate gratitude with mindfulness and compassion. Thích Nhất Hạnh encourages starting each day with a smile and acknowledging the gift of time. He writes, "Waking up this morning, I smile. Twenty-four brand new hours are before me. I vow to live fully in each moment and to look at all beings with eyes of compassion." Buddhism teaches that happiness arises from appreciation, not accumulation.[59] Gratitude doesn't depend on what we have but comes from unconditionality.

> The roots of all goodness
> lie in the soil of appreciation for goodness.
> —Tenzin Gyatso, the 14th Dalai Lama

In Confucianism, gratitude is vital to maintaining harmonious relationships and cultivating moral character. Expressing gratitude toward parents, ancestors, elders, and authority figures is deeply ingrained. Rituals and ceremonies provide structured ways to express gratitude.[60] Confucius teaches that Unconditional Gratitude is essential, emphasizing humility, reflection, and learning from experiences.

> I was complaining that I had no shoes till I met a man who had no feet.
> —Confucius

> It is better to light one small candle of gratitude than to curse the darkness.
> —Confucius

Across diverse traditions and history, great thinkers have highlighted Unconditional Gratitude as a singular force for personal well-being, healthy relationships, and a balanced society. It frees us from constantly evaluating each situation to determine how we should feel. It liberates us from the drama and uncertainty that comes with conditional gratitude, allowing us to find peace in the steadiness of appreciation that isn't tied to external circumstances.

*　*　*　*　*

In the last section, I admitted my tendency toward career comparisons. I acknowledged this first-world problem often undermines objectivity and causes worry that can lead to anxiety. Although I still catch myself surfing LinkedIn to analyze others' accomplishments, I've gotten better in middle age. Perhaps the lessons I learned after my mother's passing helped me choose gratitude more readily. Maybe the loss of the HLS project, coupled with appreciation of team accomplishments and personal career enjoyment, also contribute. Either way (or both), I generally take a more mature approach. We can all benefit from the following:

- We try to dwell only on what we can control. When we ponder the future, it's for planning, not worrying. We can't control others, so we should avoid comparing ourselves to others.
- We recognize that we make comparisons to determine whether we're as good as someone else, but in reality, there's no objective way to measure ourselves against others, because everyone's circumstances are inherently different. We can only decide what's good and better for ourselves and use individual metrics to measure our progress.
- When we fall into comparative thinking, we acknowledge the thoughts, pause, and try to question those thoughts against objective reality—asking for help from friends when needed.
- We turn toward Unconditional Gratitude by considering our unique strengths and achievements and framing others' triumphs as inspiration to reach our potential.

* * * * *

Unconditional Gratitude enables us to live with contentment rather than constant yearning. While others tally their troubles, we can count our blessings. There will be times when it's hard to find reasons to be grateful. By focusing on our constants—supportive relationships, personal strengths, and daily comforts—we can shift our perspective from one of scarcity to one of abundance. We'll still make mistakes and face setbacks, but with gratitude, we can appreciate the lessons we learn and remain mindful not to take any blessing for granted. As we practice gratitude, it becomes part of who we are. Ultimately, what matters is that we understand our need for Unconditional Gratitude and its transformative impact on our lives.

> It's not so much what we have in this life that matters.
> It's what we do with what we have.
> —Fred Rogers, "Mister Rogers"

How to Live It

IN AN EPISODE of *The Gratitude Podcast*, host Georgian Benta interviews Aaron Hale, a fourteen-year army veteran, military chef, and Explosive Ordnance Disposal (EOD) team leader who lost his vision and hearing after an explosion. Hale explains that these disabilities didn't stop him. He runs ultramarathons, owns an online fudge business, and invests in real estate. He lives life to the fullest because he chooses to embrace gratitude. In Hale's words:

> I was a US Army bomb technician, the guy that diffuses those roadside bombs. One of them detonated to take my eyes. Four years later—a complication with my injury—I contracted bacterial meningitis, and I lost my hearing. Between the meningitis and the installation of the implant, there was about half a year of being in complete darkness and complete silence. During that time, there was no communication, no information input except what I could feel. My entire world ended at my fingertips. . . .
>
> A couple of times in my life, it could have gone either way. Right after the bomb blast, learning that I'd be blind for the rest of my life. Then the meningitis and learning that I'd be deaf also. There were those things that I called my demons. That internal voice that asks, "Why me?" or "What if?" Of course, the second time around, it was "When is enough enough? When have I paid my dues? When have I had my fair share? Why is this happening to me?" All of that. . . .
>
> If you keep [going] down that path, it ends up in this self-limiting, depressing spiral and—forgive the pun—into a world of darkness. I had to flip it around. I had to make it external, less about me and [more] about others. . . . I got busy with things I could do instead of worrying about things I couldn't do any longer. Instead of saying "I can't," it was "What can I do?" . . .

I'm still a father, a husband, a son, a brother. I'm still a soldier at heart. I have all these roles to play, these hats to wear. I couldn't just sit there feeling sorry for myself. . . . I was, of course, extremely grateful for having my fellow veterans near me, supporting me, all of them fighting their own personal battles. I thought about what they were going through. Their struggles gave me hope for at least a good ending, a happy life ahead. I got busy working on that. . . .

I began having adventures. I started climbing mountains. I was kayaking whitewater. I started running marathons. That physical activity, that sense of adventure. . . . Seeing the world through my feet. That feeds the soul. . . .

It is an incredible world. Full of amazing things. Great adventures, incredible people, and just amazing experiences. Like I mentioned before, to waste time on those questions that can't be answered, the things we left behind, the things we can't do. They shut the door to creativity. They pull the rug out from gratitude and turn out the lights on opportunity. We've got to be open, we've got to be curious, and we've got to be humble, because that's when opportunity, imagination, creativity, and *gratitude come in and fill our lives.*[61]

My wife would tell you that I'm intolerant of complaints in our house. This comes from an understanding that my family and I are among the luckiest people on earth, at least in terms of our standard of living. Very few have had as much access to basic needs, comforts, and freedoms as we do today. My travels abroad have made this even more apparent. I've seen how lucky I was to be born into such favorable circumstances—something I didn't earn but just happened to receive. Beth and I try to help our kids understand this too. We've taken them on trips to other countries so they can see it for themselves, and we talk about it whenever we can.

As I write this, I know that if gratitude depended on how fortunate we are, I should be one of the most grateful people in the world. I realize some might think, *It's easy for you to say*, and they're right—I'm aware of my privilege. But we must all remember that nothing in life is guaranteed, even life itself. My mother's sudden death was painful proof of that for me. Our lives can change at any moment.

The good news is that gratitude isn't dependent on our circumstances. We can fully experience the benefits of gratitude, for ourselves and those around us, no matter what's happening in our lives. Unconditional Gratitude doesn't depend on our prospects or predicaments. It doesn't change. Striving for Unconditional Gratitude helps us maintain a steady assurance that we always have reasons to be thankful, even if they're not immediately obvious by society's standards. When it comes to Unconditional Gratitude, what matters is how deeply we embrace it in our lives and how sincerely we share it with others.

> The best way to show my gratitude
> is to accept everything, even my problems, with joy.
> —Mary Teresa Bojaxhiu, "Mother Teresa"

Personal

Unconditional Gratitude is a transformative force. No matter how it's expressed, gratitude positively impacts our well-being and relationships. One common practice is counting our blessings, which helps us focus on the positive aspects of our lives and shifts our focus toward positivity.[62] We let go of expectations and appreciate our lives as they are.

Keeping a gratitude journal is a popular way to count blessings regularly. According to Dr. Robert Emmons, psychology professor at the University of California, Davis, the benefits are remarkable. His studies involving over two thousand people show that "people are 25 percent happier and more energetic if they keep gratitude journals, have 20 percent less envy and resentment, sleep 10 percent longer each night and wake up 15 percent more refreshed, exercise 33 percent more, and show a 10 percent drop in blood pressure" compared to those who don't.[63] Another approach is a gratitude jar where we place notes whenever we feel thankful. Writing notes of appreciation compounds our gratitude beyond the limitations of our thoughts. Reading these notes reignites warm feelings of appreciation and reminds us of our many blessings.

Setting reminders is a practical way to prompt moments of gratitude throughout the day. Phone notifications or sticky notes in visible places can encourage us to pause, reflect, and express appreciation. Incorporating gratitude into daily routines, such as counting blessings at the start or end of the day, also nurtures thankfulness.[64] The more grateful we are, the more beautiful our world becomes.

Acts of kindness, whether small or significant, have powerful, positive impacts. Spending quality time, listening well, showing empathy, apologizing for mistakes, volunteering, and donating are all meaningful expressions of gratitude. The mental, physical, and emotional benefits are often greater for the givers than the receivers.

Gratitude is profoundly personal. For the religious, God is the source of everything deserving of gratitude. So Unconditional Gratitude should be easy to practice; since the Creator gives us everything, the least we can do is give thanks. Sadly, we often don't, as daily distractions overwhelm our ability to show gratitude to the Giver of Life. This should be a fundamental focus for believers of all faiths. Believers or not, we all have innumerable things to be thankful for: life, good health, family and friends, safety and security, education, employment, culture, nature, technology, and individual rights and freedoms.[65]

Thinking about how to infuse our lives with gratitude can feel intimidating. We may not know where to start, even with regularly counting our blessings. We must have mercy on ourselves. Unconditional Gratitude is an ideal—no one does everything right. We can start by choosing one practice that resonates with us and commit to it for one week. After the first week, we try another week. As we experience the benefits of gratitude, we'll naturally incorporate more practices into our lives. We'll create more moments of happiness that help us build inner strength. Most importantly, we'll intuitively share our gratitude with others. It's by sharing that we realize gratitude's greatest power.

Relational

Expressing gratitude isn't just a passing emotion or polite gesture. It's the foundation of human connection and social cohesion. It elevates our interactions, strengthens communities, and cultivates a culture of gratitude. When we acknowledge others' actions, we show them they're valued and appreciated. People who feel appreciated are likelier to engage in positive behavior and extend kindness to others. This cycle of appreciation builds social responsibility and a shared commitment to the well-being of our communities.[66]

One of the simplest ways to share gratitude is by saying thank you. Whether spoken, written, or expressed through gestures, these words strengthen relationships and deepen feelings of gratitude. Verbal expressions can be delivered in person or through other means, like phone calls or messages. Though more formal, written notes or letters of thanks are often especially appreciated because they require extra effort and are even more meaningful when personalized.

*   *   *   *   *

In the "Where We Go Wrong" section, I mentioned Southern hospitality. People not from the Southern US often wonder if the culture truly embodies this phrase. As a Southern boy, I can vouch that it does, at least where I've lived and visited, which is most of the South. We're raised to say thank you, please, sir, and ma'am; hold doors open; and give up our seats to older people. It wasn't until adulthood that I realized these practices weren't universal. Growing up in the South ingrained these values in me so deeply that even living and traveling outside the region hasn't weakened them. I see this as a cultural advantage: politeness, intuitive to me, is universally positive. Everyone likes to be thanked and treated courteously. Expressing appreciation and civility is always right.

*   *   *   *   *

Giving gifts is another tangible way to express gratitude. The thought and effort behind the gift often mean more than its monetary value. Gifts that reflect the recipient's interests or needs are particularly cherished. Public expressions of gratitude, like posting thank-you messages on social media or acknowledging someone at an event, can also be appropriate if the recipient is comfortable with public attention. Gestures like smiles, hugs, or handshakes can convey gratitude without words.[67] It's easy to underestimate the power of a smile, compliment, kind welcome, or listening ear. Though seemingly trivial to the giver, they can change a moment, a day, or a life.

> Feeling gratitude and not expressing it
> is like wrapping a present and not giving it.
> —William Arthur Ward

Unconditional Gratitude is proactive and preemptive. It involves sharing appreciation randomly, not reciprocally. Living by the principle "I am, therefore I have gratitude" demands constant thankfulness. This can feel awkward at first. Building grateful habits takes time. It's normal to forget or miss opportunities. The key is to keep trying. We begin by thanking one person each day, focusing on the positive impacts of their actions. As we consistently express appreciation, we find it becomes more natural and fulfilling. Each expression enriches our relationships, deepens our sense of well-being, and nurtures gratefulness in those around us.

As a Parent

Gratitude is an essential life skill we must impart to our children. It helps them develop inner strength, cement relationships, and establish a foundation of positivity. We can teach it by talking about and encouraging it, but mostly, we must model it. We show gratitude by recognizing kindness and expressing thanks to others. We also need to express appreciation directly to our children, explicitly acknowledging the behaviors that merit thanks so they can mentally link their actions with appreciation. We should especially connect appreciation with core family values to reinforce their importance. Moreover, we should express our gratitude for having them in our lives, letting them know they bring us joy and fulfillment simply by being who they are. This reinforces Unconditional Love, for them and us, and represents as pure an expression of Unconditional Gratitude as possible.

We often instinctively prompt our children to say thank you in public. To make our words impactful, we must back them with actions. We need to be consistently appreciative in public and private for our encouragement to have its full impact. We can instill gratitude through habits like sharing what we're thankful for before meals or bedtime, creating a family gratitude jar, and teaching our children to craft thank-you cards. We must exemplify acts of kindness and generosity with our children so they witness the positive impacts on others and themselves.

> Piglet noticed that even though he had a Very Small Heart,
> it could hold a rather large amount of Gratitude.
> —A. A Milne

*   *   *   *   *

I'm unsure if it's a Southern or motherly tradition, but Beth's mom and mine were devoted thank-you note writers. They might not have matched John Kralik's pace of one note per day, but it sure seemed like it. If you asked them, both of our mothers would've said they were taught the importance of thank-you notes by their mothers, who learned from theirs, and so on. Of course, ours intended to pass the lesson to us. After every occasion when we received gifts, they insisted that we handwrite thank-you notes to the givers. Then, they lovingly reminded us, nagged, and finally browbeat us until we complied. (To be fair, the nagging and browbeating only happened in my house. Beth learned the lesson much quicker than I did.) Naturally, Beth carries on the tradition today: when our kids receive gifts, she encourages them to write thank-you notes, then lovingly reminds them, and so on.

*   *   *   *   *

Two other essential truths about gratitude we should share with our kids:

- When expressed about the simplest tasks, appreciation has an outsize impact.
- Gratitude isn't a zero-sum game—there's plenty to go around.

Finally, we must consistently stress the importance of intangibles—relationships, experiences, learning, and personal growth—over material things. Unconditional Gratitude can't coexist with materialism. Our children's greatest joy will come from understanding the value of mental and emotional rewards rather than physical ones.

Building gratitude habits as a family takes intentionality and persistence. Amid all our demands, it can feel daunting. Parenting, like gratitude, is a constant work in progress; we need patience—with our children, but mostly with ourselves. We can begin by choosing one shared practice, like giving thanks at mealtimes. Over time, it can become a routine that strengthens our family's togetherness and each individual's resilience. Consistency is critical to making gratitude a foundational family value.

> Appreciation is a wonderful thing:
> It makes what is excellent in others belong to us as well.
> —Voltaire

At Work

Studies have found that we're less likely to show gratitude at work than anywhere else.[68] However, gratitude brings many benefits to the workplace, including improved relationships, increased motivation, and better mental and physical health. When employees feel valued, they're more motivated and enthusiastic. Acts of gratitude like thank-you emails, public acknowledgment, and appreciation lunches can become part of the culture, boosting morale, job satisfaction, communication, collaboration, and organizational effectiveness.

In the article "The Grateful Workplace," Ryan Fehr and colleagues present a model for gratitude at work. They identify three types:

- **Episodic:** Gratitude felt in response to a specific experience.
- **Persistent:** "A stable tendency to feel grateful within a particular context."
- **Collective:** "Persistent gratitude [that] is shared by the members of an organization."[69]

By itself, episodic gratitude may seem conditional or dependent on circumstances, but it's a place to start, and these forms build upon one another. Cultivating collective gratitude begins with encouraging episodic gratitude and creating an environment where gratitude thrives. Fehr proposes three initiatives to promote a grateful environment:

- Appreciation programs, such as celebrating retirements or product launches.
- Opportunities for employees to interact with those who benefit from their efforts.
- Feedback from managers focused on employees' development and growth.[70]

Regardless of the practices adopted, gratitude is essential for employee satisfaction, performance, and organizational success.

Cultivating a culture of gratitude at work may seem hard, especially if it's not the norm. The change can start with one person. We can catalyze a more positive, productive, and grateful work environment by consistently expressing appreciation and acknowledging others' efforts.

As a Leader

Appreciation is critical in positions of authority. Unfortunately, we usually fall short. A 2017 study found that many leaders don't offer praise or positive feedback—37 percent of leaders avoided giving praise altogether.[71] The researchers suggest leaders might believe their primary role is to correct mistakes, viewing praise as optional. Gratitude is never optional and shouldn't depend on work quality or timeliness. It should be given unconditionally.

Adrian Gostick and Chester Elton's book *Leading with Gratitude: Eight Leadership Practices for Extraordinary Business Results* emphasizes the importance of team morale through targeted, thoughtful rewards. Leaders should ensure gratitude is specific and public so the team understands why it's given. Vague appreciation can come across as disconnected or indifferent. Specific words tying gratitude to core values make it memorable and reinforce those values.[72,73]

Gostick and Elton explain appreciation has the longest-lasting impact on motivation, more than tangible items or cash bonuses. Of course, offering words when monetary rewards are possible will eventually be viewed negatively, but verbalizing gratitude is essential.[74]

> I often ask managers to write an e-mail of praise or thanks to a friend, family member, or colleague each morning before they start their day's work—not just because it contributes to their own happiness, but because it very literally cements a relationship.
>
> —Shawn Achor[75]

One of the most effective approaches is appreciating small-scale good deeds as much as significant accomplishments. Too often, we reserve praise for major successes, so long periods pass, making gratitude stale. Instead, we can look for daily, incremental wins, such as mentoring a team member, helping a colleague with a complex task, or showing patience with demanding customers. When feeling grateful toward a colleague or about something they've done, we must immediately let them know. Regularly expressed gratitude keeps team members engaged.[76]

Sharing specific thanks may feel uncomfortable, especially for leaders with reserved styles. Even when we know and want to do better, we can get caught up in day-to-day responsibilities and forget to express gratitude. Our teams crave authentic appreciation. Even small gestures, like short emails or texts, can be extremely effective. We can start by identifying one team member's specific contributions. Then, we set a goal of recognizing at least one member's efforts each day. As we see the impacts on morale and performance, we'll find it more natural as a regular part of our leadership approach. Making appreciation a priority transforms our leadership and our teams.

Chapter Summary

Unconditional Gratitude is the second value after Unconditional Love for many reasons. Practicing gratitude boosts resilience, reduces materialism and greed, and helps us become better friends, parents, employees, and leaders. Most importantly, gratitude is the gateway to lasting joy and contentment. Everything changes when we shift from a scarcity mindset to one of thankfulness. We open our eyes to the blessings surrounding us daily.

Conditional gratitude is a fleeting feeling when things go our way, but it changes too easily to worry, complaint, and ingratitude. The solution is constant and unshakeable gratitude that flows from who we are, not what we have. Unconditional Gratitude doesn't depend on presents or possessions. It's an enduring way of engaging with the world. We accept reality and find reasons to be thankful in every situation.

When we strive for Unconditional Gratitude in our thoughts and demonstrate it in our words and deeds, it changes us. It makes us stand out from the complaining crowd and stand above who we were before. When coupled with Unconditional Love, it forms a foundation upon which the other Unconditionals can stably build. Unconditional Gratitude is a superpower that can be ours if we're willing to work for it.

Encouragement and Questions for the Reader

At some point, you'll probably feel swamped by the struggle of Unconditional Gratitude. You'll be disappointed that your defects aren't disappearing. Don't be hard on yourself. Personal growth isn't the finish line but an ongoing odyssey. Everyone is imperfect. Advancing toward Unconditional Gratitude can be slow, but it's bold. Every grateful thought helps beat back worry. Each expression of appreciation helps curb complaint. As you consistently choose gratitude, it becomes increasingly natural and joyful, enhancing your life and the lives of those around you.

The following are questions to ask yourself. As you seek to cultivate greater gratitude, use them to help you choose one area where you can strive for unconditionality.

- Do you keep score of what you've earned versus received? What steps can you take to alter your perspective from entitled to grateful?
- Are you letting worry and complaint overshadow your blessings? What steps can you take to keep life's challenges in perspective and focus on reasons to be grateful?

- How often do you express appreciation to your loved ones for who they are, not what they do for you? How can you more frequently voice Unconditional Gratitude for and to them?

- As a parent, are you modeling Unconditional Gratitude for your children through your words and actions? What family activities can you start that instill thankfulness?

- Do you notice and acknowledge coworkers' efforts, even small ones? How can you spread gratitude to boost morale and bonds in your workplace?

- In leadership positions, do you offer specific, personalized appreciation tied to team members' efforts and shared values? How can you set the tone by intentionally expressing gratitude to a colleague at least once daily?

- What's one daily practice you can start today in pursuit of Unconditional Gratitude as a lifelong commitment and source of profound fulfillment?

> Every day, think as you wake up:
> "Today I am fortunate to have woken up.
> I am alive. I have a precious human life.
> I am not going to waste it."
> —Tenzin Gyatso, the 14th Dalai Lama

Chapter III

Unconditional Integrity

Integrity is the essence of everything successful.
—R. Buckminster Fuller

What It Is

Honesty is the first chapter of the book wisdom.
　　　　　　　　　—Thomas Jefferson

INTEGRITY IS OUR root system—the base on which character grows and keeps us standing tall. It's the anchor that holds us fast to truth against tornadic winds. It may be unseen, but it nourishes the parts of us others do see that create our identity. When our integrity is healthy and strong, our other virtues flourish. But if it weakens, our entire character withers.

In the following pages, we'll explore the meaning and importance of integrity in our personal lives, relationships, families, and work. We'll examine how the world tempts us toward compromise and mine timeless wisdom to illuminate a path of Unconditional Integrity—an unshakable foundation for a life of purpose and peace. Integrity is a choice, not an inborn trait. No one is perfect, but we become our best selves when we dare to make that choice, moment by moment, day by day. Everything depends on it. Integrity is the essence of everything successful.

The Latin word *integer*, meaning "whole" or "complete," is the root of several English words. In mathematics, integer refers to a whole number without fractions. Integrate means to combine separate elements into a whole, similar to *combine, consolidate,* or *unify.* Among these related terms, *integrity* carries the most complex meaning.

When applied to inanimate objects, integrity denotes wholeness, being undivided or unbroken. A country's territorial integrity implies its land is undivided. A building's structural integrity indicates it's sturdy, with all parts cohesively united. In technology, systems or datasets undergo integrity checking to ensure they remain uncorrupted.

When applied to a person, integrity retains its core meaning of wholeness but refers to character. A person with integrity demonstrates consistency between actions, words, and thoughts. Personal integrity signifies an undivided self. It means fulfilling promises and acting on beliefs, regardless of difficulty. Like structural integrity in buildings, personal integrity means our character is strong and tough—the severest storm can't knock us down. Integrity means we're consistent, reliable, and can be trusted. Like secure electronic systems, we're incorruptible and uncompromising. Integrity equals soundness of character.

The words *unconditional* and *integrity* aren't synonyms, but they have interesting similarities. Unconditional means unquestionable and complete. Integrity means undiminished and unblemished. But unconditional is a lack of stipulation—there are no situations where it doesn't apply—whereas integrity is standing against weakness and corruption. Unconditional is an adjective, integrity is a noun; they fit together— Unconditional Integrity. We aren't perfect, so we can only aim for flawless character. But we become our best when we aim high.

*   *   *   *   *

In 2015, Dr. Mona Hanna-Attisha, a pediatrician in Flint, Michigan, encountered an alarming spike in lead levels in her young patients' blood. Suspecting a connection to the city's recent switch to a new water source, she initiated a study. Her findings were shocking—lead levels in children had doubled, and in some areas tripled, since the change in water supply.[1]

She faced a difficult decision. Speaking out meant challenging government officials who insisted the water was safe, risking her professional reputation, and facing potential legal repercussions. Silence, on the other hand, would allow more children to suffer lead poisoning. Despite the risks, she chose to act and publicly presented her findings.[2]

The backlash was swift and harsh. State officials tried to discredit her work, accusing her of causing panic. They attacked her personally and professionally. But Dr. Hanna-Attisha refused to back down. She knew her data was sound and that children's health was at stake. Her persistence paid off. Further investigations confirmed her findings, and the Flint water crisis became national news. Her work forced the government to admit the problem and take action.[3]

Dr. Hanna-Attisha's integrity and courage in the face of intense pressure helped expose a major public health crisis and inspired others to fight for what's right. Her story shows how maintaining integrity, even at personal risk, can have far-reaching positive impacts on society.[4]

*　*　*　*　*

Unconditional Integrity is third among The Unconditionals because it's our cornerstone. It's no exaggeration to say that everything we do depends on integrity. Integrity is the most complex value in this book, but it's also one of the three most impactful on our lives. It greatly affects our decisions and how we act alone and with others, making it crucial to understand and always practice integrity. That's why it's unconditional—its importance is undeniable. We must strive to be personally whole.

Placing Unconditional Integrity here also aligns with the organization of this book. The four core life areas are inside, outside, connection, and action. Integrity is borne inside us and plays out in our hearts and heads, but it gets tested most when we interact with the outside. The world's pressures threaten to create division, expose weaknesses, and corrupt our character if given the chance. Therefore, I chose integrity to represent The Unconditionals for the outside. Outside relates to our thoughts first—before actions—but it's not confined to our inner lives. Unconditional Integrity involves both our private and public selves. Like a tree with roots hidden underground, integrity isn't directly visible to others, but it's primarily responsible for whether we produce healthy, appealing results.

> One can acquire everything in solitude—except character.
> —Marie-Henri Beyle, "Stendhal"

*　*　*　*　*

Following are two inspiring stories about integrity.

Story 1: In the 1920s, Al Capone was the most notorious organized crime boss in the United States. He made over a billion dollars through bootlegging, gambling, and sex trade while terrorizing Chicago with protection rackets and gang murder. His legal counsel, nicknamed Easy Eddie, helped keep Capone in power and out of jail. In return, Capone lavished extravagant wealth on Eddie, including an estate spanning a city block. Although involved in a world of corruption, Eddie had a soft spot for his son. He wanted to give his son what he didn't have—good morals and ethics. He wanted his son to be a man of honor, but he knew he wasn't setting a good example. Easy Eddie asked himself, "What good is it for a man to gain the whole world and lose his soul?" He decided he had to do the right thing. He embarked on a path toward redemption, confessing to authorities about Capone's criminal empire and eventually testifying as a key government witness. Sadly, the mob gunned him down in the street within a year. However, his efforts were not in vain. Easy Eddie left his son a greater inheritance than any material wealth—the gift of integrity.[5]

Story 2: During World War II, fighter pilot Butch O'Hare was flying with his squadron when he looked at his fuel gauge and realized the ground crew had not refilled his fuel tank. He wouldn't have enough fuel to complete the mission and return to the aircraft carrier. His commander ordered him to return to the ship, which he reluctantly did. As Butch headed back, he saw a Japanese squadron racing toward the American fleet. With his entire division on a mission, he knew the ships were vulnerable, and there wasn't time to recall them or warn the fleet. He decided there was only one thing he could do—try to divert the enemy planes. Ignoring his safety, he dived into the formation with guns blazing. The Japanese aircraft fired back from all angles, but Butch kept fighting. When he ran out of bullets, he tried to clip an enemy's wing to bring it down. Shocked by his bravery, the Japanese squadron changed course. Butch safely returned to the carrier, having single-handedly shot down five Japanese aircrafts, becoming the Navy's first flying ace of World War II and the first naval aviator to receive the Medal of Honor. O'Hare Airport in Chicago is named after him to honor his heroism.[6]

These stories are linked: Butch O'Hare was Easy Eddie's son. Eddie didn't just talk to Butch about integrity; he showed it through his actions. Integrity means taking action, not just talking. Eddie demonstrated integrity by giving his life for it, and his son later risked his life in a heroic act of integrity, likely saving many fellow soldiers.[7]

* * * * *

Who you are inside is what helps you make and do everything in life.
—Fred Rogers, "Mister Rogers"

Elements of Unconditional Integrity

Integrity has many parts, including honesty, moral courage, consistency, authenticity, fairness, and loyalty. Understanding each part is crucial for developing integrity.

Unconditional Integrity requires **honesty**. Some confuse integrity with honesty, thinking honesty is the key ingredient. However, integrity includes many personal qualities. Honesty is about what we say, while integrity is about how we show it. Honesty also means not deceiving, cheating, or stealing, which applies to ourselves as much as to others.

Unconditional Integrity involves having **moral courage**—doing the right thing and not doing the wrong thing, even when it's hard or inconvenient. It means knowing and living according to our values and beliefs. It's having strong morals and high ethical standards and sticking to them, like being polite when others are rude.

Inner character is far more significant a factor in success
than talent or intelligence or circumstances.
—Stephen R. Covey

Unconditional Integrity comprises **consistency** between what we think, say, and do. It's like moral courage but goes beyond doing the right things; it's also about thinking and saying the right things. It's about maintaining our values, standards, and ethics, no matter what's happening around us. Consistency builds credibility.

Unconditional Integrity includes **authenticity**, which combines consistency with truth. It means aligning our public and private lives. It's being our true selves, honest with ourselves and others and presenting ourselves to the world without pretense. It requires vulnerability and admitting imperfection, but it enables deep trust and transparency in relationships.

Unconditional Integrity contains **fairness**—being just, impartial, and equitable in our actions, decisions, and treatment of others. Fairness considers everyone's rights, dignity, and perspectives, regardless of background and free from prejudices. It's more than just following the rules— it's following the *spirit* of the rules.

Finally, Unconditional Integrity embraces **loyalty**. Loyalty is being faithful to people, affiliations, and causes. It's standing by and standing up for friends, family, and country. It also means keeping confidences and not gossiping. Its deepest meaning is enduring difficulties to honor personal commitments, sometimes drawing on moral courage. (As noted in chapter 1, this should never mean staying in unhealthy or abusive situations. Unconditional Love and Integrity are better maintained in safe, healthy environments.)

* * * * *

In September 1982, Johnson & Johnson (J&J) faced a crisis that would become a defining moment in corporate history. Seven people in Chicago died after taking Tylenol capsules laced with cyanide. The tampering had occurred after the product left J&J's facilities, but the impact was immediate and severe. Tylenol was a popular pain reliever, but after the deaths, its market share plummeted from 37 percent to 7 percent, and J&J's stock dropped more than 20 percent.[8]

CEO James Burke had to decide what to do. He could have waited for government action or tried to convince people it was a local problem. But Burke believed in always putting customers first. He ordered a nationwide recall of all thirty-one million Tylenol bottles, costing the company $100 million (over $300 million in today's dollars). J&J gave customers refunds, set up hotlines, and told the public everything they were doing. They also worked with the government to create tamper-resistant packaging, which all drug companies still use.[9]

Burke's commitment to public safety and transparent communication, even at significant cost, demonstrated remarkable integrity. He put people before profits. As he said later, "[Integrity] was our sea anchor. It kept the company pointed into the wind when the sea got rough." His ethical leadership worked. After about a year, Tylenol regained most of its market share. Burke saved lives and the company's reputation by making safety the top priority and being transparent. His actions showed that integrity anchors individuals and organizations, especially in crises.[10]

Why It Matters

What lies behind us and what lies before us
are tiny matters compared to what lies within us.[11]

AS R. BUCKMINSTER Fuller said in the quote on the first page of this chapter, integrity is the key to success. It sets successful people apart from unsuccessful ones. It's vital for personal, relational, and professional achievements, acting as our moral compass through calm and storms.

The purest rationale for Unconditional Integrity is that it makes us happy. Humans are wired to feel good about doing good.[12] It nourishes our well-being. That doesn't mean it's easy. We often fail to do things that make us happy, even though we want to. But when we manage it, integrity brings us peace. It reduces stress because we avoid hiding lies or bad behavior. With integrity, we're at peace knowing our values and priorities and having the strength to follow them. Studies show focusing on our values reduces anxiety before stressful events. Knowing our values helps us distinguish between what's urgent and what's truly essential.[13]

Integrity helps us make friends. Just as we feel good about doing good things, we also feel good when we see others do them. Many of us try to be around those who do good because it makes us feel good too. Think about how natural it is to like the movie protagonist who tries to do the right thing. Living with integrity shows strength of character that people notice. We're attracted to those who demonstrate power and resilience because we hope it will rub off on us. Our appreciation grows as the movie hero endures daunting challenges in the pursuit of justice. We want to be capable of goodness in hard times, so we're drawn to those who are.[14]

Integrity is career-enhancing. Employers want trustworthy employees who keep promises, are consistent and authentic, act fairly, and are loyal. These qualities lead to sound decision-making, reliable performance, high-quality customer service, and effective management. Employees with integrity are less likely to act unethically or make serious mistakes—or, if they do, they're likely to accept the consequences to help recover efficiently. They get along well with coworkers and follow the organization's core values.

* * * * *

Seven-year-old Tanner Munsey was playing first base during a T-ball game in Wellington, Florida. He tried to tag a runner going from first base to second but couldn't. The umpire, Laura Benson, called the runner out. Tanner immediately went to Benson and told her that he had not actually tagged the runner. She reversed her call. Tanner's coach gave him the game ball for his honesty.

Two weeks later, in another game, the reverse happened. This time, Tanner did tag the runner, but Benson—umpire for this game, too—called him safe. She looked at Tanner and asked if he tagged the runner. He told her he had. She immediately called the player out. When opposing coaches and people in the crowd complained, she explained what happened in the last game and told them she trusted Tanner's honesty.[15]

* * * * *

What Matters About Each Element of Integrity

The most important element of integrity is **honesty**. Though sometimes difficult, honesty is always best in the long run because it builds trust and avoids the stress of managing conflicting stories or maintaining a facade. A study by Notre Dame researchers showed that frequent liars experienced more mental health problems than those who were honest.[16] Honesty enables genuine connections, which are crucial for healthy and fulfilling relationships. Being known as someone who doesn't deceive, cheat, or steal, admits mistakes, and gives credit where due earns others' support and allegiance. People feel secure and respected, fostering unity and collaboration. Honesty opens doors to partnerships and leadership roles. No virtue is more universally accepted as proof of good character.

Moral courage—doing the right thing—builds inner strength and helps us withstand future challenges. It develops self-respect, self-confidence, and conviction. It deepens belief in our values. It encourages critical thinking through principled decision-making. It's an example to others, inspiring them to act on their beliefs and contribute to a more responsible community.

Consistency between our thoughts, words, and actions minimizes stress and enhances self-discipline by improving control over our emotions and decisions. Our productivity increases since we don't have to adapt to changing circumstances. Regardless of the situation, maintaining standards leads to better results and provides experiences we can build on. Consistency builds credibility, which is vital in personal and professional relationships.

> Happiness is when what you think, what you say,
> and what you do are in harmony.
> —Mahatma Gandhi

Like honesty and consistency, **authenticity** promotes emotional well-being by reducing conflict between our inner and outer selves. Authenticity helps us feel comfortable in our skin. We establish a clear identity and better understand our values and purpose. When our public and private lives align, we make decisions that reflect our true goals and feel freer to express unique perspectives. This helps us form genuine connections and meaningful relationships.

Fairness earns esteem and resolves conflicts by bringing objectivity and impartiality to disputes. Though we don't always act fairly, we always recognize fairness when we see it. Fairness enhances morale, encourages camaraderie, and promotes open communication and collaboration.

Loyalty builds trust among friends, family, and colleagues. It creates a sense of dependability, stability, and security. It enables emotional bonds that provide comfort in tough times. It encourages cooperation and shared achievements. Being faithful inspires reciprocal loyalty, creating an environment conducive to peace and collective growth.

Be loyal to those who are not present.
In doing so, you build the trust of those who are present.
—Stephen R. Covey

*   *   *   *   *

Unconditional Integrity is the backbone of who we are. It means doing what's right when it's tough, being honest and reliable, and staying true to our principles, no matter what. It leads to a more meaningful life because living by our principles fosters fulfillment. Pride and self-respect come from knowing our actions align with our beliefs. The world values the qualities of integrity because they nurture strong friendships, well-run workplaces, connected communities, and stable societies.

Despite these benefits, we often take the easy way out. While doing the right thing brings richer, longer-term rewards, doing the wrong thing offers instant gratification that's too tempting. The next section explains where we go wrong; knowing the root cause of a problem is critical to fixing it. The two sections that follow then describe why and how to focus on the satisfaction that comes from living in alignment with our values, because inner peace is worth the effort.

First they came for the socialists, and I did not speak out—
    Because I was not a socialist.
Then they came for the trade unionists, and I did not speak out—
    Because I was not a trade unionist.
Then they came for the Jews, and I did not speak out—
    Because I was not a Jew.
Then they came for me—and there was no one left to speak for me.
—Martin Niemöller[17]

Where We Go Wrong

WE'RE ATTRACTED TO integrity—something in us craves it. The problem is that other parts of us—our crafty hands, wandering feet, and careless tongues—pursue shorter-term rewards. We want integrity, but only when it's easy. We're honest—when it's simple. We're fair and loyal when it helps us. But do our thoughts and deeds match our words, especially when facing problems? Are we who we say, think, or want to be?

> Character cannot be developed in ease and quiet.
> Only through experience of trial and suffering can the soul be strengthened,
> vision cleared, ambition inspired, and success achieved.
> —Helen Keller

In chapters 1 and 2, I used *spectrum* to describe ranges of conditional emotional responses, from positive to negative. On the Spectrum of Conditional Love, we choose how to feel based on who others are or how they treat us. The Spectrum of Conditional Gratitude drives our thankfulness to depend on what we have. Love and gratitude are vulnerable to conditionality.

While the emotional natures of love and gratitude make their vulnerabilities understandable, integrity's susceptibility is less obvious. As a quality rather than an emotion, we might imagine it's immune to conditionality—but we'd be wrong. We can fail at integrity in many ways, manifesting as dishonesty, betrayal, insincerity, hypocrisy, and corruption. We know what's right but compromise our ethics based on how we interpret others' behavior or the situation, choosing to benefit ourselves at others' expense.

The Trouble with Dishonesty

The simplest and most common failure of integrity is dishonesty. Dishonesty is lying, cheating, stealing, or misrepresenting the truth to gain an advantage or avoid negative consequences. While some cheating is premeditated, most often, we do it almost without thinking; an opportunity presents itself, and we take it. Maybe the student in front of us sits sideways at her desk, making her quiz answers visible . . . so we look. Or a friend tells us about a contract his company just won that will cause the stock to skyrocket but hasn't been announced yet . . . so we decide to invest.

Dan Ariely, professor of psychology and behavioral economics at Duke University, has researched dishonesty extensively and published *The (Honest) Truth About Dishonesty*. Ariely begins by explaining a common conception about honesty: our decisions are based on subconscious risk-reward analyses, weighing the likelihood and consequences of getting caught against the potential benefits. Ariely argues that's only part of the story. His central thesis:

> Our behavior is driven by two opposing motivations. On one hand, we want to view ourselves as honest, honorable people. We want to be able to look at ourselves in the mirror and feel good about ourselves . . . . On the other hand, we want to benefit from cheating and get as much money as possible . . . . Clearly these two motivations are in conflict . . . . This is where our amazing cognitive flexibility comes into play. Thanks to this human skill, as long as we cheat by only a little bit, we can benefit from cheating and still view ourselves as marvelous human beings. This balancing act is the process of rationalization.[18]

Ariely's research shows we generally act with integrity when we're being watched, but we're more likely to cheat when we think we're not. He describes experiments where participants inflated their task performance when they thought they weren't monitored, suggesting we may compromise our integrity if we think we can avoid repercussions. His key point is something we'd rather not admit: almost all of us cheat a little, at least occasionally, but not enough to make ourselves feel guilty.[19]

You should not live one way in private and another in public.
—Publilius Syrus

Research by the International Center for Academic Integrity reveals that about 95 percent of high school students engage in academic dishonesty, and over 60 percent of university students admit to cheating.[20] Almost all of us are dishonest, and we don't improve much as we age.

We'd like to believe that, in the working world, we know right from wrong and act accordingly. The truth is . . . not so much. Job pressures can be intense; meeting expectations and achieving success can feel like life or death. Under such stress, integrity often suffers. Recent studies show that 33 percent of employees across thirteen countries witnessed misconduct at work in the past year. In the US, 30 percent of workers reported seeing rule-breaking at work.[21] Only 21 percent of employees said they work in businesses with strong ethical cultures, while 40 percent said their companies had weak ethical cultures.[22] It should be a flashing red light with a blaring siren that over 50 percent of the largest corporate bankruptcies since 1980—Enron, WorldCom, and Lehman Brothers—resulted from unethical business practices.[23]

*　　*　　*　　*　　*

Many times in my career, I've managed complex aerospace technology development projects for government customers. On one such occasion, I led an industry team working for a government project manager named Jim (neither his nor other names are real). Jim had strategic vision and good rapport with government leadership, but he hadn't previously managed large teams, and his inexperience and insecurities showed in his management style.

Jim had a close relationship with Shawn, a senior member of my team. In a private conversation, Jim confided to Shawn that he didn't want Emma, an employee at our company, involved in team meetings, saying he didn't trust her. He couldn't provide a rationale, so his distrust seemed more like personal dislike. Jim insisted the information stay private. But Shawn felt that loyalty to the team mattered more to him than it did to Jim in this case, so he told me what Jim had said. Jim never directly excluded Emma from meetings. He acted normally toward her. When asked how he felt about her, he denied any negative feelings. However, he continued to privately remind Shawn of his desire to remove Emma from the team.

The contradiction between Jim's public and private behavior put us in a bind, caught between the private wishes of our customer and fairness to one of our company employees (not to mention the potential loss of her benefit to the team). Although the dishonesty was his, he'd forced us to deal with it.

Team dynamics fundamentally shifted from that point on. When talking with Jim, we necessarily replaced openness with careful diplomacy. Although he continued leading as if nothing had changed, the project had totally changed for me. Jim had provided a textbook example of how to lose the trust of your team.

* * * * *

We'd like to believe we would intervene when witnessing dishonest behavior, but research suggests otherwise. Ariely's findings show that when we see unacceptable conduct, we often "recalibrate our internal moral compass and adopt their behavior as a model for our own." If the transgressor is an authority figure, such as a parent, boss, or teacher, we're even more likely to follow. Ariely points out that social norms around honesty are often ambiguous, so others' behavior strongly influences us. In other words, cheating is infectious.[24]

Ariely explains that the gap, real or imagined, between us and those affected by our actions makes a big difference in our behavior. "We have an incredible ability to distance ourselves in all kinds of ways from the knowledge that we are breaking the rules, especially when our actions are a few steps removed from causing direct harm to someone else."[25]

> By a lie a man throws away and, as it were, annihilates his dignity as a man.
> —Immanuel Kant

* * * * *

Just because I'm writing this book doesn't mean I have a perfect record of integrity. Here's one example of many when I've failed. As the internet went mainstream in the late 1990s, many entrepreneurs rushed to create anything dot com to cash in. However, a few turned other people's moneymakers into freeware by putting paid goods online for free. Among the most public and prolific was music. Pirated music was ubiquitous. I found sites with thousands of songs posted for anyone to download. Of course, I knew it was wrong. It was technically stealing. Yet, I did it anyway. I told myself: "Everyone else is doing it." We weren't stealing directly from shelves in a music store. In my case, I wasn't ripping the songs from compact discs and posting them. I was taking advantage of what was publicly and freely available. But we all knew we were cheating musicians and the industry. We justified our lapses of integrity because the internet created a barrier between us and the music providers, and we used that barrier like a blindfold, pretending not to know what we were doing.

*   *   *   *   *

Ariely says we shouldn't treat a single act of dishonesty as a minor infraction, as just one instance can shape how we view ourselves and others. It's common to forgive first offenses because everyone makes mistakes, but it's crucial to identify and address all acts of dishonesty, no matter how innocent they seem. Once overlooked or accepted, dishonesty can spread like a virus. As dishonesty grows, ethical behavior slackens, breeding distrust and gradually damaging the community.[26]

To be clear, integrity doesn't require always providing every aspect of the truth. Ariely calls it a white lie when we lie for another's benefit, not for selfish reasons. His classic example: few married men think the best answer to the question, "Honey, how do I look in this dress?" is always the complete truth (at least not men who hope to stay married). In certain relationships, it's understood that we tell white lies, and we expect others to tell us white lies too. White lies can help preserve relationships.[27] Dishonesty is deception for personal gain at the expense of others, with disregard for Unconditional Love and Unconditional Gratitude.

Ariely explains that we tend to cheat in little ways without consciously considering our actions. We spend time at work on social media rather than working. We don't return extra change cashiers mistakenly hand us. We sell clients products they don't need to boost our sales. We constantly look for ways to benefit from dishonesty without hurting our self-image. Ariely asks, "Where is the line?"[28]

Dishonesty can seem trivial. No one notices, and no one gets hurt. However, dishonesty is often the starting point from which we depart integrity, and it quickly leads to other failures. Once we allow ourselves a little lie, like saying we performed better on a task than we did, it's simple to slip a little more, such as manipulating data to give others more favorable but false impressions of us (like including incorrect information on our resume). It's a short step from dishonesty to deceit. From there, it's another short step to betrayal—like sharing confidential information. Then, another step to hypocrisy—saying one thing but doing another. By then, we're close to full moral compromise, letting personal benefits overwhelm our ethics. If entrusted with power, we may slide all the way to corruption, using bribery, fraud, or abuses of power for personal gain. In all these cases, we decide based on what we think is best for ourselves in the moment, not what's best for others, the world, or ourselves in the long run.

> He who permits himself to tell a lie once finds it much easier to do it a second and third time, till at length it becomes habitual; he tells lies without attending to it, and truths without the world's believing him. This falsehood of the tongue leads to that of the heart, and in time depraves all its good dispositions.
>
> —Thomas Jefferson

* * * * *

One of soccer's most famous and controversial moments occurred during the 1986 FIFA World Cup quarterfinal between Argentina and England. Beyond the inherent excitement of a match between the final eight of the most important tournament in the world's most watched sport, there was extra anticipation and animosity between the countries due to lingering political tensions from the 1982 Falklands War.[29]

Six minutes into the second half, the score was 0–0. Near the English penalty area, Argentinian Diego Maradona, the best player on the pitch, passed to teammate Jorge Valdano. Valdano tried to take on several defenders, but the ball was intercepted, deflected off several players, and kicked high into the air toward the English goal by midfielder Steve Hodge. As the ball came down just inside the penalty box, Maradona and England's goalkeeper Peter Shilton jumped to reach it. Shilton, eight inches taller than Maradona, jumped forward with his right hand while Maradona did so with both his head and left arm outstretched. Despite his height disadvantage, Maradona managed to knock the ball into the net.[30]

However, Maradona's goal was illegal. Instead of heading the ball, which is allowed, he punched it with his hand, which isn't. Maradona celebrated while glancing sideways at the nearest official. The referee didn't have a clear view and believed Maradona had legally headed it in. The English players, seeing the action more clearly, loudly protested. The referee asked a linesman, but he didn't have a better view, so he confirmed the goal. Argentina took a 1–0 lead, and Maradona, his teammates, and Argentinian fans went wild.[31]

Four minutes later, Maradona dribbled past five English players, covering over half the pitch, and scored another goal. Argentina won 2–1 and went on to win the World Cup, with Maradona playing a central role.[32]

After the match, when asked about his first goal, Maradona said he had scored "a little with the head of Maradona and a little with the hand of God." From then on, the incident was known as the hand of God goal. For years, Maradona refused to admit he had scored illegally. However, Mexican photographer Alejandro Ojeda Carbajal had perfectly captured the moment, removing all doubt that Maradona hit the ball with his hand. Finally, in his autobiography published in 2000, Maradona acknowledged his offense, saying, "Now I can say what I couldn't at that moment, what I defined at that time as The Hand of God. What hand of God? It was the hand of Diego!"[33]

Maradona is celebrated for his talent and contributions to soccer. However, the hand of God goal remains one of the most contentious moments in sports history. It has been the subject of many debates about sportsmanship and is among the most infamous public examples of disregard for integrity.[34] Ironically, Maradona's second goal of the England match (scored just four minutes after the first) is regarded as one of the greatest displays of soccer skill ever. It showed he could lead his team to victory without cheating. He could have admitted his error on the first goal and still won the match and World Cup. We'll never know.

*   *   *   *   *

Although his was more public than most, and caught on film, most of us have to admit Maradona's failure of integrity wasn't that different from our own. Whether or not we view ourselves as people of integrity, we all slip sometimes. We know better and may want to do better, but we all fail, sometimes in small ways and sometimes big. What causes us to fail is treating integrity as contingent, dependent on circumstances or others' behavior. We abandon integrity because the outcome will be better for us. That's conditionality.

I noted that we may start with little lies, but when we practice conditionality, it's easy to slip from dishonesty to betrayal, hypocrisy, moral compromise, and outright corruption. As with love and gratitude, we tend to act along a *Spectrum of Conditional Integrity*. One extreme is conditional integrity, and the other is a complete lack of it. For simplicity, I'll use the made-up word *disintegrity* as a catch-all for the opposite of integrity. From integrity to disintegrity, the spectrum is contingent on the outcomes we want for ourselves.

Like with love and gratitude, we're taught integrity is contingent. Maybe not directly—most of us are told by our parents and teachers that we should always be honest, fair, and loyal—but indirectly (by watching others), we learn integrity doesn't always produce short-term profits. We see others forsake integrity to acquire more immediate advantages. When we hear one thing but see another, we accept that integrity has limitations, and we choose behaviors along the Spectrum of Conditional Integrity based on circumstances and how we evaluate the risks and rewards of our actions. When we act conditionally, we may choose dishonesty. If we believe the benefits are great enough, we may continue to slip further from integrity until any condition seems suitable for disintegrity.

> Be more concerned with your character than your reputation,
> because your character is what you really are,
> while your reputation is merely what others think you are.
> —John Wooden

Answers in Timeless Wisdom

I SHARED A story in the last section about Jim, a government manager with a strong strategic vision but poor leadership. Jim behaved in public as if there were no issues. Privately, he told Shawn—a member of my team—that he didn't want our colleague Emma involved with the team, but he didn't provide a good reason and denied any personnel concerns to others.

We didn't want to openly act against our customer's wishes, as he was clearly capable of reacting poorly and fabricating errors to make us look bad. Neither did we want to marginalize Emma unfairly. Ultimately, we tried to do the least harm—we kept Emma out of meetings involving Jim but retained her on the project in other capacities.

I left the project soon afterward—for many reasons, but this incident was a factor. I no longer trusted Jim, and I couldn't work for someone I didn't trust. He'd demonstrated how a leader's dishonesty corrodes individual careers and team culture and effectiveness. Once broken, a team's trust is more difficult to rebuild than individual professional relationships.

In retrospect, I'm ashamed of my own weakness in the situation. I had several opportunities to act with integrity: I could've scheduled a meeting with Jim to express concerns about the impact of losing Emma, focused on team effectiveness rather than personal bias. I could've refused to participate in Jim's exclusions, continuing to involve Emma everywhere her role warranted. I might even have documented the issue and brought concerns to Jim's superiors. In any case, I didn't confront him about his dishonesty because I lacked sufficient moral courage.

Due to my failures, I was complicit in his unprofessional behavior. I didn't act with blatant disintegrity, but neither did I do everything I could or should have. My integrity was conditional. I protected myself rather than risking my relationship with Jim or my position.

* * * * *

When our integrity is conditional, we make decisions based on cost-benefit assessments, and tempting situations can lead us to fall short of our best behavior. We act based on how much we can get away with while maintaining a good self-image. Yet, our self-image shouldn't depend on our actions, and integrity failures don't define us. They stem from conditional integrity.

The solution is Unconditional Integrity. It isn't situation dependent. It isn't determined by outcomes or advantages. No instance deserves integrity more than another, and we can do nothing to earn or forfeit it. It's based on internal values. Our thoughts, words, and deeds come from personal principles, not predicaments. It's not easy, but research shows it's possible—studies have found people with a strong sense of integrity behave consistently, whether or not they're being watched. They maintain high integrity regardless of circumstances and are less likely to compromise alone or under pressure.[35]

Unconditional Integrity disconnects us from the Spectrum of Conditional Integrity. It removes us from the slippery slope that easily carries us from integrity to disintegrity. Fortunately, integrity failures don't make us bad people. Those failures come from conditional integrity. When we practice Unconditional Integrity, we decide to be different.

Ultrasuccessful college basketball coach John Wooden said, "The true test of a man's character is what he does when no one is watching." What we do when we can get away with anything says something about us, but what we do when everyone is watching can be more revealing. That's when the stakes are highest and defending our values is hardest. Unconditional Integrity means complete and consistent wholeness of character. Our actions matter, but so do our thoughts before we act and our words after. Unconditional Integrity requires treating others as equals and showing it in what we do.

Unconditional Integrity transcends time and culture. It's always been central to who we are and has guided us through moral complexities. Many influential religious and secular thinkers have spoken about it throughout history. The following paragraphs include ideas from some of these thinkers, first on overall integrity and then on its elements.

Jesus taught the importance of integrity throughout his ministry.

And you will know the truth, and the truth will set you free.
—John 8:32 (NIV)

Blessed are those who hunger and thirst for righteousness,
for they will be filled.
—Matthew 5:6 (NIV)

Righteousness is living and acting according to moral principles even when doing so is difficult. Religions connect righteousness to living in alignment with divine will or cosmic order. In Christianity and Judaism, righteousness (*tzedek* in Hebrew) involves proper conduct toward others and maintaining a right relationship with God.

Muslims are advised to have integrity in all parts of their lives. The Qur'an condemns lying and cheating, encouraging believers to seek and uphold truth. Prophet Muhammad emphasized integrity as a critical Islamic virtue:[36]

When you speak, speak the truth; . . . discharge your trust . . . .
Guard your tongue against swearing falsely,
for swearing falsely leads a man far away from faith.
—Prophet Muhammad, Hadith

He who cheats us is not of us.
—Prophet Muhammad, Hadith

The best of people are those with the most excellent character.
—Prophet Muhammad, Hadith

Confucius believed integrity is central to personal character and community. He taught the importance of keeping promises, being sincere, and maintaining credibility.[37] In Confucian philosophy, *xin* means being honest, not breaking promises, and doing what we say we will do.[38] *Lian* relates to avoiding corruption and dishonesty, committing to moral principles, knowing right from wrong, and self-control.[39]

In Buddhism, dharma is living in harmony with moral principles and behavior that reduces suffering. Siddhartha Gautama, the "Buddha," taught a framework of integrity. His Five Precepts focus on refraining from harmful actions—killing, stealing, sexual misconduct, lying, and intoxicants—to guide ethical living and create internal and societal harmony.[40]

> Three things cannot be long hidden: the sun, the moon, and the truth.
> —Buddha

Aristotle taught that integrity isn't just a set of traits but a way of life developed through consistent virtuous actions.

> Moral excellence comes about as a result of habit.
> We become just by doing just acts,
> temperate by doing temperate acts,
> brave by doing brave acts.
> —Aristotle

Stoicism is a philosophy that began in Greece around 300 BC and influenced many cultures. Marcus Aurelius, a Stoic philosopher and Roman emperor, embraced living with integrity. The qualities of integrity guided him through the challenges of ruling an empire. He left a wealth of wisdom in his *Meditations*.[41]

> If it is not right, do not do it;
> if it is not true, do not say it.
> —Marcus Aurelius

Mahatma Gandhi, leader of the Indian independence movement, promoted nonviolent resistance, justice, and truthfulness as essential elements of integrity. He earned global and historical recognition for integrity and profoundly influenced civil rights movements worldwide. He emphasized that truth is fundamental and a vital part of integrity.[42]

Truth is by nature self-evident.
As soon as you remove the cobwebs of ignorance that surround it,
it shines clear.

—Mahatma Gandhi

Wisdom about Each Element of Integrity

Integrity, wholeness of character, is best understood by examining its individual elements and the sum of its parts. Great thinkers have contributed wisdom over the centuries to help us appreciate the depth and substance of each part.

Honesty, often the first quality used to judge our character, is crucial to integrity. Others' belief in our honesty is necessary for their trust. Unconditional Integrity requires honesty with others and ourselves, as well as self-trust. Self-trust doesn't mean thinking we know everything or that we will always think, speak, and do right. It's a belief in our fundamental integrity and confidence that our thoughts, words, and deeds are grounded in solid values. It helps us become self-reliant without meaning we're independent of others. Self-trust accepts that we'll make and learn from mistakes. It avoids self-punishment, which bogs us down in regret. It acknowledges failures while reinforcing that our integrity will persevere.[43]

Self-trust is the first secret of success.
—Ralph Waldo Emerson

Moral courage is choosing to act virtuously when we have the power to do otherwise. Most injustice is committed by people who don't intend to be unjust. They simply do nothing when they witness injustice. Aristotle emphasizes the importance of both doing the right thing and not doing the wrong thing.

What it lies in our power to do, it lies in our power not to do.
—Aristotle

Moral courage demands strength and determination in uncertain situations with conflicting interests or personal risks. Inspired by Gandhi, Martin Luther King Jr. preached and exemplified moral courage in the face of discrimination.

> The ultimate measure of a man
> is not where he stands in moments of comfort and convenience,
> but where he stands at times of challenge and controversy.
> —Martin Luther King Jr.

> Our lives begin to end the day we become silent about things that matter.
> —Martin Luther King Jr.

Unconditional Integrity requires **consistency** between thoughts, words, and deeds. Marcus Aurelius promoted consistency as a critical element of integrity. It's not just that our credibility depends on consistency. It's that our thoughts define us.[44]

> The happiness of your life depends upon the quality of your thoughts.
> —Marcus Aurelius

Authenticity matches who we are with how we act. Philosopher Søren Kierkegaard examined the importance of living according to our true selves.[45]

> The most common form of despair is not being who you are.
> —Søren Kierkegaard

Fairness is distributing justice equally, independent of characteristics or circumstances. Saint Thomas Aquinas taught that cultivating virtuous habits creates righteous behavior.[46]

> Justice is a certain rectitude of mind
> whereby a man does what he ought to do
> in the circumstances confronting him.
> —Saint Thomas Aquinas

Aristotle also emphasized fairness as a crucial personal characteristic.[47]

All virtue is summed up in dealing justly.
—Aristotle

Loyalty is standing by friends, family, and country. It's a pledge of allegiance and sacred commitment.

We men and women are all in the same boat, upon a stormy sea.
We owe to each other a terrible and tragic loyalty.
—G. K. Chesterton

When integrity is conditional, cost-benefit analyses drive decisions, and tempting situations can lead us to fall short of our highest standards. In these moments, our actions are guided by how much we think we can get away with while preserving our self-image. However, our actions shouldn't define our self-image, and lapses in integrity don't determine our worth. Failures stem from conditional integrity.

Unconditional Integrity distances us from the Spectrum of Conditional Integrity. It's consistent, applying to every situation and everyone, driven by a commitment to be our best selves. By embracing it, we release ourselves from evaluating each circumstance to decide if integrity is worthwhile. It spares us from the uncertainty and inconsistency of conditionality, providing comfort in its steadfastness.

It's not the honors and the prizes and the fancy outsides of life which ultimately nourish our souls. It's the knowing that we can be trusted, that we never have to fear the truth, that the bedrock of our very being is good stuff.
—Fred Rogers, "Mister Rogers"

How to Live It

WHEN INTEGRITY IS dependent, we can slide toward dishonesty, hypocrisy, and cowardice. We see how much we can get away with. We can't trust others because we're untrustworthy ourselves. Unconditional Integrity carries us beyond the limitations of conditionality. It saves us from questioning others' motives and purifies our own. We can rest in integrity's independence.

This section provides practical steps to strive for Unconditional Integrity personally, in relationships, as parents, and professionally. We can build honest, open connections with others based on authenticity and loyalty. We can teach integrity to our kids by modeling it and helping them develop their moral compass. We can bring integrity to our jobs to create an ethical culture that drives individual and team success and lead with integrity to inspire trust and right behavior.

Personal

Integrity is essential to a fulfilled life. While we can never be perfect, we can strive to be known as people of integrity, earning it through repeated thoughts, words, and deeds.

When we're honest, we share truthfully. We don't hide details, mislead, or deceive. We admit our mistakes.

With moral courage, we defend what we believe. We speak out and act if we see unethical behavior, even if it's unpopular. We stay committed to our ethical values, handling complex or sensitive topics compassionately and seeking solutions that align with our values.

Showing consistency means upholding our values in all parts of life. We avoid contradictions. We communicate clearly.

Being authentic means we're genuine. We express thoughts and feelings sincerely. We're self-aware and try to align our thoughts, nonverbal and verbal expressions, and emotions with our values. We avoid pretending to be something we're not, embrace vulnerability, and share our true feelings. We accept ourselves.

When we're fair, we make judgments based on facts. We listen to others and consider their perspectives with empathy. We support everyone, but especially those who are marginalized or oppressed.

Loyalty means being dedicated and faithful. We offer encouragement, help, and guidance in tough and good times. We keep confidences. We prioritize the well-being and harmony of our relationships.

Pursuing Unconditional Integrity is a never-ending quest. We'll have setbacks and periods of self-doubt. We must be patient with ourselves. We can admit our stumbles, learn from them, and recommit to integrity. What counts is the pursuit.

* * * * *

I saw Andy Roddick win his first professional tennis tournament in Atlanta in 2001. As a tennis enthusiast, I was interested in watching him play, and I saw him defeat Xavier Malisse in the final. Over the years, I watched Roddick with mixed feelings. I always cheered for him because of my connection to his Atlanta win (and loyalty to American players). He played a power game and was fierce on the court, which sometimes came across as brash. His intensity often spilled out verbally, usually funny but sometimes sarcastic and argumentative. However, I grew to appreciate and respect him for more than his tennis excellence.

On May 5, 2005, at the Italian Open in Rome, Roddick played Fernando Verdasco in the round of sixteen. Roddick, ranked number three in the world, was the tournament's number one seed and heavy favorite against the number-fifty-six-ranked Verdasco.[48]

Roddick dominated early, charging to a 7–5, 5–3 lead. He had Verdasco in a desperate situation, down love-40 on serve—triple match point; Roddick had three chances to win. Verdasco missed his first serve. Players are typically conservative on second serves to avoid losing the point on service, but Verdasco was aggressive, and Roddick couldn't return it. But the linesman called the serve out. Double fault on Verdasco. Game, set, and match to Roddick.[49]

As the crowd cheered, Verdasco ran to the net to shake Roddick's hand. Roddick walked toward the net too, but he stopped to examine the mark made by Verdasco's serve. He pointed to it, saying the serve had nicked the line. He told the umpire the serve was in, not out. Though neither the umpire nor linesman had planned to check the mark, Roddick insisted the serve was in. He wiped the mark with his foot and returned to his position. Stunned, the umpire reversed the call and awarded the point to Verdasco. Slow to grasp what had happened, then surprised but appreciative, the crowd applauded Roddick's gesture. The match restarted, still double match point for Roddick.[50]

Given another chance, Verdasco quickly overcame the deficit to reach deuce. They traded points, with Roddick gaining a fourth match point, but Verdasco saved it with a sharp backhand. Verdasco then hit a forehand winner and backhand passing shot, taking the game. Roddick was still up 5–4 and serving for the match with one of the sport's most intimidating serves. However, with a floating volley that fooled a charging Roddick, Verdasco broke to force a tiebreaker, which he won. He then took the third set 6–4 for a final tally of 6–7, 7–6, 6–4.[51]

Despite the astonishing turn of events, Roddick didn't appear disappointed post-match. He downplayed his sportsmanship, joking, "Maybe I should have stood on the mark. I don't think I did anything extraordinary. If the umpire had come down and looked at the mark, he'd have seen the ball was in. I just saved him the trip."[52,53]

*　*　*　*　*

The time is always right to do what is right.
—Martin Luther King Jr.

Relational

Integrity is essential to the health and happiness of relationships. In relationships with integrity, we experience the word's full meaning—undivided, whole. We work as a team, recognizing that we do better together than apart, and we prioritize the relationship. Doing the right thing for ourselves means doing the right thing for our partner.

Relationships with integrity are honest, open, and vulnerable. We listen to our partners and consider their hopes and dreams. We build and share deep emotional connections, discussing the issues we face now and in the future. Trust isn't betrayed. Relationships built on integrity are consistent—our thoughts, words, and actions align with our partner's expectations.[54]

Authenticity comes naturally with emotional connection; when we're connected, we're comfortable being ourselves. Maintaining integrity doesn't require always agreeing with or approving of our partner's decisions, just being fair.[55]

Integrity requires loyalty (though not to unhealthy degrees), which means working through tough times. It means taking time to sort things out rather than keeping score. It means remaining committed, continuing to communicate, and pursuing mutually agreeable answers. When we're apart, loyalty is continuing to prioritize the relationship, avoiding suspicious situations and inconsistencies between words and actions. When reunited, we're transparent about our actions while apart.[56]

Finally, relational integrity depends on the first two values. It requires our relationships to be centered on love—in the forms of compassion, kindness, and respect—and on gratitude as we continually think about and express appreciation for our loved ones.

Building relationships of integrity takes time. We can start by being wholly honest and authentic with our loved ones in all matters. As we demonstrate our consistency, we'll foster the trust that builds long-lasting loyalty and cultivates mutual support and commitment.

> To be trusted is a greater compliment than being loved.
> —George MacDonald

*   *   *   *   *

In his match with Verdasco, Roddick wouldn't have been criticized for accepting the bad call. He could have kept quiet and taken the victory. Honor calls aren't expected in modern sports; officials make the calls, and players abide by those decisions. The umpire had agreed Verdasco's second serve was out. Only Roddick's insistence caused him to change the call.[57]

Roddick lost a match he had essentially won an hour earlier—with officials and the crowd convinced the final point was over and Verdasco at the net ready to concede—had it not been for his act of sportsmanship. His integrity cost him tens of thousands of dollars, perhaps much more if he had gone on to win the tournament, which was highly possible. Integrity mattered more to him than winning or money. He lost the match but preserved his integrity and set an example of sportsmanship. He defied the usual way of the world and did what he thought was right.[58,59]

Andy Roddick chose integrity regardless of the consequences. In the 1986 World Cup, Diego Maradona chose deceit. Roddick sacrificed victory for integrity without a second thought. Maradona sacrificed integrity for one goal without a second thought. The difference? While Maradona's integrity depended on the situation and what he thought was best for him, Roddick's integrity wasn't based on the match's circumstances or how his decision would affect him—it was unconditional.

As a Parent

We want our children to understand the elements of character and realize that consistently striving for them is essential to being whole as humans. But integrity is hard to explain. It's harder to teach and hardest to model. We can't be perfect parents, especially when it comes to integrity. Sometimes, we will fail, and our children will see it. We hope those times are rare. The best we can do is strive for Unconditional Integrity and trust that our children will learn its importance through our ardent pursuit of the ideal.

> It is no use to preach to [children] if you do not act decently yourself.
> —Theodore Roosevelt

Integrity is vital to a healthy parent-child relationship. Our children must know what we stand for, reinforced by words and deeds. We engage our kids in conversations about our family's values—what matters to us—and the importance of living in alignment with them. We must communicate our expectations and follow up to ensure complete comprehension. One of the most significant gifts we give our children is a moral compass.

* * * * *

When I taught basic orienteering to my son's Cub Scout den, I discovered that instruction only goes so far. No matter how much we practiced with the map and compass in the classroom, they couldn't fully grasp the concepts until they went outside, used the tools themselves, made mistakes, and experienced successes. Only then could they absorb the lessons and find their way.

The same goes for a moral compass. We give our children a moral compass and map for life, point them in the right direction, and give them a nudge. Yet, they can't fully fathom orienting themselves until they go out into the world on their own. We must allow our children age-appropriate independence to make decisions, take responsibility for their choices, and experience autonomy and accountability before entering the world full-time. They must use their moral compass, make mistakes, and experience successes to know they can.

When I led the Scouts, I didn't hand them maps and compasses, drop them in the wilderness, and let them find their way out. Similarly, we can't expect our children to read their map of values and use their moral compass to find true north right away. We walk beside them, then behind them, and finally, stay in the general area. We should foster an environment where they feel comfortable discussing questions, concerns, and mistakes without fear of judgment.

* * * * *

Parents must reinforce positive behavior. We emphasize that pursuing integrity is more valuable than personal achievement. We solidify the connection between ethical conduct and the right results. When they make mistakes, we turn them into learning opportunities; discussing what went wrong, why it happened, and how to make better choices in the future. When they encounter ethical dilemmas, we talk about the possible outcomes of their choices and help them make informed decisions. When necessary, we guide them on what to do and not do. We always remind them that we believe in their ability to decide and act with integrity.

*　*　*　*　*

During high school, our son found a website containing questions and answers on the subject of one of his classes. The site was publicly accessible and unaffiliated with his school or teacher, so he used it as a resource for an upcoming exam. However, when he took the test, he realized many questions used identical wording to the online source he'd studied. The teacher had pulled exam content directly from that website.

When he arrived home that day, our son was distraught. Although he hadn't known his teacher was using the same material he'd found online, he felt like he'd cheated. When he told me and Beth, we tried to console him. We knew he hadn't intentionally studied the teacher's exact questions. Still, he had to do something about it. He couldn't keep using the website as a study guide if the teacher continued to extract test questions from it verbatim. We advised that the best course was to speak with the teacher, disclose his discovery of the website, and explain his realization about the test questions.

The next day, he approached his teacher and revealed what he'd found. Surprisingly, the teacher admitted he already knew about the site and that students had found it. He acknowledged pulling questions directly from it but didn't tell our son to stop using it or say he'd stop using it himself. Our son faced a new dilemma. If the teacher acknowledged students knew about the site but didn't prohibit its use, was using it wrong? Was the teacher setting a trap to catch cheaters?

The issue went unresolved. The teacher continued using the site for exam questions, and our son grappled with his conscience for the rest of the semester. He sought guidance multiple times, but we couldn't give a definitive answer. While he had done the right thing by informing the teacher, the teacher's ambiguous response left the situation open-ended and uncomfortable.

I acknowledge my parental bias, but I believe the teacher acted irresponsibly. Using verbatim questions from a public source he knew students accessed was careless and lazy. By not expressly forbidding the site, he abandoned students in an ethical gray area. Moreover, his appropriation of someone else's questions constituted a form of cheating and set a poor example of integrity for his students.

*   *   *   *   *

We may feel daunted by the task of instilling integrity in our children. We shouldn't. Our children don't need greatness—they need genuineness. Consistently striving for Unconditional Integrity is a powerful example, and our lapses sometimes offer the best lessons. Our son's ethical dilemma with his teacher allowed us to encourage him to question decisions that didn't seem right and to have the courage to initiate difficult conversations. Although solutions aren't always clear-cut, they're invaluable growth opportunities.

> The one thing I want to leave my children is an honorable name.
> —Theodore Roosevelt

At Work

Like a person, a company either has or doesn't have integrity—its culture determines it. Just as integrity impacts a person's success, the level of integrity in a company's culture plays a significant role in creating and sustaining value. The Ethisphere Institute, which promotes good corporate character, annually recognizes the World's Most Ethical Companies. The companies on that list in 2018 outperformed the US Large Cap Stock Index (a measure of US companies with the highest market values) by nearly 5 percent from 2015 to 2017.[60] In other words, companies with the highest levels of integrity performed the best.

Company cultures are defined by their leaders but maintained or destroyed by their employees. The professional integrity of the workforce shapes a productive and ethical work culture. Employers know this and value integrity in new hires and current employees. Employees with high integrity make sound decisions, produce reliably, deliver high-quality customer service, and interact well with colleagues. Employers know this and value integrity in new hires and current employees.[61]

Professional integrity leads to specific behaviors in the workplace. Showing up on time, being ready to work, and giving our best effort daily demonstrate this commitment. We never lie, cheat, or steal. Open communication undergirds our work relationships—we don't spread misinformation to customers to make a sale or to coworkers to make ourselves look good. We treat others' belongings, including company property, with the same care as our own.

> Whenever you are to do a thing,
> though it can never be known but to yourself,
> ask yourself how you would act were all the world looking at you,
> and act accordingly.
> —Thomas Jefferson

Moral courage enables tough decision-making. Quality standards—personal, collective, and corporate—matter, even under pressure to compromise. Reporting inappropriate or unethical behavior requires backbone, especially when it involves friends or supervisors. Direct confrontation of issues, rather than avoidance, strengthens workplace integrity.[62]

In the workplace, consistency, authenticity, fairness, and loyalty manifest through specific actions. Strong values and adherence to company policies guide daily conduct. Respectful treatment of coworkers includes patience, emotional control, and civil discourse. Diverse viewpoints deserve consideration. The defense of right ideas, combined with resistance to gossip, builds a culture of trust, fairness, and loyalty.

Building a culture of integrity in the workplace can seem like an uphill battle, especially if unethical behavior has become normalized. Although we must have integrity because it's right, we're also an example for others. One person can't create workplace culture alone, but our actions motivate others and can be the seed from which a culture of integrity grows. With cultivation by others, it can spread, making the organization an enjoyable, fulfilling, and prosperous place to work.

As a Leader

After Unconditional Love, the most essential value for leaders is Unconditional Integrity. Leaders who achieve the most significant long-term success build their leadership on personal and professional integrity.

John C. Maxwell, author of several influential leadership books, including the bestseller *The 21 Irrefutable Laws of Leadership: Follow Them and People Will Follow You*, defines his sixth law, the law of solid ground, by saying, "Trust is the foundation of leadership." Teams trust us when we lead with integrity. He says we must "treat trust as our most precious asset" and that "no leader can break trust with his people and expect to keep influencing them."[63]

Leaders without integrity eventually fail, no matter how persuasive or resourceful they are. Without integrity, they make decisions based on greed, self-protection, or personal whims, ultimately leading to ruin. No amount of intellect or charisma can outweigh the power of trust.

Trustworthy leadership begins with self-trust, giving us confidence to stand by our decisions and communicate rationale effectively. We're honest with ourselves and our teams. Nothing should be hidden—neither actions nor outcomes. We push our teams to be trustworthy, self-reliant, and ready to collaborate.

> Few delights can equal the mere presence of one whom we trust utterly.
> —George MacDonald

Moral courage in leadership demands refusal to compromise. Strong values guide right actions, even when it's hard. We don't have to pretend to be comfortable making difficult decisions, but we make them. While we can't expect perfection in team members, we must expect them to follow rules and acknowledge errors. Ethical conduct is nonnegotiable.

*　*　*　*　*

Nelson Mandela, a South African lawyer, became involved in politics and took leading roles against apartheid in the 1940s. In 1962, he was sentenced to life in prison for advocating equal rights. In prison, he was subjected to hard labor. Under harsh wardens, prisoners were worked to exhaustion, given insufficient food, denied beds and blankets, and barred from seeing their families. Yet Mandela maintained his moral courage. When food was rationed, he insisted other prisoners eat first. When it was cold and they lacked enough clothing, he made sure the neediest stayed warm. He was consistent in his words and deeds, regardless of his treatment.[64]

Twenty-seven years after arriving, amid international pressure and fears of civil war, Mandela was released. By then, even his jailers had become supporters. The integrity he demonstrated in his words and actions won over his enemies.[65]

Mandela and the country's then president led negotiations to end apartheid. In 1994, the country held its first multiracial general election, and Mandela was elected South Africa's first Black president. Despite nearly three decades of unjust imprisonment, he focused on fostering racial reconciliation and forgiveness. He established the Truth and Reconciliation Commission, which allowed victims and perpetrators of apartheid crimes to share their stories, seek amnesty, or face prosecution. This enabled the country to confront its painful past, admit the atrocities committed, and move toward a more just and united society. Mandela's dedication to reconciliation was pivotal in South Africa's transition to democracy, and his ability to forgive his oppressors showed remarkable integrity.[66]

*   *   *   *   *

Leadership credibility grows through consistency. Standards must be established, communicated, and demonstrated; we say what we do and do what we say. Team members naturally match their behavior to consistently upheld standards. We make decisions based on rational, open information, and then we stay the course as long as our rationale holds, but if factors change, we share the new data and lead down the best path.

People are drawn to authentic leaders. Our character shows in every interaction—meetings, emails, hallways, etc.—so we don't try to be someone we're not. Also, to foster comfort as a team and confidence in their collective abilities, we welcome team diversity.

We must be fair, reasonable, and objective with all members. Our decisions must be grounded in justice.

Loyalty manifests through steadfast support of organizational policies that preclude gossip and backbiting among the team. We always support members, even when they make mistakes. A supportive culture in which everyone feels valued reduces the temptation of unethical behavior.

Incorporating strong moral values in our daily behaviors encourages similar conduct by the team. When we prioritize integrity, harmony thrives, and cooperation becomes the norm. With integrity as our foundation, leadership traits like humility, selflessness, approachability, and discernment come naturally.

We strive to embody Unconditional Integrity in our leadership to build right behaviors, but when we're constantly faced with complex ethical decisions amid dynamic circumstances, we'll sometimes fail. That's okay. Trust grows not from perfect answers but from courage aligned with values. Teams respond to honesty and consistency. Authentic communication and principle-aligned decisions earn trust. Empathetic confrontation of unethical behaviors strengthens bonds. Direct, fair resolution of issues builds credibility. Trust, once earned, transforms into loyalty, creating cultures where integrity thrives.

> Waste no more time arguing about what a good man should be. Be one.
> —Marcus Aurelius

Chapter Summary

Integrity is the cornerstone of our character and the foundation upon which we build a life of meaning, purpose, and positive impact. It isn't just about honesty; it's about consistency in our thoughts, words, and actions. It requires moral courage to do what's right even when it's hard. It demands authenticity, fairness, and loyalty in all we do.

The reality is that we all fall short of perfect integrity. Dishonesty, betrayal, and hypocrisy stem from treating integrity as conditional and justifying compromises based on circumstance. True integrity is unconditional. It transcends situations and applies to every person. When we commit to Unconditional Integrity, we free ourselves from the trap of conditionality. We find peace in knowing who we are and what we stand for. We realize our potential to earn trust, inspire others, and drive positive change. When we pursue integrity with devotion and strive to align our innermost thoughts with our outward actions, we tap into the best of our potential. We become a force for good and truth in a world that desperately needs it.

When we accept the challenge of Unconditional Integrity and exemplify it in our thoughts, words, and deeds, it differentiates us from others and our former selves. It opens new opportunities to grow toward the best we can be. When built on Unconditional Love and Unconditional Gratitude, it takes on transformative promise and power. Unconditional Integrity is a superpower that can be ours if we're willing to work for it.

Encouragement and Questions for the Reader

You may become bogged down by the burden of Unconditional Integrity, frustrated that you fail despite genuinely good intentions. Personal growth isn't the pinnacle but a perpetual pilgrimage. Progress, not perfection, is the goal. You'll improve as you pursue the ideal.

Change starts with charting the course. Choose to pursue Unconditional Integrity and set off. You develop character by navigating an ocean of daily decisions; every choice to act with integrity strengthens your resolve. When you stand firm in your convictions, you stabilize yourself for future challenges. Consistency in your thoughts, words, and actions keeps your direction clear. You'll have setbacks, but each stumble is an opportunity to find your bearings and continue. By steadily seeking Unconditional Integrity, you'll create a life of profound purpose and impact.

The following are questions to ask yourself. As you seek to cultivate greater integrity, use them to help you choose one area where you can strive for unconditionality.

* Do you live by your core values, even when no one is watching? How can you strengthen your dedication to integrity in your personal life?

- Are your thoughts, words, and actions consistent, regardless of the situation or audience? What changes will you make to ensure you don't say one thing and do another?
- When faced with ethical dilemmas in your relationships, do you have the moral courage to stand up for what's right? Will you have difficult conversations to uphold your integrity?
- As a parent, do you consistently model integrity for your children through your words and actions? Are you giving them the tools they need to develop their moral compass? How can you help them navigate ethical challenges on their own?
- Are you true to yourself at work? Do you have the courage to report unethical behavior? How can you avoid compromising your values to fit in or get ahead?
- When making decisions as a leader, do you prioritize fairness and objectivity? What can you do to prevent biases from influencing your choices?
- What's one daily practice you can start today in pursuit of Unconditional Integrity as a lifelong commitment and source of profound fulfillment?

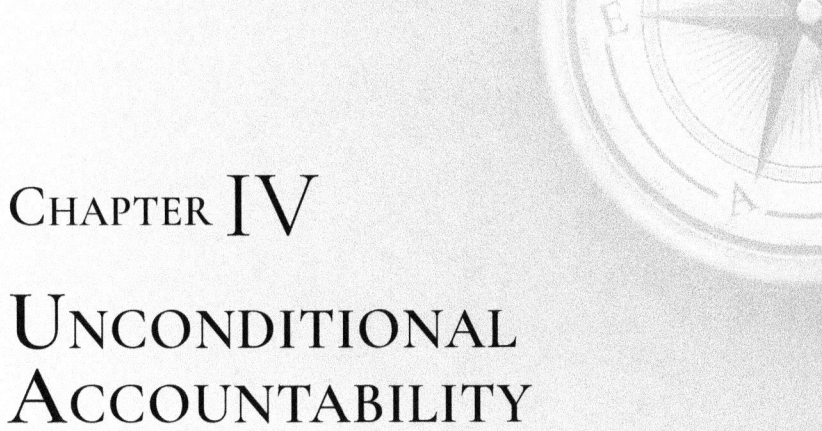

CHAPTER IV

UNCONDITIONAL ACCOUNTABILITY

I believe that accountability is the basis of all meaningful human achievement.

—Sam Silverstein

What It Is

OWN IT.

In early 2020s American slang, *own it* means either taking responsibility for our actions ("If that project you're managing fails, you have to own it.") or exhibiting something about ourselves confidently ("If you're going to wear a purple sequined jacket to a black-tie event, you've got to own it."). To own something means claiming it, acknowledging it's ours, and taking responsibility for it. These definitions capture the essence of accountability: taking ownership. It's accepting obligations and following through. Accountability combines doing what we *have to do* (our jobs), *should do* (our duties), and *say we'll do* (our commitments).

The first step in accountability is knowing our roles and responsibilities. These come from birth, culture, circumstances, and life choices. They can be divided into three categories:

- **Jobs:** Things we're legally or contractually required to do; things we *have to* do or else face consequences, such as being a:
  - Student (primary and secondary school)
  - Employee
  - Taxpayer

- **Duties:** Things we *should do* because we're born into them, result from our choices, or are the right things to do, such as being a:
  - Daughter/Son (in the *have-to* category until adulthood)
  - Sister/Brother (in the *have-to* category until adulthood)
  - Mother/Father
  - Citizen/Voter/Community Member

- **Commitments:** Things we *say we'll do*, resulting from choices about personal connections or activities, such as being a:

- Friend
- Teammate
- Student (post-secondary and beyond)
- Wife/Husband/Partner
- Supervisor/Leader

While some might argue that being a wife/husband/partner is a duty, it seems more like a commitment since we can leave this role, and many do. Similarly, mother/father allows more choice than other duties. However, once that choice is made, it's a duty—we can't stop being parents, only fail to do our duty.

Early in life, we don't choose our roles: daughter/son, sister/brother, and family member. These teach us what responsibility means and what fulfilling obligations entails. As we grow up, we take on more roles and gain control over managing our responsibilities as a student, community member, and citizen. In adulthood, we're expected to organize ourselves and choose our roles: wife/husband/partner, mother/father, and employee. When we become independent adults, we decide whether and how to handle the responsibilities for all our life roles—the jobs, duties, and commitments. For each role, we choose our level of ownership—how much we're willing to own it. That's accountability.

It is easy to dodge our responsibilities,
but we cannot dodge the consequences of dodging our responsibilities.
—Sir Josiah Stamp

*　*　*　*　*

As most children do, I began learning about accountability from my parents and teachers and watching others. My early duties were simple: personal hygiene, good manners, and cleaning my room. As I got older, my family responsibilities grew, and I made my own commitments, like friendships and joining sports teams. They taught me the value of following through and helped me build good habits. Doing chores at home gave me confidence in my ability to complete other tasks. By the time I left for college,

I'd developed a solid, though still growing, understanding of the responsibilities in various life roles and the satisfaction of doing things well.

Today, I have natural duties as a son, brother, and family member; chosen duties as a father, community member, and American citizen; jobs as an employee and taxpayer; and commitments as a husband, friend, teammate, and leader. Each role requires accountability, and I learn more every day about what that means. I'll never be perfect, but each time I complete one of my responsibilities, I experience fulfillment that only comes from accountability.

*   *   *   *   *

A critical aspect of accountability is recognizing that our actions have consequences. This involves two essential elements: free will and self-efficacy.

Free will is the ability to make decisions and take actions without being controlled by past events or other influences. It allows us to act independently and makes us responsible for the results. Actions made by free will can lead to credit or blame.[1]

Self-efficacy is the belief in the impact of our actions. It measures our confidence in our skills, not the actual skills themselves. High self-efficacy means we firmly believe that:

- Our actions can influence the result.
- We can steer the outcome toward our goal.

In other words, high self-efficacy is the conviction that we can substantially determine whether a task succeeds or fails. With high self-efficacy, we set ambitious goals, face challenges directly, view setbacks as opportunities, and persist in our pursuits. Low self-efficacy is associated with fewer goals, self-doubt, and a lack of determination.

Accepting free will and at least moderate self-efficacy is necessary for personal accountability. This book assumes free will exists and everything we do has consequences. Accountability means considering those consequences and living with them. It involves honesty with ourselves and others about our decisions and taking responsibility for the results.

Accountability requires forethought, which involves planning and imagining what could happen, both good and bad. It also requires vulnerability. We must acknowledge our actions, accept the consequences, and own the results, whether praise or criticism. Being accountable means admitting and apologizing for mistakes, giving credit where it's due, and not letting others take unfair blame. Everyone errs, so it also means remembering that everyone errs, forgiving ourselves and resolving to make better decisions in the future.

Accountability is one of The Unconditionals because owning it is a powerful factor in personal success. Unconditional Accountability begins and ends with ourselves. When we see the direct link between what we do and what we get, we realize that all successes and failures are ours. We stop making excuses. We enjoy achievements and learn from disappointments. Unconditional Accountability means owning our responsibilities without conditions.[2]

> Ninety-nine percent of all failures
> come from people who have a habit of making excuses.
> —George Washington Carver

Unconditional Accountability empowers us to be authors, not victims, of our lives. Those two options look like this:

Accountable		*Not Accountable*	
Behavior	**Thoughts**	**Behavior**	**Thoughts**
Seeks Reality	*What's happening?*	Avoids Reality	*I don't care what happens.*
Accepts Reality	*That's how it is.*	Fights Reality	*That's not how I see it.*
Owns It	*It's up to me.*	Makes Excuses	*It's not my job (or my fault).*
Finds A Solution	*What can I do?*	Waits/Hopes	*If meant to be, it'll happen.*
Takes Action	*I'll do it.*	Blames Others	*If you would do your job!*[3]

There are legitimate victims in the world who bear no responsibility for harms inflicted on them and deserve compassion and support. For the rest of us, feeling like a victim is more about attitude than circumstances. We must remove our veil of victimhood and be accountable.

* * * * *

In the aftermath of the Oklahoma City bombing, Bud Welch grappled with the tragic loss of his daughter Julie. Rather than succumbing to hate and blame, Welch made the difficult choice to meet with the father of Timothy McVeigh, the perpetrator of the attack. By extending empathy and seeking to understand, Welch took accountability for his own healing journey. He showed that even when senseless tragedy strikes, we can be accountable for how we respond.[4]

* * * * *

Successful people understand their roles, know their actions directly affect outcomes, and take responsibility. They face reality, accept it, and own the consequences of their choices. They consider the impact of their behavior and act in ways that lead to positive results.

Unconditional Accountability requires self-discipline to follow through on obligations, keep our word, and admit when we need to change. Self-discipline helps us avoid excuses, confess faults, and find solutions when we make mistakes. We also need self-discipline to own our emotions, thoughts, and words, but it's better to build the habit than live with the remorse of unchecked, hurtful words. As the saying goes, there are two pains in life: the pain of discipline and the pain of regret. The difference is that discipline weighs ounces while regret weighs tons.

Unconditional Accountability implies a commitment to excellence—doing our best in all responsibilities. This closely relates to Unconditional Endeavor, which will be discussed in the next chapter. Accountability means striving for excellence in everything we're responsible for.

Unconditional Accountability also means being determined to push through challenges. It requires us to overcome any obstacles to complete a task—this is perseverance. Perseverance is also a key part of endeavor, so it's covered more fully in the next chapter.

Achieving Unconditional Accountability in all situations is impossible. Being human means occasionally falling short. However, the ideal is worth pursuing. Committing to it means engaging our head, heart, and hands in owning our choices. If we consistently consider consequences, use discipline to act with good intentions, take responsibility for results, do our best, and persevere, we will succeed.

> Never, ever, blame others for what befalls you, . . .
> Trust you, and only you, to be responsible for your own life.
> —Diane von Furstenberg

Chapter 2 was about inside, chapter 3 was about outside, and this chapter is about connection because accountability is meaningless alone; obligations become relevant when we interact with others. Naturally, we want to collaborate effectively for collective benefit. It's fundamental to contributing to a well-functioning world. Our accountability profoundly impacts those around us, shared resources, our community, and the world.

* * * * *

Johnson & Johnson CEO James Burke's response to the 1982 Tylenol crisis (see chapter 3) exemplifies accountability in action. When seven people died from cyanide-laced capsules, Burke didn't wait for government directives or try to minimize corporate responsibility, even though the tampering occurred after the products left J&J's facilities. He immediately ordered a recall of thirty-one million bottles, established customer hotlines, and maintained transparency about the company's actions. Rather than deflecting blame, he took ownership of both the crisis and its solution. His accountability not only saved lives but also restored public trust.[5]

* * * * *

Accountability vs. Integrity

The topics of this chapter and the last one are closely linked. Integrity is thinking, saying, and doing the right things according to our values and living those values in the world. Accountability is thinking, saying, and doing what we're supposed to do according to our jobs, duties, and commitments. The two principles overlap in certain ways. When we practice accountability, we consider the consequences of our actions, doing so with integrity by following our moral and ethical principles. Also, accountability means we're responsible for our thoughts, words, and actions, which relates to integrity's element of consistency—our thoughts, words, and actions must align with our values. We can't have Unconditional Integrity without personal accountability, and we can't have Unconditional Accountability without personal integrity.

However, the two are distinct from each other. The critical difference lies in *ownership* and what each word implies that we own:

- Integrity is owning our thoughts, words, and actions and keeping them aligned with our values. For example, if honesty is a cherished value, integrity requires that we think and speak the truth and act honestly.
- Accountability is owning our thoughts, words, and actions regarding our life roles and fulfilling the responsibilities of each role (son/daughter, father/mother, employee/supervisor, leader, priest/pastor/imam/rabbi, politician, etc.) For example, as an employee, accountability requires that we follow company policies and complete our assigned tasks on time.

Sometimes, the two principles might conflict with each other. For example, suppose a journalist discovers corruption within her news organization. Integrity—her values of honesty and justice—require her to expose the wrongdoing. Conversely, accountability—her role as an employee—requires discretion and doing what's best for the company. She must decide how to balance the two principles and whether one might outweigh the other in certain areas.

Therefore, it's crucial to understand Unconditional Accountability separately from Unconditional Integrity.

* * * * *

Martin Luther King Jr. and Mahatma Gandhi exemplified integrity and accountability in their commitment to justice and equality. Dr. King built his leadership of the civil rights movement on a foundation of personal integrity. He held himself accountable to his nonviolence and civil disobedience principles, even in the face of threats and imprisonment. His "Letter from a Birmingham Jail" affirmed his commitment to both, as he argued that "one has a moral responsibility to disobey unjust laws."[6] Similarly, Gandhi led India's struggle for independence with adherence to truth, nonviolence, and self-discipline. He endured hunger strikes to show his willingness to suffer the consequences of challenging injustice. Like King, his ideas often blended personal accountability with integrity; he said, "To believe in something, and not to live it, is dishonest."[7] These two leaders demonstrate that combined commitment to Unconditional Integrity and Accountability can incite positive change in communities and even nations.

* * * * *

Accountability vs. Responsibility

Responsibility is also closely connected with accountability. Many people confuse or use them interchangeably. They're related but distinct concepts.

Responsibility is the obligation to perform a task. The task may be given, come from a life role, or voluntarily be undertaken. It doesn't require thinking about the consequences of the task, only completing it and meeting deadlines and standards.

Accountability is the obligation to ensure a task is performed. It's being answerable for the assigned work and its results. We aren't required to carry out the task ourselves; we only need to ensure it gets done and own the outcome. It involves understanding how actions affect stakeholders, goals, and objectives. If goals are not met, accountability requires transparency about the failure, evaluating the reasons, and committing to improvement.

Commitment is an act, not a word.
—Jean-Paul Sartre

While we can assign, delegate, or share responsibilities, we can't share accountability. When we accept a role, we're accountable for ensuring the responsibilities associated with that role are performed. For example, when I became a father, I became accountable for the responsibilities of fatherhood. Whether or not I carry out those responsibilities and how well they're achieved depends on me. I'm the only person who can own and answer for them.

Why It Matters

Once upon a time, there were four people named Everybody, Somebody, Anybody, and Nobody. There was an important job to be done. Everybody was asked to do it. Everybody was sure Somebody would do it. Anybody could have done it, but Nobody did it. Somebody got angry because it was Everybody's job. Everybody thought Anybody could do it, but Nobody realized Everybody wouldn't do it. In the end, Everybody blamed Somebody when Nobody did what Anybody could have.

—Charles Osgood

WHAT'S MISSING FROM the story above? Accountability. No one is assigned or takes responsibility because none of the characters are accountable. Eventually, "Nobody did it," which is a play on words but points to the fundamental problem: Without accountability, there's no ownership or clarity, emotions run high, there's finger-pointing, and nothing gets done. If one of the characters is accountable, not only does the job get done, but outcomes are considered, decisions are transparent, actions are performed optimally, and credit (or blame) is fairly given.

Accountability is an essential personal trait. We need it to fulfill our responsibilities in our families, workplaces, and communities. It compels us to try to meet expectations, not procrastinate, and be punctual. We admit mistakes, learn from them, and strive to improve.[8]

Accountability makes us reliable, doing what we say we'll do. Keeping promises earns respect and strengthens relationships. Reliability boosts our reputation, leading to personal growth and career opportunities.

Accountability fosters a culture that identifies issues, addresses concerns, and finds solutions. A pillar of professionalism, it promotes commitment to life roles, performance standards, and principles. It spurs cooperation and a shared sense of responsibility, helping teamwork thrive.[9]

In society, it makes business and government work and keeps daily life running smoothly. Accountability creates connections across the world that are essential to Earth's long-term health and safety.

Although we may understand all the benefits of accountability, we still struggle to pursue it. The next section explains where we go wrong. When we know what causes our mistakes, we can work toward resolving them. The two sections that follow explain how Unconditional Accountability helps us take control of our lives. It unlocks the traps of blame and self-pity and supplies the power to own our outcomes.[10]

Where We Go Wrong

ACCOUNTABILITY IS CHOOSING to be in control of our lives. It's considering consequences and taking responsibility for emotions, thoughts, words, and actions. However, it's not easy, so most of us practice conditional accountability.

In the first three chapters, I described a spectrum covering typical conditional responses to people and circumstances. I explained we choose how to feel on the Spectrum of Conditional Love based on who others are or how they treat us, how to feel on the Spectrum of Conditional Gratitude based on what we have, and how to behave on the Spectrum of Conditional Integrity based on circumstances and how we evaluate the costs and benefits of our actions.

There's a *Spectrum of Conditional Accountability* too. When our accountability is conditional, we only own our outcomes *if* they turn out how we want. If not, we quickly abandon accountability and slide down the spectrum toward unaccountability.

* * * * *

On December 3, 1984, a toxic gas leak at a Union Carbide pesticide plant in Bhopal, India, killed thousands of people and injured hundreds of thousands more in what was the world's worst industrial disaster to date. In the aftermath, Warren Anderson, the company's CEO, flew to India and was arrested. He was quickly released on bail and immediately left the country.[11]

Union Carbide denied responsibility, claiming sabotage by a disgruntled employee. However, investigations revealed that the plant had major deficiencies, including broken and malfunctioning safety systems, poor maintenance, minimal safety training, and cost-cutting measures that compromised safety protocols.[12]

Although he was charged with homicide, Anderson didn't face trial. He never returned to India despite multiple extradition requests by the country's authorities. He lived freely in the US until he died in 2014. Union Carbide ultimately paid a settlement of $470 million in 1989 (about $2,200 per victim) while maintaining they had no liability. The company was later acquired by Dow Chemical, which also denied responsibility for cleaning up the site or compensating victims.[13]

The site remains contaminated, and many survivors and their descendants still suffer health issues. The case stands as a stark example of corporate evasion of accountability for a preventable catastrophe that led to massive human suffering.[14]

> Without accountability, there's no civilization.
> —Abhijit Naskar

* * * * *

The Trouble with Unaccountability

We allow unaccountability into our lives in many ways, from innocent to immoral. Seven common ways fall along the Spectrum of Conditional Accountability, from mildest to most severe; we'll call them the seven D's:[15]

- Daftness
- Disregard
- Diffusion
- Deflection
- Denial
- Default
- Dereliction

In the following paragraphs, I include descriptions of the seven D's, along with a couple of sentences on how Warren Anderson and Union Carbide failed at each of them.

Accountability is the line of control between human and animal behavior.

—Abhijit Naskar

Daftness

One issue with accountability is simply that we're daft or clueless. We don't know whether certain jobs, duties, or commitments belong to us or what their responsibilities are. We don't know how to follow through or grasp the consequences of our choices and lack the skills to predict what could happen. The best way to learn accountability is often through a role model. Without one, we can lack self-awareness.[16] But can we be self-aware enough to know we're not self-aware? We can ask ourselves: "Can others count on me to do what I say? Do others see me as reliable? How can I tell?"

Union Carbide CEO Anderson displayed astounding daftness by visiting India without a solid legal strategy, leading to his arrest and hasty escape. His impulsive approach heightened suspicions of guilt and damaged the company's credibility.[17]

Disregard

The first step to avoiding accountability with little effort is disregard. Disregard is a lack of concern. We ignore responsibilities, treating duties as unworthy of consideration. A prime example is littering in public spaces; it's selfish, lazy, and a blatant breach of personal accountability—a complete lack of ownership.

Union Carbide displayed indifference to repeated warnings about safety hazards at the Bhopal plant, including a 1982 safety audit that identified many serious risks. Their disregard continued after the disaster, when they ignored the survivors' suffering.[18]

Diffusion

After disregard, we slip to diffusion. Diffusion is downplaying the importance of our duties. We don't ignore duties or pretend they don't exist; we act to diminish them, saying, "What's the big deal?" We point out that many avoid accountability, so it must be acceptable. For example, if criticized for littering, we claim, "Everybody does it."

Union Carbide spread responsibility across multiple levels of management and between Indian and American operations, making it impossible to hold any single entity accountable. Anderson exploited this organizational complexity to shield himself from personal liability.[19]

> Weaseling out of things is important to learn.
> It's what separates us from the animals . . . except the weasel.
> —Homer Simpson

Deflection

The next step is deflection. Deflection is shifting focus to someone or something else and diverting attention from our responsibilities. We search for someone who seems more flawed than we are: "What about that guy? He's getting away with something much worse." Continuing with the littering example, if we deflect, we say, "At least I don't throw trash out my car window onto the road, like that couple in front of us!"

When faced with evidence of negligence, Union Carbide pointed fingers at a supposed disgruntled employee saboteur while also blaming the Indian government and local workers.[20]

Denial

If deflection doesn't work, we turn to denial, or rejection of reality. Denial means refusing to acknowledge our commitments, as if they don't exist. We often deny accountability to guard our ego. We see accountability as a threat to our self-image. We want to protect the perception of perfection. Appearing flawless can feel more important than acknowledging and addressing issues, so we avoid risk by not accepting accountability.

I'm convinced one of the chemicals that comes with puberty infuses our bodies with expertise in denial. All teens seem to know the tactics and phrases. (Not my teenagers, of course. Mine are angels.) Aiming to manipulate their parents, they make excuses, blame others, and play the victim with phrases like "No one understands what I'm going through,"

"Why do bad things always happen to me?" and "There's nothing I can do to fix this."

In all fairness to teenagers, adults aren't immune to denial. We also fear embarrassment and go to great lengths to hide our mistakes, just in more professionally acceptable ways. For example, if a work project we're managing fails, we criticize our colleagues because we don't want to be seen as a failure, even though we were responsible for oversight.

Anderson and the company denied wrongdoing despite overwhelming evidence of safety failures. The CEO declared, "Union Carbide has done nothing wrong," even as thousands lay dead and many more were dying.[21]

Default

As we slide more toward unaccountability, we default on our commitments. Default is ducking our responsibilities and not doing what we're supposed to do. Default takes many forms and has many causes. If we aren't reliable, whether from laziness, procrastination, or lack of follow-through, we erode and can eventually eliminate others' trust in us.

One common cause of unaccountability is poor self-discipline. We may genuinely want to act responsibly but lack the discipline to do so. Our craving for instant gratification outweighs our desire for long-term rewards. Another cause, evasion, is a more deliberate, actively avoiding accountability to escape the consequences of our actions. We evade to dodge discomfort, as taking responsibility can be emotionally challenging. When our brain senses potential negative emotions, it signals us to run the other way.

Whatever their cause, the results of defaulting are the same: we fail to keep our promises and become wholly undependable and unreliable.

Union Carbide defaulted on its moral and legal obligations by providing inadequate compensation and refusing to clean up the site. It also withheld critical information about the composition of the leaked gases, hampering medical treatment efforts and preventing doctors from providing proper care to victims.[22]

Wisdom stems from personal accountability.
We all make mistakes; own them. . . learn from them.
Don't throw away the lesson by blaming others.
—Steve Maraboli

Dereliction

Derelict sometimes describes a house in deplorable condition due to disuse and neglect. The same can be said of us if we refuse to accept accountability. Dereliction is extreme unaccountability—open, shameless neglect of our duties. It isn't ignoring or downplaying but acknowledging responsibilities while refusing to do anything about them. Dereliction is worse than irresponsible; it's corrupt. If we go so far as opposing our obligations, dereliction can become delinquent, even criminal.

Anderson abandoned his duty as CEO by fleeing India and spending the rest of his life avoiding justice, while Union Carbide abandoned its responsibility to the community by selling the company to Dow Chemical without fairly dealing with the devastating consequences.[23]

Entitlement

I introduced entitlement in the chapter 2 discussion of gratitude. While some say entitlement is the opposite of gratitude, I believe it stems from a lack of personal accountability. Although it doesn't start with a *D*, it belongs to the abovementioned seven issues. (Plus, isn't it fitting for entitlement to be awarded a place with the others despite not following the same rule?)

We all want success, but it's only possible when secured by accountability. With entitlement, we expect success without earning it. We're quick to take credit (often overinflated), but we reject blame. We avoid the responsibilities that come with roles like student, employee, or citizen but still expect the benefits.[24] We expect to receive more than we give, assume output should exceed input, and presume preference without performance.[25]

High living standards in developed nations have created privileged environments that lead to a sense of entitlement.[26] Childhood consultant

Karen Deerwester says, "It took decades of consumerism and wealth, super kids, supersized egos, and hypervigilant parents to amp up to current levels of entitlement behavior."[27] In chapter 2, I blame first-world problems for unwarranted worry. First-world expectations can be blamed for rampant entitlement.

In the workplace, entitled employees suffer from a "disconnect between what [they] expect to achieve and what they're capable of achieving."[28] They expect more praise, rewards, and perks than their skill levels, workloads, performance, or company policies suggest are reasonable or consistent with their colleagues.[29]

> Don't go around saying the world owes you a living.
> The world owes you nothing. It was here first.
> —Robert Jones Burdette

So what? What's the harm in the seven D's and entitlement? What happens if we're unaccountable? When we don't take responsibility for our actions, we lose others' trust, damaging relationships. We struggle with guilt and increased stress. If our unaccountability slips into dereliction and delinquency, we can face life-altering legal troubles.

When employees neglect critical tasks, the impact ripples across the organization. Jobs go unfinished, deadlines are missed, and productivity suffers. Coworkers feel resentment and start finger-pointing. Mediocrity becomes acceptable. Unaccountability sabotages morale and causes disengagement, leading to poor decision-making, failures, and financial and personnel losses.

* * * * *

While watching television recently, I saw an advertisement for a local roofing company. My eyes usually glaze over during commercials, but this one grabbed my attention with the most understated catchphrase I've ever heard: "We Show Up." I laughed out loud. I doubt the business was claiming their greatest strength is arriving for appointments. They likely discovered that many of their roofing competitors do struggle to arrive, on time or at all, for scheduled jobs. Evidently, the problem is so prevalent that the company believes it can separate itself from the pack simply by showing up—so they plainly say so. I hope the commercial doesn't reflect how rare the most basic displays of accountability have become, but I'm afraid it does.

*   *   *   *   *

In a culture of unaccountability, it's impossible to trust others. We see public figures who lack accountability, undermining our confidence in institutions and governance. We see powerful people avoid consequences, perpetuating inequality and injustice. If unaccountability seeps into all parts of society, it can erode our norms and values and create chaos.

> Failing to hold someone accountable is ultimately an act of selfishness.
>
> —Patrick Lencioni

At their core, the seven D's and entitlement are about selfishness. By putting ourselves first, we act without regard for our responsibilities, don't consider the consequences of our actions, and fail to own our outcomes. The damage might be minimal if the consequences are confined to personal problems, but as noted above, that's seldom the case. We live in an interconnected world. The unaccountability of one affects us all.

Accountability in the Commons

In 1968, ecologist Garrett Hardin introduced an influential economic theory in his article "The Tragedy of the Commons." This theory describes a situation where multiple people can access a shared resource called a *common*. Hardin suggests that every person, acting independently and rationally, will use the common as much as possible for their benefit. When everyone does this, the common becomes depleted or spoiled, which is bad for all users—hence the tragedy.[30] According to this theory, selfishness overcomes accountability.

For many years, Hardin's theory was widely accepted. Most believed that people would inevitably overuse and destroy shared resources because our short-term self-interests always outweigh the long-term common good. However, in 2009, political economist Elinor Ostrom won the Nobel Prize in Economics for her book *Governing the Commons: The Evolution of Institutions for Collective Action*. She disproved Hardin's theory through field studies in small, local communities. Ostrom found that people can cooperate to create rules that sustain shared resources economically and ecologically. They monitor usage and enforce rules to prevent the destruction of commons.[31] In other words, accountability can triumph over selfishness.

Both theories, tragedy and triumph, hold truth. It's easy to find real-world examples of depletion and sustainment of shared resources. We're prone to prioritize self-interest over the common good, but we also have the ability—and, with effort, the willpower—to support the common good through accountability.

Consider shared public spaces like roads and waiting lines. When driving, we share the road with many others whose interests and issues we often don't know or care about. Similarly, when waiting in line—at a fast-food counter, bank, or grocery store—we share the queue with strangers. In both cases, we want to get through with as little trouble as possible.

However, if one person chooses self-interest over accountability in these commons, it spoils the resource for everyone. Reckless driving, ignoring road signs, or exhibiting road rage turns a safe, convenient transportation method into a dangerous one. Cutting in line or behaving rudely in a queue creates anger and disorder. Refusing to act with accountability in shared spaces depletes the common resource and hinders society's effective operation.

> It is wrong and immoral to seek to escape the consequences of one's acts.
> —Mahatma Gandhi

Accountability extends beyond our jobs, duties, and commitments to how we behave in almost any situation. We're highly interdependent across our families, friends, and communities, so our words and actions can impact others in unexpected ways. We must understand how our choices affect the well-being of others, locally and globally. In a shared environment, including virtual ones, our responsibilities are collective. This doesn't mean the responsibilities fall to Everybody. As noted above, with that approach, they are done by Nobody. It means we—all of us who share that environment—equally bear the responsibilities. We hold ourselves and others accountable to avoid a tragedy of the commons, which would ruin it for everyone.[32]

* * * * *

Some may say I'm petty or outdated, but I view silence as a common good. I love the sounds of nature—birds chirping, streams bubbling, or steady rain falling—but air that's free of noise made by man or machine is sacred. I acknowledge that industrial clatter is inevitable, and I value human sounds as much as anyone (my wife doesn't appreciate some human sounds as much as I do), but I think we should minimize the sounds we make whenever possible. For me, the point is respecting others' right to silence.

I get it—making a racket is part of being human, so we have to be able to handle a little hubbub without getting grumpy. I agree. I also believe that sound-making is a freedom everyone should enjoy. Having said that, most of us carry our creation of commotion beyond what's reasonable, as we do with most common goods. Most importantly, we ignore that those around us have as much right to their sound space as we do, and we fill ours and theirs with whatever hullabaloo we produce. Examples that irk me are people playing music, watching social media videos, or conducting personal phone calls in speaker mode, loudly, and in public. While everyone should be allowed to savor their entertainment and conduct personal conversations, so should those in the vicinity be able to choose their own sounds without interference.

Like others described in this section, man-made sound pollution is caused by self-interest overriding accountability. One individual prioritizes immediate personal benefit over long-term, collective well-being, diminishing a shared resource. It typically involves otherwise considerate people who don't recognize the impacts of their actions on others.

* * * * *

A common most of us frequently share is the internet. Unfortunately, the virtual nature of online platforms makes them exceptionally vulnerable to misconduct. Easy anonymity, digital detachment, and lack of regulation weaken or eliminate the barriers to bad behavior that exist face-to-face. Without accountability, cyberbullying, spreading misinformation, hacking, identity theft, and other destructive practices prosper with few to no repercussions.[33]

Even in-person communities, where identities and actions are visible, can be overrun by mischief and injustice. We often ignore discrimination, marginalization, unfair resource distribution, overconsumption, and unequal access to opportunities, but they preserve societal imbalances. These tragedies continue to exist because we consider accountability conditional. We choose our accountability based on whether or not we think it will benefit us. Often, we think it won't, so we prioritize self-interest over social responsibility.[34] As Ostrom shows, we can think long-term and choose in favor of the commons. Unfortunately, conditional accountability condemns us to suffer more tragedies than triumphs.

The root of our accountability problem, like with the first three values, is our belief that it must be conditional. This belief lets us off the hook. It leads us to abandon accountability if circumstances don't go our way.

The Spectrum of Conditional Accountability seems to come naturally, but we learn it from others. We see others prioritize self-protection over accountability and slide down the spectrum from disregard to dereliction. We witness unaccountability daily, making it seem more acceptable, but we know better.

With all the ways we learn to avoid accountability, it's easy to fail at it regularly. However, these failures don't define us. They stem from a belief in conditional accountability. We can choose a new belief. We can decide our identity isn't conditional and that we won't live conditionally.

Answers in Timeless Wisdom

THE SOLUTION IS Unconditional Accountability. It isn't dependent. It's based on principles. It's not afraid of outcomes because it always applies. We can break from the Spectrum of Conditional Accountability and avoid the slippery slope from accountable to unaccountable. When we practice unconditionality, we can't suddenly slip back onto the spectrum. Unconditional Accountability is isolated, and as long as we genuinely strive for it, we're immune to conditionality. Unconditional Accountability becomes part of who we are.

Adopting Unconditional Accountability requires an intentional, rational decision to change our thinking and living. Self-awareness and self-discipline are essential. We don't stop making mistakes, but we take responsibility for them and work to make amends. We admit when we've fallen short, seek ways to right our wrongs, and learn from our experiences. Holding ourselves to the highest standards, we steadily grow into our best selves.

*   *   *   *   *

The Parable of the Talents

A man going on a journey . . . called his servants and entrusted his property to them. To one he gave five talents of money, to another two talents, and to another one talent, each according to his ability. Then he went on his journey. The man who had received the five talents went at once and put his money to work and gained five more. So also, the one with the two talents gained two more. But the man who had received the one talent went off, dug a hole in the ground and hid his master's money. After a long time, the master of those servants returned and settled accounts with them. The man who had received the five talents brought the other five. "Master," he said, "you entrusted me with five talents. See, I have gained five more." His master replied, "Well done, good and faithful servant!

You have been faithful with a few things; I will put you in charge of many things. Come and share your master's happiness!" The man with the two talents also came. "Master," he said, "you entrusted me with two talents; see, I have gained two more." His master replied, "Well done, good and faithful servant! You have been faithful with a few things; I will put you in charge of many things. Come and share your master's happiness!" Then the man who had received the one talent came. "Master," he said, "I knew that you are a hard man, harvesting where you have not sown and gathering where you have not scattered seed. I was afraid and went out and hid your talent in the ground. See, here is what belongs to you." His master replied, "You wicked, lazy servant! You knew that I harvest where I have not sown and gather where I have not scattered seed? Well then, you should have put my money on deposit with the bankers, so that when I returned I would have received it back with interest. Take the talent from him and give it to the one who has the ten talents."
—Matthew 25:14–30 (NIV)

The Parable of the Talents is a well-known biblical story. Jesus uses it to illustrate the importance of wisely using our God-given abilities. It's also a lesson in accountability, encouraging us to be responsible for our duties and opportunities. A master gives each servant a responsibility—to take care of his talents. Back then, a denarius was a typical day's wage. A talent was worth about six thousand denarii, or around sixteen-and-a-half years of wages. This made the master's trust in his servants significant, even for the servant given only one talent.[35] The master expected accountability.

Stewardship means taking care of something, like money, property, or an organization. It means being responsible for it despite not legally owning it. In the parable, the master entrusts his servants with stewardship of talents. The straightforward interpretation is that God entrusts all people with stewardship of talents. Our modern meaning of *talent* (natural ability) perfectly fits this parable. God gives us all skills and abilities—some seemingly have more numerous, visible, or desirable ones, but we all have them. God gives everyone different skills and expects us to be good stewards.[36]

The parable also suggests we should use our skills to do good things. The servants given five and two talents knew they were expected to steward the money like the owner would—to keep it safe and leverage it into more. However, the servant who started with one talent was afraid and buried the money. He understood he needed to keep it safe, but fear overwhelmed him, so he didn't use what he was given to do good. So, his master punished him. The parable teaches that we shouldn't waste our skills by hiding or not trying to grow them. God expects us to be accountable for our talents by overcoming our fears and working to increase them.[37]

The parable is a depiction of Christian beliefs about accountability. Just as the servants were held accountable for doing all they could with their given talents, we're held accountable according to our abilities. When we're faithful with our responsibilities, we receive more. When we do our best with what we've been given, our talents and responsibilities will increase. As the parable makes clear, we're not all given equal talents, but we're accountable for ours and expected to put them to work for positive results.[38]

*   *   *   *   *

This section cites historical great thinkers who explored Unconditional Accountability. Although they developed their ideas decades or centuries ago, their insights remain profoundly relevant. The answers lie in our core values, which define us.

Accountability is woven into the fabric of Islam, just like in Christianity. The Qur'an and the teachings of Prophet Muhammad provide principles of accountability. The Qur'an says that every action is recorded, and we will be rewarded or punished based on those actions. It emphasizes adhering to moral values and being accountable for our behaviors in private and public life. Islam places particular emphasis on intentions, teaching that our deeds are judged not only by their outward appearance but also by the purity of our intentions. We're accountable for both the results of our actions and the motivations behind them. Like Christianity, Islam emphasizes stewardship. Muslims are taught to be accountable for their talents and to take care of their finances, the environment, and other resources. Islam also encourages communal accountability, meaning we're responsible for our actions and the well-being of our communities.[39] In Prophet Muhammad's teachings on accountability, he emphasizes self-awareness and urges us to assess our behaviors before judging others. He also highlights intention in determining the moral value of actions, saying that we're accountable for our deeds and intentions.[40]

> Take account of yourselves before you are taken to account.
> —Prophet Muhammad, Hadith

> Actions are judged by their intentions,
> and everyone will be rewarded according to their intention.
> —Prophet Muhammad, Hadith

Judaism places significant emphasis on personal accountability. Passages from the Mishnah stress that we must take responsibility for ourselves and others, be accountable for our actions, and not seek rewards for doing good because good deeds are valuable on their own.[41]

> If I am not for myself, who will be for me?
> And if I am only for myself, what am I? And if not now, when?
> —Pirkei Avot 1:14

> The reward of a good deed is the deed itself.
> —Pirkei Avot 4:2

Philosopher Jean-Paul Sartre's works deeply explore accountability. He asserts that we're responsible for determining our values and creating meaning in our existence. Existentialism, for which Sartre is best known, posits that we're responsible agents with free will to make choices. With this freedom, we're accountable for the consequences of those choices. He suggests free will is both a blessing and a curse: We can choose who and what we want to be, but we bear responsibility for our lives and the consequences of our actions. We're accountable for shaping our existence. He says we choose our values and how to live, but our choices determine our identity and moral character.

Man is condemned to be free;
because once thrown into the world, he is responsible for everything he does.
—Jean-Paul Sartre

I am my own existence, and I am made responsible for it entirely.
—Jean-Paul Sartre

We are our choices.
—Jean-Paul Sartre[42]

Sartre believes there is great power in personal agency—the ability to make decisions for ourselves. We're responsible for what we can control and how we respond to things outside our control. Accountability means we're in charge of creating meaning and purpose for our lives amid successes and challenges, in good times and bad.

Freedom is what you do with what's been done to you.
—Jean-Paul Sartre[43]

*   *   *   *   *

In chapter 1, I shared the story of Nicholas Winton, who organized transportation for hundreds of Czech children to escape the Nazis. He had no official responsibility for these children, yet he took accountability for their safety and well-being, working tirelessly and at personal risk to secure their passage to England. His actions exemplify the accountability that Sartre advocates as essential to human existence.[44]

*   *   *   *   *

We make the decisions that create our realities. Unfortunately, many of us choose to do nothing and let the world happen to us. But indecision is a decision—it's deciding not to act and allowing the world to control our lives. We might think that not making hard choices means we dodge responsibilities. That's wrong. Only we can be held accountable for our own lives. Since we're free to act, we bear the responsibility for action and inaction. This doesn't mean it's our fault when bad things happen due to factors outside our control, but it does mean we're free to choose how to react, and our actions or lack thereof impact the long-term consequences.

Wisdom about Each Element of Accountability

Like integrity, the elements of accountability are worth studying individually, and great thinkers have provided timeless insights to help us do so. The following paragraphs address them: reliability, accepting responsibility, considering consequences, taking blame and credit, transparency, and self-discipline.

Reliability means doing what we're supposed to do. It means following through on commitments, delivering on obligations, and honoring agreements. Immanuel Kant believed our actions should be guided by duty, not driven by desires or outcomes. He said we must act according to moral principles regardless of personal consequences. Like Islamic belief, Kant asserted that the morality of an action isn't solely determined by its consequences but by its intention and the principles guiding it. He thought we're accountable for completing our commitments and respecting the dignity and autonomy of others.[45]

Although outcomes shouldn't drive our actions, we must **accept responsibility** for them. We may understand that accountability is taking responsibility for actions and owning outcomes, but we must also realize that actions come from decisions. Since we live with the consequences of choices that impact our lives, letting others make those choices for us seems nonsensical. It also doesn't make sense to let others decide how we feel about things that happen to us. In her bestseller *13 Things Mentally Strong People Don't Do*, psychotherapist Amy Morin writes about mental strength, which is the ability to control our thoughts, behaviors, and emotions. Like physical strength, mental strength requires exercise—and courage. If we don't have the courage to be accountable for actions that might fail, then we don't have the courage to succeed.[46]

Reinhold Niebuhr says that because we're responsible for making good decisions in complex and challenging situations, we must constantly **consider the consequences** of our actions and recognize the results may not be what we expect.[47]

All human sin seems so much worse in its consequences than in its intentions.
—Reinhold Niebuhr

Stephen R. Covey, author of the bestseller *The 7 Habits of Highly Effective People*, explores the role of accountability in achieving personal and professional success. He says that when we make our decisions, we create our circumstances. So when we take responsibility for those circumstances, we can develop solutions.[48]

> We are not a product of our circumstances; we are a product of our decisions.
> —Stephen R. Covey

> When you take proactive responsibility for your problems,
> you empower yourself to create the solutions.
> —Stephen R. Covey

In chapter 3, I described how Dr. Mona Hanna-Attisha exposed the Flint water crisis, risking her reputation and career to protect the city's children from lead poisoning. She weighed the consequences of speaking out against powerful interests versus remaining silent and allowing the damage to continue unchecked. By choosing to prioritize the health and welfare of Flint's families over her comfort and security, she exemplified the principled accountability advocated by Niebuhr and Covey.[49]

*　*　*　*　*

We don't like to admit mistakes because we don't like how they make us feel. When we consider the consequences and have the mental strength to take responsibility for ourselves, we can accept whatever happens, whether it means **taking blame or credit**. If we make errors, we must readily admit and rectify them and take steps to prevent similar mistakes in the future. John C. Maxwell, leadership expert and author of *The 21 Irrefutable Laws of Leadership* and *The 360 Degree Leader*, emphasizes that learning from mistakes and taking corrective action is essential for personal growth. Blaming others robs us of the opportunity to learn and improve. Accountability, on the other hand, produces wisdom.

A man must be big enough to admit his mistakes,
smart enough to profit from them, and strong enough to correct them.
—John C. Maxwell[50]

Openly sharing information about our actions and their results is crucial to accountability. **Transparency** builds trust and helps others understand the context and reasons for our actions. In the previous section, I noted that, unfortunately, the lack of transparency common in many online communities can make unaccountability pervasive. To reduce toxic behavior online, we need to start with ourselves. We must first assess our actions and their impacts and address any that fall short of full accountability. Then, we must pressure those we influence to take responsibility for themselves and others in pursuit of an accountable digital environment.

Self-discipline helps us follow through, no matter the consequences. It keeps us focused on our goals and reminds us to manage our inward thoughts and emotions and outward actions. If we don't control what we think, we can't control what we do. Self-discipline helps us to think first and act afterward. It also enables self-regulation, which means adapting our behaviors to align with our standards. When we can self-regulate, we're more likely to be accountable, even when alone, because our values guide our actions.

* * * * *

In the last section, I claimed silence is a common good and decried needless noise like loud music and phone calls on speaker mode in public. Some may say calling those annoyances an accountability issue is an overstatement. I think not. We can equate sound pollution with any other type of pollution. Creating an unnecessarily noisy environment is the same as tossing trash on the ground or pumping toxic chemicals into the air: laziness and selfishness ruin a shared resource. Sound pollution doesn't receive the attention of other types, so it may occur due to lack of awareness. More likely, though, is a lack of accountability. Accountability requires thinking about consequences, but not only consequences to ourselves; we must consider the impacts of our actions (or lack of action) on others and their surroundings. We must recognize that exercising our freedoms can infringe on the same freedoms of others and try, whenever possible, to minimize that infringement so that others may choose their own uninterrupted experiences.

*　　*　　*　　*　　*

Avoiding Entitlement

The best tool to combat entitlement is accountability. When we take responsibility for our thoughts, words, and actions and own the outcomes, we eliminate unjustified expectations, face reality, and move toward true success.[51] A comparison of accountable and entitled behaviors looks like this:

Accountability	Entitlement
Accepts hardships and setbacks as normal	Never expects to face hardships or setbacks
Waits in line like everyone else	Cuts in line since needs are more important
Expects standard service, pays normal price	Demands greater service, deeper discounts
Acknowledges exam grades are earned	Complains about grades when didn't study[52]

*　　*　　*　　*　　*

In chapter 3, I told the story of Easy Eddie, a lawyer who managed Al Capone's illegal activities. Despite profiting from his association with Capone, Eddie didn't believe he was above the law. Instead, he was accountable for his misdeeds and cooperated with authorities, ultimately paying with his life. He rejected the entitlement mentality typical among his associates, choosing a more honorable, accountable path.[53]

*　　*　　*　　*　　*

Always Add Value

Unconditional Accountability requires us to approach every job or project expecting to have a positive impact. It must be part of every commitment. Another phrase for having a positive impact is *adding value*. When we add value, we improve a situation or leave something better than we found it.

We can add value in many ways. Each of us has skills and expertise that make us distinct. We may bring creativity, innovation, or a fresh perspective from life experiences. We may add value through a positive attitude that uplifts others or be adaptable, calm under pressure, strong problem-solvers, multilingual, or have deep cultural understanding. Our emotional intelligence, leadership abilities, and other attributes may enable us to add value.[54]

Accountability for adding value ties back to the Parable of the Talents. Like the servants were held accountable for doing all they could with the talents given to them, we're accountable for stewardship of our unique qualities, abilities, and experiences. We must use our talents to add value, not hide or fail to grow them.

> Let no one ever come to you without leaving better.
> —Mary Teresa Bojaxhiu, "Mother Teresa"

> Try not to become a man of success but rather to become a man of value.
> —Albert Einstein

*   *   *   *   *

Earlier in this chapter, I shared about Army veteran Aaron Hale, who refused to let his loss of sight and hearing keep him from adding value. He continued to serve by raising awareness, advocating for fellow veterans, and inspiring others through his resilience. His determination to contribute and refusal to be defined by his disabilities exemplify the always add value mindset that's central to accountability.[55]

*   *   *   *   *

With conditional accountability, we only own our outcomes *if* things turn out how we want. We reject responsibility for undesirable results, abandoning accountability and sliding toward unaccountability. Unconditional Accountability helps us bear our responsibilities, regardless of their weight. It releases us from the strain and regret of unaccountability and brings peace through independent, consistent commitment.

We're accountable for what we think, say, do, feel, and how we behave and respond. Since we own all aspects of ourselves, we might as well proactively create the lives we desire and take responsibility for the results. We can approach decision-making with self-awareness and seek to understand potential consequences.

How to Live It

IN 2010, A catastrophic mine collapse in Chile trapped thirty-three miners seven hundred meters underground, five kilometers from the mine's entrance. With limited food and water, the miners faced a dire situation. Yet, against all odds, every miner was rescued sixty-nine days later. Their survival hinged on one crucial factor: personal and collective accountability. They recognized their responsibility for their own safety and well-being and took decisive action. They rationed their meager supplies, worked together to maintain hope and community, and stayed calm through meditation. Most critically, they refused to give up. Each miner was accountable for his own and his fellow miners' survival. This story exemplifies Unconditional Accountability—taking full responsibility not just for our actions but for our very lives. The miners demonstrated the power of accountability. By taking ownership of our lives, we can overcome any adversity.[56]

Don't blame your parents, don't blame your boyfriend, don't blame the weather.
Accept the reality, embrace the challenge, and deal with it.
Be in charge of your own life.
—Diane von Furstenberg

* * * * *

When accountability is dependent, we slide toward diffusion, deflection, denial, selfishness, ego, and entitlement. We reject responsibility for results unless they're favorable for us. If not, we quickly abandon accountability and begin to slide down the spectrum toward unaccountability. With Unconditional Accountability, we won't slide. We own our outcomes, whatever they are. We rest in constant, complete accountability.

This section provides instructive ideas on becoming accountable personally, in relationships, as a parent, at work, and as a leader.

Personal

In his book *Make the Leap: Think Better, Train Better, Run Faster*, Bryan Green presents a path to peak performance, emphasizing one key factor: "Accountability is what sets great athletes and great teams apart." He outlines a five-stage approach: Show Up, Execution, Evaluation, Planning, and True Accountability.[57]

Green's framework for athletic accountability translates powerfully to other areas of life. Just as athletes fall short of their potential when they blame coaches, training programs, or bad luck, we fail to reach our goals when we aren't responsible for our results. Accountability means preparing diligently, adhering to the plan, and exerting necessary effort. These practices don't guarantee success, but they create the conditions for progress and open doors to new opportunities. I've adapted Green's stages into a four-step path to personal accountability using the acronym ACCO (not coincidentally the first four letters of *accountability*):

- **Step 1: Acknowledge:** This step is about acknowledging that our obligations—jobs, duties, and commitments—are part of our life roles. We recognize that the obligations are ours. We're present, and we participate.
- **Step 2: Consequences:** In this step, we consider the consequences. We take responsibility for ourselves and recognize that we create our lives by what we think, say, and do. We think before speaking or acting and reflect on good and bad possibilities.
- **Step 3: Complete:** This step requires reliability—doing what we're supposed to do. We're dependable, keep our word, and follow through.
- **Step 4: Own:** In this step, we accept the results of our actions, whether deserving of blame or credit. We confess shortcomings and admit wrongdoings when no one is watching. If we make errors, we correct them and work to prevent similar ones in the future.

Achieving personal accountability requires transparency, self-discipline, and commitment to do our best. We must be honest with ourselves and others when we fail to meet a goal. We declare failure and explore ways to improve. Self-discipline helps us overcome the pull of short-term self-interest by sticking to our long-term, healthier goals. It also helps us manage our inner thoughts, feelings, and outer actions to maintain personal consistency.

*   *   *   *   *

Despite their dire circumstances, the trapped Chilean miners demonstrated clear-headed accountability. They didn't allow themselves to become overwhelmed and throw up their hands. They didn't disregard their plight; they actively worked to find a solution. They didn't downplay the severity of the situation or diffuse responsibility but took ownership as a unified team. They focused on doing what had to be done. By taking ownership of their situation and working together toward a solution, they exemplified how accountability empowers individuals and teams to overcome obstacles even in seemingly hopeless circumstances.[58]

*   *   *   *   *

Personal accountability is strongest when it aligns with personal integrity. The two support each other, and moral courage lies at their intersection. We consider the consequences of our actions based on our ethical values, and moral courage provides the strength to act according to those values, no matter the consequences. By backing our beliefs and owning our outcomes, we can persist through challenges, knowing our actions match our ethics.

Sometimes, our ever-growing list of responsibilities feels weighty. Each job, duty, and commitment feels like another stone in a backpack we must constantly carry. It's important to remember that not every stone can be a gem—no one handles all those responsibilities perfectly. We should go easy on ourselves. Cultivating personal accountability is a process, not an endpoint. We can't polish every stone at the same time. We should choose one and appreciate each step in the right direction. As we advance our accountability, we'll see personal and professional growth.

If practiced to habituation, the four steps of ACCO can help us achieve accountability. We should be able to proudly say, "I'm totally accountable for what happens in my life. I take responsibility for what surrounds me and how successful or unsuccessful I am or will become, personally and professionally. I don't attack or criticize others. I don't blame external circumstances for what I don't like. I can realize my dreams and aspirations while living a healthy, prosperous, fulfilled life and serving others."

* * * * *

The trapped miners embodied accountability under extreme duress. Rather than denying their reality or defaulting to despair, they owned their situation. They accepted its gravity and took action by rationing their supplies, maintaining hope through emotional support, and staying calm. They didn't make excuses but did everything in their power to survive. By focusing on what was within their control, supporting one another, and working toward rescue, they showed how accountability enables us to survive and thrive with resourcefulness and resolve.[59]

Relational

Being accountable in relationships means recognizing that our words, decisions, and behaviors affect others, especially those with whom we have close or regular interactions. We accept responsibility for these consequences, but it's not easy. We often struggle with personal accountability and overlook its impacts on others. Following are important ways to build and maintain accountability in relationships.[60]

First, it's critical to understand our roles and responsibilities in the relationship. Most people have multiple roles in life, each with different responsibilities. For example, being a mother at home and a supervisor at work may have some similarities but also essential differences, especially regarding how we interact and the consequences of our actions. Sometimes, we can have more than one role in a relationship with a single person. For example, we might be both a father and a coach to the same child, requiring us to consider proper behaviors in different contexts.

Next, the core of accountability is doing what we're supposed to do. We fulfill the duties of our roles in the relationship. Others must trust that we'll follow through, and we can only earn that trust by meeting their expectations.

Then, we must have self-awareness. Accountability requires understanding our thoughts and feelings and stepping outside ourselves to objectively review our words and actions and their impact on our relationships. It doesn't matter if our partner is oversensitive, someone else contributed to the problem, or outside factors interfered. We must set aside our pride and own the outcomes of our words and actions, whether they're within our control or not.[61]

> We may honestly admit to ourselves
> that we are at least partly to blame for the problem.
> —Stephen R. Covey

A complicating factor with relationship accountability is that feelings are involved, and feelings can get hurt. When our partner is hurt by something we said or did, owning it means we apologize. Apologies are critical and deserve a chapter of their own, but that's for another author and another book. What's essential is to apologize genuinely, meaning we accept responsibility, no matter what. Unconditional means there are no caveats or restrictions, no *ifs* or *if onlys*. The apology must be clear and complete. Finally, we must commit to improving, repairing what's broken, or fixing the issue, no matter how small our contribution. We must be transparent and truthful in our desire to make amends. Our partner needs to believe a change can happen.[62]

Another critical difference from personal accountability is that, in relationships, we must listen. Again, the art of listening could fill its own book. What's vital is listening with love and an open mind to hear the meaning of our partner's words. Accountability means we listen to understand our partner's perspective. We can't own the outcomes if we don't understand them. If necessary, we ask questions to ensure we fully grasp their perspective, interpretation, frame of mind, or experience. Only then can we respond. Again: listen first; respond after.[63]

Also: respond—don't react. Reactions tend to be sudden, knee-jerk responses that come from biases or prejudices of the unconscious mind, driven by our human instinct to protect ourselves. They may not consider consequences. Responses consider our and others' well-being. In other words, responses are accountable; reactions are not.[64]

> You are not only responsible for what you say,
> but also for what you do not say.
> —Martin Luther

*   *   *   *   *

Trapped seven hundred meters underground in apparently hopeless circumstances, it would have been understandable for the Chilean miners to abandon accountability. However, instead of neglecting their sudden and somber obligations, they fulfilled them with tenacity. They took responsibility for their own and each other's well-being and followed through on their commitment to sacrifice for their shared goal of survival. They lived due to the power of their personal and collective accountability.[65]

*   *   *   *   *

Accountability in relationships requires that we're open to compromise.[66] A compromise is a collaboration in which both parties' views are heard and a mutually beneficial solution is found. Of course, a compromise starts with Unconditional Love between partners, Unconditional Gratitude for the relationship, and Unconditional Integrity in our desire for mutual benefit. We listen first, then respond (not react), and we both take responsibility for our contributions to the issue. Finally, we demonstrate willingness and ability to give and take. The goal is to find a compromise that accounts for the values and needs of both parties and can be put into practice so that both can move forward.[67]

Accountability can't survive secrets. Open, frequent communication is the most critical part of any relationship—personal or professional. Communication establishes common ground and builds trust that how we think, talk, and act will be interpreted reasonably and that we will understand each other's behaviors. If we're committed to accountability, we must be willing to ask for input on how our words or actions are coming across and then listen and be open to criticism. Accountability requires continuous improvement.[68]

Finding an accountability partner is one of the fastest ways to build accountability. An accountability partner can be a spouse, peer, mentor, or coach. It should be someone who knows us well or is willing to know us, is willing to invest time and energy into the relationship, can be encouraging, and, most importantly, can be honest. Honesty and vulnerability are essential. As we experience the connection that comes from accountability, we may be encouraged to apply it more broadly.

> True happiness consists of precisely carrying out one's duty.
> —Cândido Mariano da Silva Rondon[69]

As a Parent

No matter how well we manage our lives before having kids, parenting requires leveling up. Our responsibilities increase, and when our kids grow into their own commitments, we often manage theirs too. Parental accountability is like personal accountability, but it feels weightier, like we're carrying our kids' backpacks as well as our own. Teaching it involves fostering responsibility, helping them understand the consequences of their actions, and encouraging a sense of ownership. One way to teach it is to model it. We talk openly about decisions we must make and discuss possible outcomes. We demonstrate self-discipline by collecting as much data as is justified and then deciding and accepting responsibility. When we make mistakes, we admit them. When appropriate, we openly apologize and make amends. These actions communicate the value we place on accountability and display the behaviors involved.

* * * * *

I'm often reminded by my own actions that I'm an imperfect parent. The worst is when I realize too late that I've reacted too harshly in an argument with my kids. There's no lousier feeling in the world than seeing my little girl cry because I yelled unjustifiably; it's like punching myself in the gut and smashing a frying pan in my face at the same time.

My daughter is stubborn, which she gets from me, but I hope she also accepts another lesson—how to apologize. There are few excuses for shouting at children, and it pains me to admit I have. Apologies don't wholly clear my conscience, but they're necessary, and thankfully, my kids are gracious. We should all seek our children's forgiveness whenever it's warranted.

*   *   *   *   *

The best way to teach accountability is to let them learn firsthand. We must first establish a framework, communicating expected behaviors and explaining family rules and task boundaries. Most importantly, we help them grasp the potential short- and long-term consequences of their actions. We do our best to provide a foundation of Unconditional Love, Gratitude, and Integrity. Then, we must let them go. Ownership means nothing without independence. For them to learn accountability, they must learn to trust themselves.

> The mediocre teacher tells. The good teacher explains.
> The superior teacher demonstrates. The great teacher inspires.
> —William Arthur Ward

We delegate age-appropriate tasks to allow our children to share family responsibilities and learn accountability. We can develop daily and weekly chore routines and assign activities as they arise. We reinforce the concept that everyone contributes to the family. We can create a behavior chart for young children to visually track and reward positive behaviors. This helps to tangibly connect action with accountability. As they grow older, we can implement a behavior contract that outlines expectations, consequences, and rewards, or we can assign tasks with incentives (e.g., allowance) and punishments to underpin their understanding.

Throughout their childhood, we continue to guide them on accountability. We encourage open communication so they feel comfortable discussing their questions, actions, and mistakes without fear of judgment. When asked, we advise them on making responsible choices and addressing issues. Occasionally, we may hold family meetings to reemphasize expectations, rules, and boundaries. We empower them to share their thoughts, supporting our belief in them and fostering a sense of involvement. It's critical that we address mistakes and celebrate successes in a loving environment. We praise responsible behavior, whatever the results. Finally, we enforce appropriate apologies when they make mistakes to teach the importance of accountability in maintaining healthy relationships.

> It's a mistake not to give people a chance to learn
> to depend on themselves while they are young.
> —Walt Disney

Parents often feel pressured to have all the answers. We can relax; no one is perfectly accountable, and our children don't need us to be. Some of the most potent lessons come from our mistakes. When we fall short, openly admitting our errors and committing to do better teaches that pursuing Unconditional Accountability is a lifelong process. By consistently trying to own our choices and outcomes, we provide powerful examples for our kids.

At Work

Remember the story of Everybody, Somebody, Anybody, and Nobody? When no one takes responsibility, tasks go undone. It's a cautionary tale highlighting why accountability is vital at work. It's easy to say success is everyone's responsibility or that delivering excellent customer experience is a collective effort. However, without good governance—a clear understanding of who does what, how, and when—crucial work slips through the cracks. Accountability sustains trust and positive relationships with coworkers, customers, and stakeholders. The most valuable elements of accountability at work are reliability, responsibility, transparency, and self-discipline.

For Employees

Employee accountability starts with doing what we're supposed to do. As noted above, we must clearly understand our roles and responsibilities. If we're unsure, it's on us to get clarification. Once we know our responsibilities, we must own the job. From project manager to pipe fitter, we're all accountable for our performance.

An accountable employee consistently demonstrates a strong work ethic, arriving on time, working a full day, and staying late if necessary. Owning a job means bringing energy and enthusiasm to work, recognizing that some days, just getting to work and having a positive attitude may be all we can muster. It's working efficiently, effectively, and diligently until a task is done, overcoming challenges, and making no excuses. It means owning the grunt work along with the glory. Most importantly, we insist on delivering work that we're proud of.[70]

*   *   *   *   *

The Johnson & Johnson Tylenol crisis demonstrates organizational accountability. When faced with contaminated products, CEO James Burke didn't deflect responsibility or wait for government action. Instead, he immediately pulled all Tylenol products nationwide at a cost of $100 million. This demonstrated organizational accountability—all employees understood their roles in protecting public safety above profits.[71]

*   *   *   *   *

> Responsibility equals accountability equals ownership.
> And a sense of ownership is the most powerful weapon
> a team or organization can have.
>
> —Pat Summitt

For Employers

The first step in enabling accountability is clearly defining roles, responsibilities, and expectations. This ensures everyone understands their parts in delivering a customer experience. When managers are transparent about expectations and advancement criteria, employees can trust that their efforts will be fairly rewarded. Setting clear expectations also counteracts entitlement. With responsibilities defined, managers can focus on building trust, creating candor, and breaking down silos to foster a collaborative workplace. Treating each employee as a valued contributor cultivates ownership and a sense of community. Accountability empowers employees to exercise autonomy, work efficiently, reduce errors, and perform at their best.[72,73]

As a Leader

Establishing accountability in our teams starts with us as leaders. First, we must demonstrate personal accountability by embodying the principles we expect from others. Then, we must communicate the expectation to all team members.

The most critical factor in team accountability is trust, which hinges on reliability. If we say we'll do something, we must follow through, no matter what gets in the way. Our teams must trust that we'll guide them toward collective goals without undermining their interests. In turn, we must trust our teams to own their areas of responsibility. Micromanagement breeds stress, hinders productivity, and erodes motivation and pride.[74] When team members feel trusted and valued, they naturally take more ownership and strive to exceed expectations.

* * * * *

Jocko Willink and Leif Babin, US Navy SEAL officers who led the Iraq War's most highly decorated special forces unit, wrote a book about personal and leadership accountability: *Extreme Ownership: How U.S. Navy SEALs Lead and Win*. As the title indicates, the book's theme is the necessity of taking full responsibility for our actions. The authors were sent in 2006 to help secure Ramadi, an insurgent-held city. They share riveting accounts of heroism, loss, and victory from the most violent and dangerous battlefield in Iraq. Willink, Babin, and their fellow warriors learned firsthand the principles that determine a team's success or failure. They draw on these insights to illustrate how readers can apply battle-tested principles to their lives.[75]

As one would expect, *Extreme Ownership* pulls no punches. A core message is that leadership is the most significant factor in any team's performance. The authors distill this truth into a powerful maxim: "There are no bad teams, only bad leaders."[76] This message is stark, simple, and spot-on. In any context—combat, business, or daily life—the buck stops with the leader. Neither circumstances, team composition, nor resources determine outcomes.

> In any organization,
> all responsibility for success and failure rests with the leader.
> The leader must own everything in his or her world.
> There is no one else to blame.
> —Jocko Willink and Leif Babin[77]

* * * * *

Holding ourselves accountable for team outcomes is a hallmark of strong leadership. We own the results of our team's actions, positive or negative. When the team succeeds, we share the credit; when the team fails, we take the blame. We delegate responsibility, grant autonomy in decision-making, and hold ourselves ultimately accountable. This approach strengthens team bonds and unites us in the pursuit of shared goals.[78]

Another aspect of team accountability is transparency. Team members want a clear vision of desired results and a road map to reach those goals.[79] Good leaders help them see the big picture and understand how their actions impact the team. Regularly measuring progress against individual and team goals keeps the team focused and committed.[80] We further motivate the team by tying accountability to incentives and consequences.

* * * * *

Willink and Babin powerfully present key principles of leadership accountability. They explain it's the leader's job to find ways to hurdle obstacles and achieve objectives. Developing a plan and ensuring the team executes it to completion falls squarely on the leader's shoulders.

Admitting mistakes, taking ownership,
and developing a plan to overcome challenges
are integral to any successful team.
—Jocko Willink and Leif Babin[81]

Willink and Babin call on leaders to look to themselves first and always for solutions. They remind us that team performance hinges on standards and expectations leaders establish.

When things go wrong, look in the mirror and ask yourself:
"What can I do to make things better?"
—Jocko Willink and Leif Babin[82]

When setting expectations, no matter what has been said or written, if substandard performance is accepted and no one is held accountable—if there are no consequences—that poor performance becomes the new standard.
—Jocko Willink and Leif Babin[83]

*   *   *   *   *

Accountable leaders must exercise discipline to maintain the team's focus. When we're distracted by urgent items, we divert energy from long-term, important activities. Accountability demands that we keep our team's end goal in mind.[84]

Accountable leaders also actively take responsibility for areas that need improvement. We leverage feedback to devise solutions and spur growth. These insights deepen our collective understanding of team strengths and weaknesses. Seeking feedback demonstrates trust and fuels empowerment, engagement, and motivation.[85]

*   *   *   *   *

Willink and Babin reinforce the vital role that discipline plays in a leader's accountability. Through stories from their military service, they describe how discipline is cultivated, why it's essential to personal success, and how it elevates team performance:

I realized very quickly that discipline was not only the most important quality for an individual but also for a team. . . . Just as an individual excels when he or she exercises self-discipline, a unit that has tighter and more-disciplined procedures and processes will excel and win. . . . Instead of making us more rigid and unable to improvise, this discipline actually made us more flexible, more adaptable, and more efficient. It allowed us to be creative. When we wanted to change plans midstream on an operation, we didn't have to recreate an entire plan. We had the freedom to work within the framework of our disciplined procedures. . . . When things went wrong and the fog of war set in, we fell back on our disciplined procedures to carry us through the toughest challenges on the battlefield.[86]

Finally, they explain that leadership is a constant balancing act. It requires developing and sustaining behaviors and skills that don't come naturally. It involves discerning when to apply seemingly contradictory approaches. Accountable leadership demands ongoing self-reflection and openness to feedback to maintain equilibrium and optimal team performance.[87]

By owning team outcomes, proactively seeking solutions, setting high standards, and relentlessly driving toward team goals, leaders exhibit accountability for collective success. We can enable the team to adapt and excel in the most challenging situations by leading with accountability and empowering members to reach their potential through a shared commitment to ownership and responsibility.

*   *   *   *   *

Constantly modeling the behaviors we wish to see in our teams is hard. We must accept that we'll fail and acknowledge our mistakes but continue pursuing the ideal. Our teams don't need infallibility; they need dependability. From the ways we communicate to how we handle setbacks, we should support an environment where everyone feels ownership. Seeing us strive, they'll be inspired to meet our standards. A leader's accountability catalyzes an engaged, motivated, productive, and high-performing team.

Chapter Summary

Accountability is crucial for success in our personal lives, relationships, work, and leadership roles. Yet, too often, we find ourselves slipping into the trap of conditional accountability—taking responsibility when things go our way and quickly abandoning ownership and descending into blame, excuses, and entitlement when results fall short. This approach condemns us to mediocrity, at best.

True fulfillment comes from striving for Unconditional Accountability—considering the consequences of our actions, exercising self-discipline to act with good intentions, and taking responsibility for outcomes, good or bad. It requires humility to own our mistakes, willingness to admit shortcomings, and determination to make amends. Most of all, it demands ignoring our instinct for self-preservation and short-term comfort to pursue what's right, even when it's hard.

When we aim for Unconditional Accountability, it distinguishes us from those who deflect and deny their responsibilities. It remakes us into our best selves and paves new pathways to reach our potential. Combined with Unconditional Love, Gratitude, and Integrity, it becomes transformative. Unconditional Accountability is a superpower that can be ours if we're willing to work for it.

Encouragement and Questions for the Reader

Eventually, you'll be humbled by the charge of Unconditional Accountability. You'll fall prey to one of the seven D's or entitlement, and you'll feel like a failure. Take heart—no one does everything right. Growth happens gradually, with regular reversals, but if you continue to pursue unconditionality, you'll improve.

Every decision to own your actions and outcomes plants a seed of accountability. Every time you follow through on a commitment waters that seed. Taking blame and giving credit when they're due helps accountability take root inside you. When you demonstrate self-discipline, your accountability blossoms, and others can see the fruit of your efforts. Cultivating accountability isn't easy, but it's rewarding—it leads to personal fulfillment, inspires others, and helps you reach your greatest potential.

The following are questions to ask yourself. As you seek to cultivate greater accountability, use them to help you choose one area where you can strive for unconditionality.

- Do you uphold your commitments, even when they become difficult or inconvenient? Where can you build trust with others by consistently following through?

- When things don't turn out as you hoped, do you take responsibility for the results of your choices, or do you make excuses and blame circumstances or other people? How can you practice owning all your outcomes, good and bad?

- When having hard conversations, do you listen to others' perspectives before responding? What can you do to listen more deeply and look for win-win solutions?

- Do you model personal responsibility for your children? Where can you give them age-appropriate opportunities to be accountable and learn from natural consequences?

- Do you take ownership of the quality and timeliness of your work? How can you be more open to feedback and use it to improve?

- In leadership positions, do you set clear expectations for team members? Do you take responsibility for team outcomes while sharing credit for successes? How can you hold yourself and team members accountable fairly and consistently?

- What's one daily practice you can start today in pursuit of Unconditional Accountability as a lifelong commitment and source of profound fulfillment?

CHAPTER V

UNCONDITIONAL ENDEAVOR

We have to do the best we can.
This is our sacred human responsibility.
—Albert Einstein

The secret of success lies in forming the habit of doing things
that failures don't like to do.
—Albert E. N. Gray

What It Is

A POTBELLIED STOVE heated a little country schoolhouse in Kansas. Thirteen-year-old Floyd and his eight-year-old brother Glenn came to school early each day to start the fire and warm the room before their teacher and classmates arrived. One day, Floyd accidentally put in gasoline instead of kerosene, and the stove exploded. By the time anyone reached the building, it was engulfed in flames. Floyd died. Glenn was dragged out, more dead than alive. Severe burns devastated the lower half of his body. He was taken to a nearby hospital.[1]

From his bed, barely conscious, Glenn faintly heard a doctor talking to his parents. The doctor said Glenn would surely die, which was for the best given his condition. But Glenn didn't want to die. He chose to survive. To the doctor's amazement, he did.[2]

When he was out of mortal danger, Glenn again heard the doctor talking to his parents. This time, the doctor said the fire had destroyed so much flesh in his lower limbs that he recommended amputating Glenn's legs. Still barely able to communicate, Glenn managed to convey distress, and his parents decided against amputation. The doctor said Glenn would never be able to use his legs. At home, after being released from the hospital, Glenn would sit in bed, his thin legs dangling lifelessly from the side. Once more, he made a choice. He would walk.[3]

> I think it was at that very moment
> that I made one of the biggest decisions of my life.
> I'm NOT going to be an invalid!
> I remember saying over and over,
> "I will walk! I will walk!"
> —Glenn Cunningham

One day, Glenn's mother wheeled him outside for fresh air. Determined not to sit in his wheelchair helpless, he threw himself from the chair onto the ground and, dragging himself across the yard, made his way to the picket fence at the edge of their lot. Straining, Glenn pulled himself to an upright position. Then, slowly, painfully, and clinging to the fence with one arm, he swung one leg in front of the other. Grasp by grasp and post by post, he willed himself down the length of the fence. He did it again the next day. And the next. He struggled along the fence every day until he wore a path around the yard.[4]

Twenty-two months after the schoolhouse explosion, Glenn took his first steps on his own (again). Gradually, he began walking to school. He taught himself to run again through sheer determination and despite the pain. Eventually, the pain subsided, and he started running consistently. He ran to school for the pure joy of it. In high school, he made the track team. Then he set high school records for the mile run. He was offered a scholarship to run track for the University of Kansas, but although he did attend and joined the team, he refused any money, preferring to pay his own way.[5]

In 1932, during his sophomore year at KU, Glenn was among the world's fastest runners. He earned a spot on the Olympic team. He ran the 1,500-meter event in Los Angeles but finished fourth due to a severe cold. In 1933, he won the Sullivan medal as the most outstanding athlete at the collegiate or Olympic level in the United States for his achievements in middle-distance running. On June 16, 1934, Glenn Cunningham ran the mile in 4:06.7 minutes, breaking the world record. His record stood for three years; at one point, he held seven of the top thirteen fastest-recorded times for the mile.[6]

In 1936, his fellow US Olympic athletes in Berlin voted Glenn the Most Popular Athlete. He earned a master's degree from the University of Iowa and a doctorate from New York University. When the 1940 Olympics were canceled, he retired from running and taught college in Iowa. During World War II, he served two years in the US Navy. After the war, he founded and ran the Glenn Cunningham Youth Ranch, where he and his wife raised nearly ten thousand troubled and underprivileged children over thirty years.[7]

As a boy, he was not expected to survive. He was told he'd never walk. Glenn chose otherwise. Dr. Glenn Cunningham, the world record runner, demonstrated that we can create the lives we want to live through Unconditional Endeavor.[8]

> In running, it is man against himself, the cruelest of opponents.
> The other runners are not the real enemies.
> His adversary lies within him,
> in his ability with brain and heart to master himself and his emotions.
> —Glenn Cunningham

* * * * *

An endeavor is an attempt to achieve something. It's an exertion of energy toward a goal. It's work. Unlike the other Unconditionals, most of us don't have preconceived notions about endeavor. One reason is that it's not just a concept—it's a process with many elements. However, that process is crucial to our well-being and fulfillment.

Endeavor is about the importance of trying. But it's not just about trying; it's also about doing. And it's not just about trying and doing; it's about doing with purpose and excellence. And it's not just about doing with purpose and excellence; it's about striving to improve. Unconditional Endeavor is about living life to the fullest, reaching our potential, experiencing everything possible, and making the most of what we have. It's growing what we have and what we can do through purpose and excellence and always striving to improve.

Throughout this book, I've said that I chose the order of The Unconditionals based on how they sustain, shape, and harmonize our lives. They're all nonnegotiable values that must be pursued to live our best life. None is more important than the others. However, they're interdependent and build on each other. Endeavor is last because it brings the other four to life. The first four are active on their own. We live them privately in our thoughts and publicly in our words and deeds. They can exist and flourish without endeavor. We can survive without endeavor. Ascetics may avoid endeavor but still feel fulfilled. But to live in the world, we must engage; we must act. Living isn't just breathing and interacting. It's doing, striving, endeavoring.

Think of The Unconditionals like a hand, where each is one of the fingers. Each is vital for its purpose, and each becomes more useful by working with the others. Losing any would reduce dexterity and ability. In this metaphor, Unconditional Endeavor is the thumb. Endeavor equips us to grab hold of our lives, seize our moment, and secure our place in the world.

Imagine we all live on a fast-moving, open-air train hurtling down the tracks. The view is best near the front, and we want to advance to see it, but the wind whips past our ears and pushes against us, making it hard to hold our ground, let alone forge ahead. The train cars have sturdy handholds that we can use to brace ourselves and pull forward. Again, thinking of The Unconditionals as our hand, we use the first four Unconditionals (our fingers) to grab a handhold, wrapping around in one direction. We rely on those values that constitute who we are to withstand the buffeting winds and provide stability. Endeavor (our thumb) wraps around in the other direction, completing the grip. We count on this value for action—the Unconditional that helps us know how to do what we do—to grasp the handholds. Endeavor empowers us to endure headwinds and gives us the confidence to reach for the next opportunity. Extending the metaphor, endeavor enables us to accomplish meaningful things: hold hands, make a fist, clench for a firm handshake, and grip a shovel.

I know of no more encouraging fact than
the unquestionable ability of man to elevate his life by conscious endeavor.
—Henry David Thoreau

* * * * *

Elements of Unconditional Endeavor

This chapter is the longest, taking nearly as many pages as all the others combined. It isn't because Unconditional Endeavor is the most important. There's just more to endeavor.

Endeavors touch all parts of our lives. They range from common to captivating, easy to exhausting. The endeavor process has ten elements, and each deserves discussion. I'll provide details in the following sections, but I'll introduce the elements here:

- Purpose
- Attitude
- Preparation
- Effort
- Focus
- Excellence
- Individuality
- Perseverance
- Practice
- Growth

One may ask, "Why these ten elements?" Fair question. After thorough study and consideration, I believe these are the fundamental building blocks of endeavor. We may debate whether others should be included or some shouldn't make the list, but it's as reasonable a list as I've seen or can devise.

A friend asked me to create an acrostic to help him remember the elements of endeavor. Ten is a large number for an acrostic, but I agree that having one is more helpful than not. Using the letters *PAPEFEIPPG* and artificial intelligence–inspired creativity, I came up with:

<u>P</u>aper <u>A</u>irplanes <u>P</u>ushed <u>E</u>astward <u>F</u>ly <u>E</u>legantly
<u>I</u>nto <u>P</u>eaceful <u>P</u>lum <u>G</u>roves.

Even if it's not the best acrostic ever, it met my three main criteria: 1) each letter appears in the intended sequence, 2) it forms a complete sentence, and 3) it flows naturally while creating an engaging and vivid mental image. Readers can determine for themselves whether it works. In case it's of additional benefit to anyone, I've created a simple graphic to go with the acrostic:

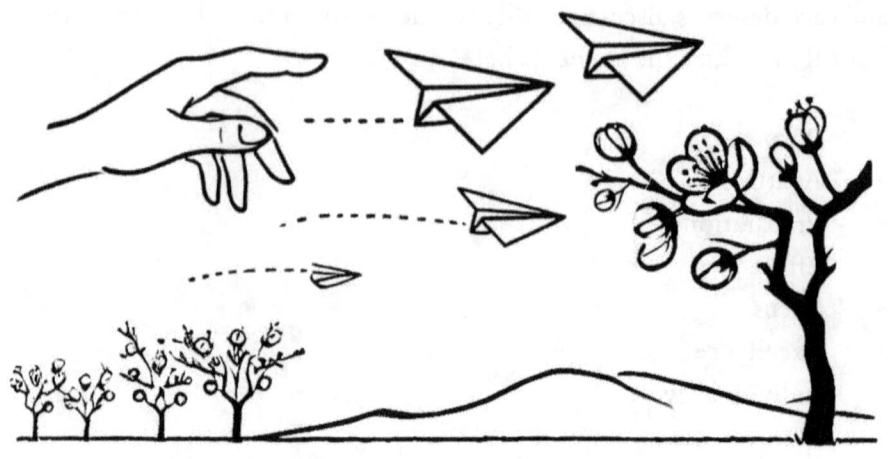

Graphic for the acrostic: Paper Airplanes Pushed Eastward Fly Elegantly
Into Peaceful Plum Groves

When we pursue Unconditional Love, Gratitude, Integrity, and Accountability, we don't just imagine ourselves progressing toward those ideals. We use the process of endeavor to make progress. Endeavor is the mechanism. The others are about how to act; endeavor is action itself.

Unconditional Endeavor is the great discriminator because, of The Unconditionals, it's the most directly connected to personal and professional achievement. This is not achievement for the sake of wealth or status; it's achievement for the sake of fulfillment. Unconditional requires commitment, pursuing something to its fullest extent. Unconditional Endeavor means striving for self-improvement and practicing to eliminate errors. It's doing our best and constantly working to get better. It's aspiring to reach our greatest potential.

When we aim for Unconditional Endeavor, we express all its elements enthusiastically. In its most positive form, purpose becomes passion. At its best, attitude is optimism. Focus turns into faithfulness and fervor.

Unconditional Endeavor also asks much of us. It demands drive and discipline. It calls for commitment, constancy, perseverance, and practice. Most of all, it requires hard work.

The rest of this chapter thoroughly explains the elements of endeavor, why they matter, and where we go wrong. It then provides answers found in timeless wisdom and offers ideas for living to the fullest. Through Unconditional Endeavor, we can make the most of who we are, what we have, and what we can do.

Virtues are acquired through endeavor, which rests wholly upon yourself.
—Sidney Lanier

Why It Matters

UNCONDITIONAL ENDEAVOR IS the culmination of The Unconditionals. It involves all the building blocks of personal growth and fulfillment. When we combine it with the other four Unconditionals, we can reach our highest potential and effectiveness.

* * * * *

Walter was born in Chicago in 1901. At sixteen, he tried to join the army to fight in World War I but was turned down because he was too young. Later that year, he dropped out of school and forged his birth certificate to join the Red Cross as an ambulance driver, but he arrived in France after the war had ended. At eighteen, he was laid off from a job as a newspaper advertising illustrator because the editor said he lacked imagination and creativity. At twenty, he started an art company with a friend in Kansas City, but it went bankrupt. At twenty-one, he moved to Hollywood to become a live-action film director, but he failed at that too. At twenty-six, he created his first movie star, Oswald the Lucky Rabbit, but his producer stole almost all his employees' and Oswald's rights. In 1928, after so many failures, he introduced his most famous character, Mickey Mouse, and Walt Disney was on his way to building one of history's most successful companies.[9]

All our dreams can come true, if we have the courage to pursue them.
—Walt Disney

* * * * *

The elements of endeavor are the ingredients of accomplishment. Each is elaborate and essential. We can tackle tasks without engaging all ten, but we need all for the hardest projects. We must learn and use them all. (Remember the acrostic: **P**aper **A**irplanes **P**ushed **E**astward **F**ly **E**legantly

<u>I</u>nto <u>P</u>eaceful <u>P</u>lum <u>G</u>roves.) Applying them in endeavors makes all the difference.

Purpose

Endeavor begins with purpose. It's our reason and rationale, our idea and intention, our direction and determination. Purpose is endeavor's catalyst.

A strong sense of purpose is often linked with ambition. In some cultures or contexts, ambition has a negative connotation. Although uncontrolled or misdirected ambition can lead to misplaced motivations, inappropriate goals, and harmful actions, it's fundamentally a desire to do or achieve something, so ambition should be a positive, supportive part of purpose.

Each enterprise we undertake follows the same endeavor process, so each one needs purpose. For most daily tasks, the process is simple, and our purpose can be basic; most don't need big goals with mission statements or motivational posters. However, sometimes, we encounter special projects that deserve more. We must pay close attention to all steps in the endeavor process; for these, our purpose must be strong and clear.

Walt Disney's early career shows how unwavering purpose inspires incredible endeavors. Despite repeated rejections and failures, he remained focused on innovating in animation. When his Oswald character was stolen, Disney created Mickey Mouse, launching an entertainment empire. His story demonstrates how clarity and consistency of purpose drive us to succeed.[10]

Attitude

Attitude is our disposition or outlook. It's called our frame of mind because it's our window to the world.[11] It sets our emotional status and mental perspective, influencing how we perceive and respond to events. It's also the first nonphysical thing people notice about us. When we maintain a consistent attitude, it becomes part of our personality and identity.[12]

Attitude is our most important control knob for quality of life. It defines self-perception, plays a significant role in our decision-making, and impacts our approach to challenges and ability to learn and grow.

Chapter 2 explains that an optimistic attitude offers emotional benefits. By focusing on good things, we interpret events positively and attract positive experiences. It keeps negative thoughts at bay and makes us feel better about ourselves and our lives.[13,14] Studies have repeatedly shown that a positive attitude improves mental health by reducing stress, depression, and alcohol abuse.[15] It also boosts physical health by lowering blood sugar and cholesterol, strengthening immunity, and reducing the risk of infections and cancer.[16] Optimism enhances emotional, mental, and physical well-being, all vital to successful endeavors.

> It is our attitude at the beginning of a difficult task which,
> more than anything else, will affect its successful outcome.
> —William James

Attitude affects how we communicate and relate to others. A positive attitude promotes respect, understanding, and cooperation, which are essential for effective teamwork. Optimism is a magnet, drawing positive people to us. In contrast, negative attitudes lead to misunderstandings and conflicts, hindering collaboration. Attitudes are also contagious—positive attitudes uplift while negative attitudes discourage. Positivity is crucial for team effectiveness in endeavors.

Attitude activates the other elements of endeavor. A positive attitude fosters open-mindedness and increases the likelihood of finding creative and effective solutions. It encourages goal-setting and harder, better work. It supports our ability to adapt, learn from setbacks, and endure tough times. It makes big tasks seem less daunting. Conversely, negative thoughts associated with a bad attitude can drain our motivation and halt progress.[17] Overall, attitude is crucial to any endeavor.

* * * * *

Helen Keller was born in Northwest Alabama in 1880. At nineteen months old, she contracted an illness that left her deaf and blind. Before she learned to speak, she was suddenly imprisoned in a world of total darkness and silence. Her family sought help and found the Perkins Institute for the Blind in South Boston. The school's director asked Anne

Sullivan, a twenty-year-old alumna, to become Keller's teacher. Sullivan came to live with the Kellers when Helen was seven and began teaching her sign language. As Helen mastered the manual alphabet and learned to communicate richly with the world, her previously dark and silent existence transformed into one filled with positivity and possibility. A year later, they went to the Perkins Institute for Helen to attend school. She learned to read, write, speak, and understand others' speech by feeling the lips and throat of the speaker. Keller attended specialist and mainstream schools and graduated Phi Beta Kappa from Radcliffe College of Harvard University as the first deafblind person in the US to earn a Bachelor of Arts degree. She became a world-famous speaker, author, and advocate for disability rights, labor rights, women's suffrage, and world peace. In 1999, Keller was listed in "*Time* 100 Persons Of The Century." Streets are named after her in the US, Switzerland, Spain, Portugal, France, Austria, and Israel.[18]

Keller is one of modern American history's best models of optimism. She exemplifies a positive attitude as an essential element of Unconditional Endeavor.

> Optimism is the faith that leads to achievement.
> —Helen Keller[19]

Preparation

Preparation can be a process on its own. We start every task by understanding its requirements, constraints, and desired outcomes. Then, we develop an approach and identify necessary resources. We organize the resources to complete the task. Finally, we establish methods to manage progress and keep it on track.

Being prepared means thinking through and practicing how to act or react in any situation so we're not surprised. We must plan for success. Awesome accomplishments are always preceded by pedestrian preparation.

While we often view preparation as dispensable, it's an essential element of endeavor. The less familiar and more complex the endeavor, the more important preparation becomes. Its significance lies in our ability to control it. We can't always predict or manipulate a task's events, but if we're prepared, we can better handle whatever happens.

Many of us skip preparation because it takes time. We focus on the effort because that's what we remember most. In the long run, though, preparation saves time. Planning backup options takes much less time and yields better results than fixing problems on the spot. Preparation decreases stress and fatigue by reducing the likelihood of being overwhelmed by events. It boosts productivity by allowing us to spend more time doing and less time redoing.[20] As explained in the discussion of the *Extreme Ownership* book, preparation creates flexibility. Planning frees mental space for creative thinking by removing the need to consider the next move constantly. It also increases resilience since imagining possible problems and solutions beforehand makes them less intimidating when they occur.[21] Finally, preparation builds our confidence because we first walk the path in our minds, providing a clear mental guide.

Ultimately, preparation dramatically increases our chances of a successful endeavor. It's proactive rather than reactive. It's strategic. Genius is the result of experience plus preparation.

＊　　＊　　＊　　＊　　＊

As a rocket scientist, I believe the most extraordinary engineering endeavor of the twentieth century was the Apollo program that landed humans on the Moon. It's astonishing today to realize that it was almost exactly eleven years from the formal establishment of NASA on July 29, 1958, to the first steps on the Moon on July 20, 1969. Such an accomplishment was possible only by fully employing all elements of endeavor. A vital part of Apollo's success was meticulous preparation. Rigorous quality control and redundancy were built into every component. Planners crafted comprehensive procedures. Astronauts spent hundreds of hours in simulators, training on every aspect of the mission. Everyone involved—from the technicians who closed the hatch before launch to the Navy frogmen who pulled the crew from the ocean after splashdown—rehearsed relentlessly. They thought of every imaginable contingency, created solutions, and ran and reran the scenarios until everyone knew them by heart. This exhaustive preparation enabled them to achieve their audacious goal on a staggeringly compressed timeline. They modeled how preparation paves the way for stellar achievement.[22]

* * * * *

Effort

Although all elements of endeavor are important, effort is its essence. Effort is the work. In most dictionaries, *effort* is used to define *endeavor*; they're often considered interchangeable. Here, I'm using a broad meaning of endeavor to include the other elements discussed in this chapter, and I'm using a narrow definition of effort. Effort is activity. It's doing.

Effort transforms aspirations into outcomes through physical or mental exertion. The quality and quantity of effort are the main factors that determine the impact (and sometimes the completion) of any endeavor. Ability matters, but it comes from consistent effort. Experience also matters, but it comes from ability and more effort. Only continued effort, plus ability and experience, can lead to success. In other words, success mainly depends on how hard we try—our results are directly proportional to our effort.

> Far and away the best prize that life offers
> is the chance to work hard at work worth doing.
> —Theodore Roosevelt

Effort is essential for learning and improving. When we do something, we learn (or we should). It also helps us care more; whether an effort is physical, mental, or both, it almost always engenders emotional investment. We love whatever we pour our heart into. Putting in effort also builds work ethic and confidence. When we work hard, we become more capable, content, and confident to do it again. As we gain knowledge, ability, and experience, we grow personally. Finally, effort fosters fulfillment. Doing work increases our chances of reaching our goals and experiencing success.

*   *   *   *   *

Teedie was a sickly, scrawny child plagued by colds, coughs, nausea, cramps, headaches, and fevers. The worst was his severe asthma, which made him feel like he was drowning at night. Doctors tried many treatments, but nothing worked. His parents worried he wouldn't live to see adulthood. But Teedie had a strong, determined mind.[23]

As a teenager, Teedie's father told him, "You have the mind, but you have not the body, and without the help of the body, the mind can't go as far as it should. You must make your body." Revering his father and wanting to become strong, Teedie started exercising intensely. His family turned part of their house into a gym, where he spent hours hanging from still rings and parallel bars. He lifted weights daily and took boxing lessons from a prizefighter. Teedie became incredibly energetic, both mentally and physically.[24]

Teedie overcame his health problems through hard work, a determination that shaped the rest of his life. Although he was from New York City, he loved nature. As a young man, he took trips out West, developing a cowboy persona defined by robust masculinity. When his wife and mother died on the same night, the devastated Teedie recuperated by buying and running a Dakota cattle ranch. He was appointed assistant secretary of the navy and played a vital role in a US naval victory over Spain before resigning to form and lead the Rough Riders, a group that fought in Cuba during the Spanish-American War. Six weeks after returning as a war hero, he was nominated and elected governor of New York. Less than two years later, he became vice president. After President William McKinley died, Teedie, now called Theodore, Roosevelt was sworn in as the twenty-sixth president of the United States. Historians and the public consistently rank him as one of the greatest presidents in American history.[25,26] The scrawny boy who built himself into the model of masculinity extolled hard work throughout his life.

Focus

Focus can have many meanings, but as an element of endeavor, it means being present, engaged, and immersed. It requires diligence and alertness. Endeavors necessitate applying our energies toward a goal and avoiding distractions.

* * * * *

In July 1991, Bill Gates Sr. and his wife, Mary, hosted a dinner party. Their guests included their son, Bill Jr., and Warren Buffett. Gates Jr. was the founder and chairman of Microsoft, while Buffett held the same roles at Berkshire Hathaway, the world's most successful holding company. For several years, they had alternated as the world's richest person. During dinner, the hosts asked what factor was most critical to their success. Both Gates Jr. and Buffett quickly replied, "Focus."[27]

> Only through focus can you do world-class things,
> no matter how capable you are.
> —Bill Gates

* * * * *

Focus is one of the best ways to improve the quality of our effort. It makes our work more accurate, thorough, and thoughtful. Focus helps us use our time more effectively and reduce stress. It improves learning by helping us absorb information, remember it better, and build expertise faster. Focus enables us to analyze problems deeply, imagine innovative solutions, and make clear, confident decisions. When with others, focus improves communication and understanding. It enriches every endeavor and increases our chances of success. The champion is often a person with similar talent but superior focus.

Excellence

If effort is the motor of endeavor, excellence is the oil. It's the difference between a grind and a high-powered operation. Excellence has long been considered one of the vital virtues. It's typically defined as being exceptional, outstanding, or superior—surpassing average or ordinary. In seeking excellence, we strive for our highest competence, skill, effectiveness, and achievement. Excellence isn't an ability. It's a mindset.

Pursuing excellence is imperative to Unconditional Endeavor. Unconditional means we commit ourselves to excellence in all we do. We set and work to achieve high standards and constantly seek to improve. Importantly, when I refer to being superior, I mean achieving superiority over our previous selves. Endeavor isn't about just showing up. It's dedicating ourselves to a task and not just completing it but doing it to the best of our abilities.

> Excellence is an art won by training and habituation.
> We do not act rightly because we have virtue or excellence,
> but we rather have those because we have acted rightly.
> We are what we repeatedly do.
> Excellence, then, is not an act but a habit.
> —Aristotle

It's human nature to treat tasks differently. We mentally rank the importance of daily tasks, performing unconscious triage. Even if we do our best on tasks we consider important, we often give less to those we think are insignificant. That's not unconditional. Unconditional Endeavor means doing our best on every task. It establishes an expectation of always giving our all and builds self-confidence to perform optimally.[28] We create the habit with little things to achieve excellence in big things. (Of course, tasks like making coffee or taking out the trash are truly trivial and need only completion—unless you're a barista or garbage collector. The meaningful ones require our best.)

*　*　*　*　*

After his brutal injury, Glenn Cunningham embodied multiple elements of endeavor. His purpose to walk again, tireless effort in rehabilitation, and unwavering focus were remarkable. But what makes his story extraordinary is his excellence. Not content with walking, he pushed himself to become one of history's greatest runners, winning Olympic medals, setting world records, and earning recognition as America's most outstanding amateur athlete. He stands out not because he overcame adversity but because he did it with such excellence.[29]

*   *   *   *   *

Excellence governs the prowess, potency, and productivity of our endeavors. As such, excellence is closely linked with integrity and accountability. When we have integrity, we're committed to doing things the right way, directly supporting the pursuit of excellence. For instance, someone with integrity won't cut corners to achieve faster results. Excellence connects with accountability because owning our actions drives us to do our best. For example, when we have to answer openly for our work, we'll ensure it meets the highest standards. Excellence is both a driver and an outcome—it pushes us to maintain integrity and accountability while being enhanced by these qualities.

Striving for excellence inspires trust. Others respect and rely on those who are committed to excellence. Excellence also motivates; just as we feel good about doing good and seeing good being done, we feel good when we see something done well. It sets an example. Excellence in a team is a strong advantage. Organizational excellence leads to high-quality products and solutions, sparks innovation, and boosts customer satisfaction.

Whether our endeavors are educational, professional, or personal, excellence increases the chances of success. It creates opportunities and leads to recognition and rewards. Most importantly, it heightens our sense of accomplishment, strengthens our self-esteem, and gives our lives meaning. Doing everything with excellence brings real satisfaction.

Individuality

Individuality is the uniqueness we bring to a task. It's our distinction. Our approach to any endeavor will differ from anyone else's and will be influenced by our specific skills, particular past, and current circumstances—that's our individuality.

> The things that make me different are the things that make me.
> —A. A. Milne

Embracing our individuality has many benefits. Accepting who we are helps us be true to ourselves and align with our values and purpose. Accepting our individuality also boosts our self-confidence and helps us avoid comparing ourselves to others. Individuality promotes healthy relationships because we approach others with authenticity and openness. Being honest about individuality allows us to admit our weaknesses and grow personally. In short, embracing and celebrating our individuality helps us become the best version of ourselves.[30]

Complex endeavors often involve experimentation and exploration. Individuality can inspire innovative solutions. For everyday endeavors, distinct perspectives produce better answers. Differences add value.

Imagination is our most exclusive property, and it's acquired by our individuality. When we use our individuality to solve problems, the results are personal and powerful. Self-expression, when appreciated, boosts self-confidence. Being ourselves increases accountability, sparks initiative, and evokes enthusiasm. Individuality improves personal, organizational,[31] and leadership performance.[32]

* * * * *

As shown in chapter 1, Fred Rogers used his individuality to make a profound impact. Early in his career, when most children's programming featured slapstick comedy, Rogers took a different approach. He focused on emotional intelligence, addressing children's fears and uncertainties. Despite skepticism from network executives, he insisted on using silence, slowness, and simplicity to create a sense of safety. His commitment to his uniqueness revolutionized children's television. He showed that embracing individuality isn't just about standing out but standing up for what we believe in.[33,34]

Perseverance

Perseverance is resolution and resilience—continuing to work hard when challenges arise and recovering from adversity. It's staying focused on our purpose through all phases of a project. Perseverance doesn't mean avoiding obstacles; they're inevitable. It means continuing to work despite obstacles. It's acknowledging but finding ways over, around, or through them—not giving up before reaching our goals. Perseverance is a pivotal part of endeavor.

Perseverance builds character, strengthens resolve, and forges mental toughness. It enables us to handle changes and challenges by increasing courage and confidence. Perseverance supports mental health.[35] When we overcome barriers, our brains release dopamine—the feel-good neurotransmitter—reducing stress, reinforcing the benefits of extra effort, and making perseverance easier the next time.[36] Perseverance also teaches us. By overcoming obstacles, we expand our abilities and discover strengths we didn't know we had. We learn to adapt and try new approaches, increasing creativity. While completing a task is naturally rewarding, overcoming adversity to achieve a goal is deeply satisfying.

* * * * *

Thomas Edison was the most prolific inventor in US history. No other American has matched his 1,093 patents. The force behind his innovation and entrepreneurship was perseverance. He's best known for inventing the light bulb, which he famously attempted thousands of times before succeeding.[37]

> Many of life's failures are people who did not realize
> how close they were to success when they gave up.
> —Thomas Edison

Edison's contributions extended far beyond the light bulb. He invented the phonograph, motion picture camera, and other devices in numerous fields, including electric power generation, home construction, mass communication, sound recording, and chemical production. He created the world's first film studio and discovered effects that led to radio. His work even anticipated technologies that wouldn't be developed for over a century, like solar and wind energy. He researched electric vehicle batteries, anticipating the electric cars of the early 2000s.[38] Edison was among the first to apply scientific principles, large laboratories, and extensive teams to the invention process. He systemized innovation by establishing the first industrial research laboratory, revolutionizing how businesses work. Due to his extraordinary combination of ingenuity and indefatigability, Edison impacted modern engineering and science more than any other American.

> Nothing is impossible. We merely don't know how to do it yet.
> —Thomas Edison

Practice

In endeavor, practice is closely connected to effort and perseverance. If effort is oversimplified as *try* and perseverance as *try, try again*, practice is *again, and again, and again*. It's doing something repeatedly to improve our skills. A sports team's or musician's practice is the classic example. For one-time tasks, we execute the endeavor process with effort and excellence. Repetitive tasks, especially complex or closely watched ones, require practice. It's an action, not just an idea.

The point of practice is progress. That progress takes different forms, depending on the endeavor. We practice to improve, deepen knowledge until tasks become habitual, and reduce weaknesses and mistakes. For endeavors culminating in performances, especially public ones like in athletics and music, we often practice more than we perform. But we should take practice as seriously as performance in many cases, not just for public performances.[39,40] It's not the time we practice that counts. It's what we put into our practice.

Expertise and success take time. No shortcuts exist. Sometimes, we feel we aren't progressing; we practice regularly without improvement. Then, a breakthrough. Breakthroughs come from discipline—showing up when we don't feel like it, continuing when we're exhausted, and not quitting when we want to concede. They happen when we've done the work and are present in the moment. They happen because we practice.

The combined elements of purpose, attitude, preparation, effort, focus, excellence, individuality, and perseverance comprise an endeavor cycle. Practice, then, is the iteration of that cycle, a rerun of all elements of an endeavor. Those initial elements may be enough to complete some endeavors; some may be finished their first time through without practice. However, Unconditional Endeavor must include practice because it's necessary for improvement. Improvement is central to the final element of endeavor—growth.

Growth

Unconditional Endeavor is about reaching our potential, and growth is its object and natural result. Growth requires believing we can learn and change through endeavor and practice, commitment to excellence, openness to knowledge and experience, and pursuing learning opportunities. Growth happens when we're challenged. Without challenges, we become complacent or lazy. If we tackle a tough task and do it well, it becomes enjoyable . . . for a while. We must continue challenging ourselves by increasing its complexity to keep enjoying it. Instead of constantly competing with others, we should compete with ourselves, trying to push past our previous limits. Fulfillment comes not from winning or reaching for perfection but from personal growth.

*   *   *   *   *

Edison is remembered for his many successes, but he also failed a lot, and he failed big. After making a name for himself with the telegraph, his first patented invention was the electrographic vote recorder. He thought he'd developed a fortune-making machine, but when he took it to Washington, there was no interest. Politicians didn't want to change the traditional process.[41] Other major failures included the electric pen (an early copy machine), the talking doll (which was pulled from sale after a few months), ore mills and separators, the Edison Home Service Club (an early music-sharing service), and the home projecting kinetoscope. One of his most successful inventions, the phonograph, took nearly a decade and many trials to perfect.[42] In addition to dogged persistence, Edison had a fantastically robust growth mindset.

> If we all did the things we are really capable of doing,
> we would literally astound ourselves.
> —Thomas Edison[43]

In 1961, Reader's Digest published an article by Edison's son, Charles. He recalled a massive fire in 1914 that destroyed his father's lab complex. His father calmly walked over and said, "Go get your mother and all her friends. They'll never see a fire like this again." When Charles protested, Thomas said, "It's all right. We've just got rid of a lot of rubbish."[44]

Edison exemplified many elements of Unconditional Endeavor. He had a grand purpose, positive attitude, incredible work ethic, and bulldozer-like perseverance, but his most lasting impact was his dedication to growth. He thrived on failures because he didn't see them as such. He built on them to improve his inventions and himself. Ultimately, his growth mindset improved the world.

* * * * *

Although we may know all the aspects of endeavor and their merits, we don't always act on them. The next section illustrates all the ways we go wrong. Then, the following two sections offer solutions from timeless wisdom and how we can apply those solutions in our lives. When we learn to pursue Unconditional Endeavor, we can make the most of our capabilities and resources to reach our highest potential and greatest fulfillment.

Where We Go Wrong

ENDEAVOR IS ABOUT making the most of ourselves and striving to improve. It activates and applies the other four Unconditionals in our daily engagements. For example, an endeavor may require respecting team members (Love), accepting what we have to work with (Gratitude), making fair decisions (Integrity), and owning the outcome (Accountability).

Even if we engage the other Unconditionals effectively, they only provide a foundation for endeavor. It has its own requirements and must be considered separately. Worthwhile achievements often depend on applying all elements of endeavor effectively. That's hard, so most of us approach endeavors conditionally. It isn't that we don't know better; we just choose to compromise our standards.

In the first four chapters, I described spectra that cover our typical conditional responses. Similarly, we can imagine a *Spectrum of Conditional Endeavor*. On one end is conditional endeavor; on the other is lack of endeavor. In this chapter's first section, I described endeavor as "action itself." So, endeavor's opposite should be called "inaction."

The Trouble with Inaction

Inaction is failure to respond to a situation or take steps toward achieving a goal. Sometimes, inaction is called for, such as when we have no knowledge, skill, or experience but have knowledgeable, skilled, or experienced companions with control of the situation. But when we're faced with an endeavor that requires our involvement, inaction is useless.

At our best, we're motivated and engaged to act, and we make progress. However, if our endeavor is conditional, we experience doubt and frustration when we encounter obstacles. Setbacks cause doubt to grow into fear. We dial back our engagement, avoid challenges, and feel pessimistic, degenerating into apathy and withdrawal. Over time, inaction leads to atrophy of our abilities. The following table shows the best and worst of all elements of endeavor:

	Highest Levels → Action	Lowest Levels → Inaction
Purpose	Committed to meaningful goals	Aimless; no drive to achieve anything
Attitude	Positive outlook; invincible optimism	Constantly negative; defeated; hopeless
Preparation	Carefully plan for known and unknown	Ill-equipped; absence of forethought
Effort	Dedicate time, energy, and resources	Lethargy; absence of work
Focus	Single-minded concentration	Inability or unwillingness to concentrate
Excellence	Pursue highest possible standard	Poor quality; fail at basic standards
Individuality	Authentic uniqueness; distinction	Lack of personal identity; conformity
Perseverance	Enduring resolve; overcomes adversity	Avoids challenges; accepts failures
Practice	Deliberate, disciplined repetition	Disinterest in improvement
Growth	Transformative progress	Accepts stagnation, regression, atrophy

We can easily slide down the spectrum toward inaction. It happens when we address one or more elements conditionally. We only incorporate those elements *if* we think the conditions are favorable or *if* we expect the benefits to outweigh the costs. Without the right conditions or sufficient benefits, we're likely to sacrifice one or more elements, and endeavors either fall short of our best or fail completely. All ten elements are essential to Unconditional Endeavor:

- Endeavor without purpose is like traveling without a map—directionless.
- Endeavor without attitude is like sailing without wind—spiritless.

- Endeavor without preparation is like building without a blueprint—orderless.
- Endeavor without effort is like farming without water—fruitless.
- Endeavor without focus is like sculpting without a chisel—graceless.
- Endeavor without excellence is like cooking without seasoning—valueless.
- Endeavor without individuality is like singing without changing notes—colorless.
- Endeavor without perseverance is like climbing without a peak—pointless.
- Endeavor without practice is like speaking without words—powerless.
- Endeavor without growth is like pouring into a cup without a bottom—meaningless.

The following paragraphs explain the potential pitfalls of each of these elements in detail.

* * * * *

On January 28, 1986, my school had a snow day. I only remember because it was one of those days we remember exactly where we were. We remember those days by their tragedies.

That morning, the space shuttle *Challenger* disintegrated seventy-three seconds after launch, killing all seven crew members. A four-month investigation discovered that O-ring seals in a solid rocket booster failed due to cold temperatures, leaking hot gases and leading to an explosion. Furthermore, the investigation found that NASA engineers had warned about critical O-ring vulnerabilities in cold weather, but management dismissed their concerns to stay on schedule. Leadership's decision to proceed with the launch despite the warnings showed failures across multiple elements of endeavor. Their purpose was skewed toward schedule versus safety. Their attitude had shifted from reasonably cautious to overly optimistic about risks. Preparation was insufficient, as they disregarded data about O-ring performance in cold conditions. Focus waned from their primary responsibility of crew safety. Also, the engineers lacked perseverance to stand firm—those who initially opposed the launch backed down under management pressure. The tragedy demonstrates how allowing conditional approaches to endeavor's elements can cause catastrophic consequences.[45]

Purpose

When we have meaningful purpose, we strive for something greater than gratifying our ego, and an endeavor becomes a labor of love. Yet endeavors can quickly go off track. Laziness and apathy are ruthless demons; the slightest crack in our commitment lets them seep in and poison our passion. Many endeavors fail not for lack of skill, knowledge, or courage but for want of purpose.

Our most frequent failures of purpose are nonexistent purpose, unclear purpose, flawed purpose, and another's purpose. The first two lead to a lack of motivation, direction, or both. With the third, our purpose could be unethical, false, misguided, or simply wrong, but in any case, it leads us to the wrong outcome. The fourth needs more discussion because it's the hardest to recognize. We might accept someone else's purpose if we're insecure, exhausted, lazy, or indifferent. For small tasks, it may not matter. But if we default to that approach, we'll eventually question the purpose. No matter how similar we are to someone, our ideas and dreams are unique. If we adopt another's purpose, we'll eventually feel like something's missing—or worse, feel like a failure.[46,47]

> If a man does not keep pace with his companions,
> perhaps it is because he hears a different drummer.
> Let him step to the music which he hears, however measured or far away.
> —Henry David Thoreau

We must choose our own definition of success. It might be earning a lot of money, becoming a CEO, traveling the world, or making a difference in the community. If our purpose aligns with our passion, the chances are greater that we'll succeed.

Our purpose is conditional when we don't set goals, our values don't align with the goals, we depend on others to tell us what to do, or we don't believe in or understand the mission. We don't know where we're headed, and we end up in a different place than we intended.

* * * * *

When I was in eighth grade, one of the major assignments of the year was to complete a project on any science, technology, or engineering topic. I chose a project on space stations. President Reagan had called for the creation of space station *Freedom* in his 1984 State of the Union address. NASA produced many designs before settling on the final configuration of what would become the International Space Station (ISS), the first component of which was launched into orbit in 1998. NASA's photographic-quality conceptual graphics and slick public brochures formed the core of my research materials. The project's centerpiece was my station design, based on naive notions of its requirements. I only recall that my version looked quite like NASA's latest, as I didn't know enough to challenge what the professionals had done.

Completing the project kindled an interest in a space career. I decided that I wanted to go to space myself. I wanted to be an astronaut.

> We cannot achieve our wildest dreams by remaining who we are.
> —John C. Maxwell

I maintained my interest in becoming an astronaut throughout high school, choosing a university and major that would further these aims. After my sophomore year, I was selected for an internship at NASA's Langley Research Center in Hampton, Virginia, where I analyzed optimal dates and trajectories for Mars missions. While at Langley, I realized I had better access to official resources than I might have for a long time. So I decided to call NASA's chief health and medical officer—the astronauts' doctor—at Johnson Space Center in Houston, Texas. I had written out several questions so I'd be ready if I reached the doctor or someone knowledgeable. However, only one question truly mattered: What were the vision requirements to pass the astronaut physical?

My eyesight was never good. I wore glasses starting in second or third grade, and they grew thicker as I got older. In eighth grade, I switched to contacts, which slowed my vision's deterioration. But by college, I needed correction to see even the top few lines on the eye chart without squinting. When I called the medical office, I knew my eyesight was borderline at best, but until I talked to the man himself, I held out hope that I could sneak in under the wire.

When I finally spoke to someone in the right office, my hopes were quickly dashed. My eyesight was well under the requirement. Correction by glasses or contacts wasn't accepted. At that time, vision correction by laser surgery wasn't mainstream, so NASA didn't allow that either. The rest of my questions didn't matter. I was disqualified because of poor eyesight.

I was crushed. My dream of becoming an astronaut was dead. I had no chance, not because of anything I could control but due to a physical flaw. This created a personal crisis. What would I do? My life plan was shredded, and my career purpose was shattered.

Fortunately, I was able to pull out of what could have been a devastating nosedive. I stepped back and looked at the big picture. I was spending the summer working at one of the premier space research facilities in the world. I was being paid to study Mars missions. My mentor was a key team member for NASA's Mars *Pathfinder*, which landed on the red planet four years later and provided the world with astonishing, inspiring images. If I couldn't become an astronaut, I could do the next best thing: conceive, design, and build spacecraft that astronauts use to explore the cosmos. I could be an aerospace engineer. That became my new purpose. It defined and determined my career.

That summer, I thought I was prevented from becoming an astronaut because of weak eyes—poor vision. Today, I realize my problem wasn't a physical limitation. It was the self-limitation of an unclear purpose. I didn't sacrifice enough to establish a clear purpose—I had poor vision of a different kind.

Attitude

A positive attitude is valuable but challenging. Our brains are wired to focus on negative experiences due to our fight-or-flight instinct. Scientific evidence shows adverse events trigger stronger brain responses than positive ones, affecting our thoughts and behaviors more powerfully. Maintaining positive thoughts requires effort to go against our nature.[48,49,50]

> Everything can be taken from a man but one thing:
> the last of human freedoms—
> to choose one's attitude in any given set of circumstances,
> to choose one's own way.
> —Viktor Frankl

While negative thoughts are inevitable, persistent negativity creates pessimism. Pessimism extends beyond negativity—it focuses on problems, expects bad outcomes, sees struggles in simple tasks, and predicts failures. Forecasting failure undermines our efforts, so pessimism is often self-fulfilling. It's unhealthy and destructive. It drains motivation, stops progress, and is linked to anxiety, depression, sleep disorders, hostility, high blood pressure, and heart disease.[51] Like a virus, it can infect others and create a negative environment.

Several factors cause pessimism. Low self-esteem leads us to interpret adverse events as results of our shortcomings and fill our minds with negative self-talk.[52] Comparing ourselves to others—about money, friends, looks, or possessions—breeds feelings of inadequacy, jealousy, and depression.[53] Fear, especially of failure, can make us avoid risks and hide behind negativity.[54] Stress can push anyone, even optimists, toward pessimism by creating anxiety and irritability. Growing up or living in a toxic environment may lead to emotional scars that make pessimism the default mode.[55]

A conditional attitude expects things to always go our way, only remaining positive when good things happen. This leads to cynicism when faced with challenges, leaving us struggling with gratitude while expecting the worst.

* * * * *

Before her family visited the Perkins Institute in Boston, several teachers had attempted to work with Helen Keller. Most quickly concluded her case was hopeless. One teacher declared after just a few weeks that Helen was "mentally defective" and impossible to educate. Another lasted only days before deciding the task was too difficult. Their negative attitudes became self-fulfilling prophecies—believing they couldn't succeed, they didn't try hard enough to find effective teaching methods. When Anne Sullivan arrived, she approached the same challenges with a fundamentally different attitude, believing that Helen could learn despite her disabilities. When she had her first breakthrough with Keller, Sullivan famously said, "My heart is singing for joy this morning. A miracle has happened! The light of understanding has shone upon my little pupil's mind, and behold, all things are changed." The contrast between Sullivan's optimism and her predecessors' defeatism demonstrates how attitude can determine whether we overcome obstacles or not.[56]

Preparation

As mentioned earlier, preparation saves time and leads to better results in the long run, but that's easy to forget in the moment. If we're tired, lazy, or apathetic, we might skip or cut corners on preparation. Without a plan, we might get lucky and succeed, but we're more likely to stumble when we encounter obstacles, slowing our progress or stopping it altogether.

Even when we do commit to preparation, we often prepare poorly. We may develop an incomplete plan that lacks steps or schedules, leading to disorganization and ineffectiveness. We may not gather the necessary resources, like money, tools, or personnel. Or we may lack the required skills or knowledge, resulting in poor performance or failure. Our preparation is conditional when we don't take an endeavor seriously or invest the necessary time. We overestimate our ability to complete the task, and our execution becomes chaotic at best.

By failing to prepare, you are preparing to fail.
—Benjamin Franklin

*   *   *   *   *

Earlier in this chapter, I talked about how critical extensive preparation was to the success of the Apollo space program; unfortunately, NASA had to learn that lesson the hardest way imaginable. On January 27, 1967, during what should have been a routine ground test, astronauts Gus Grissom, Ed White, and Roger Chaffee died in a fire inside the Apollo 1 command module. The subsequent investigation revealed critical preparation failures. In the rush to meet President Kennedy's end-of-decade lunar landing goal, NASA approved a capsule design without understanding its dangers. Among the worst: its atmosphere was pure oxygen, and it contained several flammable materials; its hatch took ninety seconds to open from the inside; and the procedures for the test hadn't classified it as hazardous, despite having the astronauts sealed inside with power on. Their failure to prepare adequately for avoidable risks cost three lives. The tragedy led to significant design changes and safety improvements that ultimately enabled the successful Moon landings, but it remains a stark reminder that preparation isn't just about planning so that things will go right; it's also about anticipating what could go wrong and finding solutions before starting.[57]

Effort

Effort is the core of any endeavor. Without effort, skill is squandered possibility, and experience is wasted opportunity. So why do we often fall short of giving enough effort? Low self-efficacy, or a lack of belief in our ability to perform tasks successfully, is one cause. If we doubt our capacity to make a meaningful impact, we might choose not to invest effort at all. Lack of accountability is another. When there are no expectations, directions, or deadlines, or when we don't hold ourselves accountable, we lose our willingness to give effort.[58]

Hard work spotlights the character of people:
some turn up their sleeves, some turn up their noses,
and some don't turn up at all.

—Sam Ewing

Procrastination stops effort when we prioritize quick pleasure over long-term purpose. We produce rushed, subpar work and miss deadlines. If we believe we lack the time, money, or skills to do the job well, we might not work hard or even start. Being stressed or overwhelmed by a task's scope or complexity can be paralyzing and prevent progress.[59] Any or several of these common problems can hinder our ability or willingness to put in our best effort.

If our effort is based on benefiting ourselves, it's conditional. We hold back if we aren't sure it will pay off. We're stuck in the mud, unable to create momentum. Our production is pitiful, and we don't meet expectations.

*   *   *   *   *

During the 1930s, Winston Churchill recognized the growing Nazi threat earlier than most. However, his effort to sound the alarm was inconsistent. He gave passionate speeches in Parliament about German rearmament, but he often retreated to his country home at Chartwell to write histories and newspaper columns while the crisis deepened. He was regularly supplied intelligence about Hitler's military buildup, but his response was sporadic, sometimes delaying action for months. Only near the end of the decade did he sustain the effort to convince Britain of the danger. By then, valuable years had been lost. Churchill's erratic effort demonstrates how even one of history's greatest leaders failed to pursue Unconditional Endeavor.[60]

Focus

Focus is about prioritization and time management. Prioritization is choosing what to pay attention to and in what order versus what to ignore or postpone. Time management is deciding how much time to dedicate to an activity based on our priorities and sticking to that schedule. Prioritization can fail when we overvalue urgent but unimportant tasks at the expense of important but nonurgent ones. Time management breaks down when we consistently underestimate how long tasks will take, leading to missed deadlines and stress.

The most common way we lose focus is distractions. They divert our attention and reduce the quality of our effort. Other focus factors include insufficient sleep, lack of physical activity, poor eating habits, and personal conditions (medical, psychological, or cognitive).[61] Failing to promptly address these issues keeps us from stretching for Unconditional Endeavor.

> Unless a person knows how to give order to his or her thoughts,
> attention will be attracted to whatever is most problematic at the moment.
> —Mihaly Csikszentmihalyi

Our focus is conditional if we don't want to dedicate ourselves to the most critical tasks. When we don't understand or believe in the mission or priorities, we allow our focus to fade. We flail around, spend time on the wrong things, get bogged down and distracted, and forget our purpose.

* * * * *

Nikola Tesla was a brilliant inventor and contemporary of Thomas Edison. In fact, Tesla was the visionary behind alternating current (AC) electricity, which was superior to Edison's direct current (DC) at long-distance power distribution and eventually became the world's standard. Yet Tesla suffered from inconsistent focus. While his incredible mind generated many innovations, he got bogged down in distractions and minutiae. He often jumped from one project to another, prioritizing the allure of new ideas over the hard work of bringing existing projects to fruition. He also struggled with time management, pouring countless hours into grandiose visions that never materialized while neglecting more pressing concerns. He fixated on far-fetched concepts like death rays to the detriment of more practical work. His eating and sleeping habits were erratic, and he'd work for days before crashing from exhaustion. With better focus and balance,

Tesla's impact could have been even more extraordinary. He exemplifies how even immense talent can be undermined by a lack of focus.[62]

Excellence

Striving for excellence means always doing our best, but that's hard. Feeling tired, unmotivated, pessimistic, distracted, overwhelmed, or lazy are excuses that keep us from doing our best. Unconditional Endeavor doesn't accept excuses. The secret to overcoming excuses is a commitment to excellence. Excellence raises our effort beyond what excuses can subdue.

> Do what you can where you are with what you've got.
> —Theodore Roosevelt

Sometimes, factors like illness or uncontrollable constraints prevent us from doing our best. Those aren't excuses. They're reasons any rational person would agree prevent peak performance. Doing our best means giving the most we can, accounting for present circumstances. Of course, we can't often measure our best, so deceiving others and ourselves is easy. Only we can know. We must rely on our integrity and hold ourselves accountable.

Trying to do *our* best isn't the same as trying to be *the* best. The former strives for the highest personal excellence. It's focused on accomplishment and growth. The latter can mean aiming for perfection. Perfectionism is believing we can look, speak, act, feel, or be perfect and behaving as if that's the goal. It's driven by social pressures or the expectations of others or ourselves. We seek perfection to feel accepted, valued, and successful and avoid judgment or blame. Unfortunately, perfection is subjective, and when judged by a perfectionist, results are never good enough.[63] It creates disappointment (even when others see success), anxiety, and depression.[64] We think perfection will give us protection, but it usually leads to self-rejection.

* * * * *

I've struggled with perfectionism and aiming to be *the* best at the expense of becoming *my* best. As a child, I had a stereotypical firstborn's desire to please, producing good manners and grades. I was rarely satisfied with success, however, and I could be devastated by anything less than perfection. I saw myself as motivated by excellence, but in retrospect, I was often motivated by the prospect of beating others more than doing my best. When I compared myself to others who were better at things than I was, I struggled. Since I'd built my identity on winning, I felt lost, sidetracked by the realization that I wasn't *the* best. My first-or-last mindset caused me to latch on to excuses, as if others had more opportunities or better training.

My need to be *the* best continued into college. In every situation, I compared myself to others, and I experienced positive or negative feelings. The negativity usually lasted longer. When I made my first academic B, I was distraught. Self-questioning ruined my holiday break. If I didn't receive the highest grade, how could I be a winner?

I wish I could claim to have overcome perfectionism in college or early in my career. Alas, only through experience and maturity did I realize that trying to be *the* best is fruitless and harmful. I still regress, but I finally have the core understanding: what matters is doing *our* best.

*   *   *   *   *

Trying to be *the* best can also mean striving for more success than others. For most of us, there's no way to measure who, what, when, or where something or someone is *the* best. Most of our endeavors are dependent on the performer and the environment. Where we can objectively compare performance, like sports, we do so only to determine a game's winner. Sadly, many of us treat all endeavors like competitions, becoming obsessed with being *the* best.

When we try to be *the* best, we focus on winning—a zero-sum game where one person's win is another's loss. We're constantly concerned with our place in the race. We want to be first, so we think of and do for ourselves first. If we don't win, we think we've failed. When we win, the joy is short-lived, as we immediately move to the next zero-sum game. This obsession with winning is all-consuming and causes stress and chronic health problems.[65,66]

Doing *our* best is a positive-sum game. It's pursuing success on our terms by setting challenging goals that push us to grow. We aim for our best in each moment and can be genuinely happy for others' accomplishments.[67]

Doing our best doesn't mean avoiding competition or ignoring wins and losses. It means measuring success by our standards, not others'. Competition can be a motivator for continued improvement. If we have a chance to win, we should try. It can bring out the best in us.

Games are meant to be fun diversions that offer challenges. We should approach them like any endeavor by giving our best. Emphasizing winning over doing our best can sap the fun, increase stress, and turn opponents into adversaries. It changes games into me-first, zero-sum battles where no one wins. I'm not advocating a participation trophy philosophy. Games with objective metrics and clear winners are part of life, but focusing on external comparisons generates adverse outcomes. Games themselves don't drive win-or-fail mentalities. Only we can allow ourselves to miss the point of Unconditional Endeavor: always doing our best, learning, and growing. Results are steps toward Unconditional Endeavor, not final outcomes.

> "Did I win? Did I lose?" Those are the wrong questions.
> The correct question is: "Did I make my best effort?"
> If so . . . you may be outscored, but you will never lose.
> —John Wooden

Doing our best is inspirational and affirming. When we choose not to do our best or put winning ahead of learning, our excellence becomes conditional. If achievement, praise, and rewards are our only drivers, we think solely about what we get from the task, and we give up if we believe we can't win.

* * * * *

Earlier in this chapter, I explained how the space shuttle *Challenger* disaster was a failure of purpose, attitude, preparation, focus, and perseverance.

It was also a failure of excellence. NASA leadership ignored clear technical evidence of the risks to the O-rings in cold weather to preserve a façade of excellence—trying to maintain an ambitious flight schedule. It underscores that excellence isn't about appearance; it requires the courage to acknowledge and address weaknesses, even when doing so challenges short-term goals.[68]

> Don't bother just to be better than your contemporaries or predecessors.
> Try to be better than yourself.
>
> —William Faulkner

Individuality

We start life unaware of ourselves as individuals. Eventually, we become conscious of our identity, which consists of the qualities and characteristics that define us. Individuality is the unique perspective—based on our principles, passions, personality, proficiencies, and past—that we bring to any endeavor. But we aren't all comfortable with being different. The struggle between conformity and individuality is a defining dimension of our teenage years. Combined with rapid brain development and dramatic hormonal changes, this struggle can be confusing and painful. Some people never fully resolve it and remain uneasy throughout their lives. Those who come to terms with their individuality do so at different ages and with varied outcomes.

The importance of individuality varies across cultures. In some societies, like America's, individuals who break norms and become pioneers are celebrated. Other cultures discourage standing out, promoting the idea that the nail that sticks up will be hammered down. Most modern societies balance individuality with shared practices and community. Cultures with strict rules and tight control become restrictive. Societies where everyone thinks, acts, and looks the same stifle imagination. Individuality expressed through creativity is vital to progress.

Our individuality is conditional if we're too scared or selfish to share ourselves. We can't distinguish our endeavors from others'. We minimize our positive impact.

Perseverance

To overcome barriers, we must understand what they are. The truth is that we create most barriers ourselves. They're either a) imagined or b) real but exaggerated in our minds. If we recognize them as self-created, we can find ways to overcome them and focus on real obstacles.

Self-doubt makes us question our abilities. Self-pity focuses on real or imagined suffering. Fear is a natural survival response but limits risk-taking. Negative retrospection dwells on past mistakes. Indifference is a lack of motivation that blocks effort. Impatience desires quick results and instant gratification. Even if we overcome these mental barriers, objective obstacles outside our control can still lead to failure. Failure has negative consequences and is seen as a sign of incompetence, so fear of failure can prevent starting or persisting. Quitting, after one try or many, results in surrendering to failure. When perseverance is conditional, we're stopped by these barriers. We only accept easy tasks, quit quickly, or stop trying altogether.

> Our greatest weakness lies in giving up.
> The most certain way to succeed is always to try just one more time.
> —Thomas Edison

* * * * *

Walt Disney's early career illustrates the potential trap of conditional thinking and how to overcome it. After multiple failures (being laid off for "lack of imagination," bankruptcy, losing his first successful character), he could have decided success depended on circumstances and that they'd always be against him. Instead, he stayed committed to his vision, pursued Unconditional Endeavor, and created Mickey Mouse.[69]

Practice

If we're honest, few would say we enjoy practicing. First, we don't want to do the work. Practice requires giving the same effort as the real endeavor—many times over. Next, noticeable improvements demand patience through many practice sessions, but we don't like to wait. We also don't like doing things we're not good at, but practicing can force us to re-live mistakes. For solo endeavors, practice can be lonely. It often focuses on little things to improve the big things, and the little things can seem tedious.

We think we can get by without practice, but if we don't practice, we don't improve or grow. The point of practice is progress. Our practice is conditional when it depends on seeing rapid results. Impatience or laziness leads to stopping if improvements aren't frequent and obvious. We try to get by with the minimum, and we don't improve. Our endeavors are lethargic because our results don't change, and we eventually lose interest. Those who excel understand that practice is paramount.

> If I skip practice for a day, I notice . . .
> If I skip practice for two days, my wife notices . . .
> If I skip practice for three days, the world notices.
> —Vladimir Horowitz

*　　*　　*　　*　　*

The Soviet space program's practice protocols in the 1960s were critically flawed in skill development. Cosmonauts were trained through rigid repetition that prioritized perfect adherence to predetermined procedures over adaptive problem-solving. This approach suppressed individual creativity and critical thinking, transforming practice from a tool of mastery into a constraint that ultimately undermined mission success and technological innovation.[70]

Growth

Growth is the foremost benefit of any endeavor. Without growth, endeavor is stagnant. To grow, we must push ourselves beyond what we've already mastered. It's tempting to think big and take big steps, especially with grand goals. But if we get lost in dreams of the result and attempt giant leaps, we often fail and feel depleted and defeated. Also, constantly concentrating on results can lead to a lack of life balance, stress, and burnout.

Growth becomes conditional when we expect it to be easy, are unwilling to push ourselves, demand quick results, or try to take a few big steps to reach our goal. It's also conditional when it's all about the outcome. We might complete endeavors, but we don't experience significant success, and we aren't fulfilled.

* * * * *

Adam Neumann co-founded WeWork with Miguel McKelvey in 2010. WeWork reimagined workplace environments, offering flexible, shared office spaces to businesses and individuals. Neumann, the CEO, pursued an aggressive scaling strategy, attracted billions in venture capital investments, and spent those billions by prioritizing growth over profitability. The company rapidly expanded from a single coworking space to a global brand. In 2019, when it announced a plan for an Initial Public Offering (IPO) of company stock, it was valued at $47 billion. However, the IPO attempt opened WeWork's books and business model to closer scrutiny and exposed fundamental flaws, revealing a narrative of inflated valuation and unsustainable expansion. Within weeks, its value plummeted, Neumann was ousted, and the company's dream of transformative growth collapsed. The episode vividly shows how chasing grand visions without embracing the elements of endeavor can lead to spectacular failure.[71]

* * * * *

Nothing in the world is worth having or worth doing
unless it means effort, pain, difficulty . . .
I have never in my life envied a human being who led an easy life.
I have envied a great many people who led difficult lives and led them well.
—Theodore Roosevelt

Answers in Timeless Wisdom

MOST OF US spend our lives performing projects along the Spectrum of Conditional Endeavor, approaching one or more elements of endeavor conditionally. We wait to see if circumstances are favorable before deciding how intensely to dedicate ourselves. When our conditions are met, we perform at our best, enthusiastically involve every element of endeavor, and achieve meaningful progress. When they aren't, we do less than we can and struggle. We doubt our abilities when facing obstacles, and our doubts turn into fears when obstacles become failures. We withdraw from challenging endeavors, sliding down the spectrum toward inaction.

The problem stems from the belief that endeavors are inherently conditional. We grow up watching others pursue tasks with pessimism, poor planning, lackluster effort, and a tendency to quit when challenges arise. Society reinforces taking the path of least resistance. However, short-term results based on conditional decisions don't lead to meaningful success, personal growth, or long-term fulfillment.

We can choose a different path: Unconditional Endeavor. It requires a decision to change our ways of thinking and acting. We must fight instinctive fears and temporary comforts to pursue endeavors without contingencies. Embracing Unconditional Endeavor means giving our all without expecting rewards or recognition. It's fueled by passion and self-belief. It's learning from failures and never giving up on what matters to us. It's not just about success—it's about embracing the journey and finding fulfillment in the endeavor. By choosing this path, we continually evolve toward our best selves.

*   *   *   *   *

Remember, Unconditional Endeavor is like the thumb that helps us grab hold of life. It's how we get things done. It's not just about doing the work. It's about understanding what a task requires, approaching it with the right mindset, and seeing it through. It involves knowing what the task is for, having the proper perspective, planning effectively, working hard, giving it our attention, doing our best, bringing our unique qualities, solving problems, improving through practice, and continuously striving for better results. Unconditional Endeavor means incorporating all these elements and performing them at the highest level, which produces the best rewards: personal growth and fulfillment.

Great thinkers have long explored the elements of Unconditional Endeavor. Though from centuries past, their insights remain relevant, as the challenges we face echo those of previous generations. The answers lie in our core values.

> It is the doer of deeds who actually counts in the battle for life,
> and not the man who looks on and says how the fight ought to be fought,
> without himself sharing the stress and the danger.
> —Theodore Roosevelt

* * * * *

Henry Ford is famous for developing the assembly line method of manufacturing, which made automobiles affordable for the middle class and revolutionized transportation, industry, and how people lived from the early twentieth century onward. He started from humble beginnings, born on a farm in what's now Dearborn, Michigan. He wasn't interested in farming. He loved machines. In the late 1890s, he helped develop some of the first primitive cars. He didn't invent the car—then called horseless carriages—but he preferred working for himself over working for others, and he had vision.[72]

Ford excelled at explaining his vision and found investors to start a car company. However, he initially struggled with running businesses, and his first two companies failed. Despite these setbacks, he kept building cars. Eventually, his cars attracted new investors, and in 1903, before his fortieth birthday, he started the Ford Motor Company.[73]

In 1906, Ford's Model N became the bestselling car in the US, but cars were luxuries, unaffordable to most. Ford envisioned a different world, one unimaginable to others in his day. He said, "I will build a car for the great multitude. It will be large enough for the family but small enough for the individual to run and care for. It will be constructed of the best materials, by the best men to be hired, after the simplest designs that modern engineering can devise. But it will be so low in price that no man making a good salary will be unable to own one."[74]

In 1908, Ford introduced the Model T. It became so popular that the company quickly sold all the cars it could make. However, Ford aimed to make all the cars he could sell. He led the company to increase production and decrease costs dramatically. The assembly line was not his only innovation. He doubled wages (to five dollars per day), enabling him to hire and retain the best workers and allowing his employees to afford cars for their families. His company started the five-day, forty-hour work week. The company's marketing set the standards for the future of advertising. Ford's innovations grew Model T sales from fifteen thousand in 1907 to nearly one million in 1919. The company eventually sold over fifteen million. More importantly, it transformed global business and how people lived and worked.[75]

Ford is most often associated with modernizing manufacturing and developing better ways to do things (endeavors). What differentiated him from his peers and made his endeavors uniquely successful, though, was his vision—his purpose.[76]

> Whether you think you can, or you think you can't—you're right.
> —Henry Ford

Wisdom about Each Element of Endeavor

Purpose

Purpose is our North Star. It's the reason we take on tasks, and it motivates us to finish what we start. If attitude sours, preparation is poor, effort weakens, focus blurs, excellence wanes, or perseverance relents, purpose can keep us going. Our purpose must be based on truth and consistent with our values. Otherwise, if another aspect falters, we may question our purpose, and the endeavor will fail.

Some of the most successful people throughout history have dreamed of (and eventually achieved) seemingly impossible things. Helen Keller dreamed of communicating with the world. Martin Luther King Jr. dreamed of ending segregation. Bill Gates dreamed that every home would have a personal computer. Their dreams were big, considered crazy by many in their times, but grounded in the truth and values of the dreamers. They didn't know how they'd reach their goals, but they had visions of success and worked toward them.[77] For big successes, we must dream big; it's the first step toward turning great ideas into reality. As Keller, King, and Gates did, we must clearly envision that future reality. Everything we create starts as an idea, and we make it so by willful action. The same is true of our dreams: we first have the dream (the purpose), then we summon the energy to make it happen. *Thought + action = manifestation.*

In Stephen Covey's *The 7 Habits of Highly Effective People*, the second habit is Begin with the End in Mind. This means starting with a clear understanding of our destination. Purpose is the envisioned end state. It's the realization of a dream.

> All things are created twice. There's a mental or first creation, and a physical or second creation to all things. Take the construction of a home, for example. You create it in every detail before you ever hammer the first nail into place. . . . Then you reduce it to blueprint and develop construction plans. . . . You have to make sure that the blueprint, the first creation, is really what you want, that you've thought everything through. Then you put it into bricks and mortar. . . . You begin with the end in mind.
>
> —Stephen R. Covey[78]

The things that usually keep us from creating the reality we want are the limitations we put on ourselves. We can open paths to success by dreaming big and removing self-imposed restrictions. Henry Ford did this. Despite numerous obstacles and early failures, he was resilient, constantly improving. He overcame experts' skepticism and financial burdens through steadfast belief in his vision. He created his reality.

The critical characteristics of a purpose are:

- It must be clear (coherent and comprehensible).
- It must be compelling (concrete and credible).
- It must be consistent (constant and changeless).

After we establish a mental image of our future reality, we need more than energy to move forward. We need self-confidence. Self-confidence is like faith: It allows us to believe something is true without tangible proof. It convinces us we can succeed before we prove it. We're ready to begin any endeavor with a clear, compelling, consistent purpose bolstered by self-confidence.

Our purpose is our compass. To properly use a compass, we need to know our starting point. *Right now, who am I? What are my values?* We must understand our current situation and how we got here. Once we know where we are, we must know our heading. We don't want to realize, too late, that we've been going in the wrong direction. Knowing where we're headed comes from a clear, compelling, consistent purpose.

Whether setting personal goals, leading a team project, or embarking on a new career path, we should dream boldly. If we align our purpose with our values, it will ignite a passion within us. As we take steps toward that purpose, our motivation increases, we find resilience we didn't know we had, and we can have greater impacts than we thought possible.

> Purpose provides activation energy for living.
> —Mihaly Csikszentmihalyi

Attitude

Helen Keller embodied the power of optimism. She wrote and spoke profoundly about our prerogative to choose positivity against all odds. Of the twelve books and several articles she wrote and published, perhaps the most relevant to attitude for endeavor is called "Optimism: An Essay," from which the following fantastic quotation is taken:

My optimism is grounded in two worlds, myself and what is about me. I demand that the world be good, and lo, it obeys. I proclaim the world good, and facts range themselves to prove my proclamation overwhelmingly true. . . . I am never discouraged by absence of good. I never can be argued into hopelessness. Doubt and mistrust are the mere panic of timid imagination, which the steadfast heart will conquer, and the large mind transcend.[79]

*　*　*　*　*

Attitude is a choice: This is one of the most powerful truths of human existence, but our skeptical, lazy minds often don't fully understand it. We're wired to react to external stimuli, and most of us accept what that approach gives us instead of challenging ourselves mentally. When we don't get the results we want, we often do nothing. If we try to change things—like our relationships, jobs, behaviors, or habits—but our outcomes remain the same, we may give up, assuming we're victims of our circumstances.

Psychologist and philosopher William James explored the relationships between attitude, consciousness, and behavior. His work on the psychology of personal belief greatly impacted our understanding of how attitudes shape our thoughts, decisions, and actions.[80]

> Believe that life is worth living, and your belief will help create the fact.
> —William James[81]

We can choose or change our circumstances by altering our attitude. To shape our situation with our attitude, we must understand how to wield this power effectively. The key lies not in blind positivity but in an outlook called realistic optimism. It doesn't ignore negatives but believes we can create positive results that outweigh them. It plays to strengths while working on weaknesses. It rejects pessimistic predictions, reframes limiting beliefs, and admits that every day may not be good but believes something good can be found every day.[82]

*　*　*　*　*

Twin brothers were studied by psychologists because they were attitudinal opposites—one was an extreme pessimist and the other an eternal optimist. The researchers devised an experiment to determine how deep these traits ran. They put the pessimist in a room filled with toys, games, sports equipment, and more. They put the optimist in a room full of horse manure. When they checked on the pessimist, he was crying in the corner. When asked what was wrong, he said, "I know all these toys will break, the batteries will run out, other kids will be jealous and steal them, and I'll hurt myself playing with them!" When they checked on the optimist, he was excitedly digging through the manure, throwing it around the room with joy. When asked what he was doing, he replied, "With all this horse sh*t, there must be a pony in here somewhere!"

* * * * *

Paraphrasing Henry Ford: both pessimists and optimists are usually correct. Pessimists believe something's impossible, so they unconsciously look for ways to prove themselves right. Optimists believe something's possible and find ways to make it happen.

Choosing a positive attitude can feel unrealistic, especially when faced with personal setbacks or external obstacles. As explained in chapter 2, the best place to start is gratitude. We acknowledge the good in our life, however faint and insignificant it may seem. This shift in perspective can be small but, over time, can profoundly impact our overall outlook. With practice, optimism can become our default mode.

Preparation

Preparation for small, daily tasks doesn't take much mental energy. Still, when we fail to plan—like forgetting to buy a fresh tube of toothpaste or package of toilet paper before running out—we very much appreciate the importance of preparation. For major tasks, preparation is vital. Humans have understood this since the beginning of history. Over twenty-five-hundred years ago, Confucius shared wisdom that's still relevant:

Success depends upon previous preparation,
and without such preparation, there is sure to be failure.

When dealing with daunting deadlines, preparation can seem like a luxury. Also, the world prioritizes progress over planning, so we feel pressured to take quick action. However, preparation is critical to success. Those who aren't natural planners should start small by defining priorities or building in time buffers for the unexpected. When we plan, we anticipate potential roadblocks and find alternate routes, avoiding significant stress and other setbacks.

*   *   *   *   *

Winston Churchill's political career enabled him to personally promote the power of preparation. As First Lord of the Admiralty before World War I, he oversaw the modernization of the British navy, converting it from coal to oil power, commissioning new dreadnoughts, and developing naval aviation. This ensured the fleet was well equipped when war broke out in 1914. Later, as Prime Minister during World War II, his foresight proved pivotal on two fronts. First, he supported the establishment of the Ultra intelligence program at Bletchley Park to break German codes, providing critical intelligence. Second, he cultivated a close alliance with the US, which was instrumental in the war's outcome. Churchill understood that victory is often secured long before the first battle begins, in the unglamorous work of laying strong foundations. His example reminds us that whether we're leading nations or our own lives, preparation is necessary to handle whatever comes.[83,84]

Effort

Effort is the action, activity, and energy of endeavor. Earlier in this chapter, I gave an equation for making things happen: *thought + action = manifestation*. Purpose creates the thought; effort provides the action. If purpose is our compass, pointing us toward our goal, effort is our ship, carrying us across the ocean of endeavor. Dreaming isn't enough; we must move in the direction of our dreams.

The most potent aspect of effort is that it creates value. It develops products, processes, services, and knowledge. The added value isn't always proportional to the effort—with better skills and experience, we can create more value with less effort—but it fosters personal, team, and community progress.[85]

All the world's major religions emphatically edify effort as an ethical responsibility. The Book of Proverbs in the Hebrew and Christian Bible contains maxims about hard work's spiritual, physical, and financial benefits, despite being written over twenty-five-hundred years ago.

> The lazy have strong desires but receive nothing;
> the appetite of the diligent is satisfied.
> —Proverbs 13:4 (Common English Version)

> There is profit in hard work, but mere talk leads to poverty.
> —Proverbs 14:23 (CEV)

"An-Najm," the fifty-third chapter of the Qur'an, also endorses effort's value.

> Man will not get anything unless he works hard.
> —Qur'an 53:39

Effort was also among Confucius's most frequent topics.

> A superior man is modest in his speech but exceeds in his actions.
> —Confucius

William James wrote extensively about effort's importance in achieving goals. In a lecture to the American Philosophical Association in 1906, later called "The Energies of Men," he said mental effort (using will to control thinking) and physical effort (consistently working hard) are necessary for success and fulfillment.[86]

> Every good that is worth possessing must be paid for in strokes of daily effort.
> —William James

Do every day or two something for no other reason than its difficulty, so that,
when the hour of dire need draws nigh,
it may find you not unnerved and untrained to stand the test.

—William James

*　*　*　*　*

Growing up, I had a few regular chores. I mowed the yard and helped when Dad rotated the tires or changed the oil, but my first experience with real work came as a teenager when I took on odd jobs for others. I mowed several yards from spring to fall, raked leaves for a few families at the end of the season, and did some labor-intensive (but very unskilled) landscaping. I didn't make much money, but it was enough for baseball cards and other little things I wanted.

I got my first real job early in high school, working for a small construction company, initially on weekends and holidays, then through the summer. To be clear, I didn't do any actual construction. That would have required skill. I started off mowing yards. As I gained the owner's trust, I was given other tasks, like sweeping and picking up debris around the sites. Eventually, I helped with a few heavy lifting jobs, like carrying roof shingles up ladders.

I remember one task most vividly. The fun part was that I got to drive a dump truck—not an industrial-grade, big-time construction site one, but a dump truck nonetheless. The not-so-fun part was that the bed was filled with mulch. My job, sometimes with a partner, was to pick up a truckload, drive it to a homesite, and spread the mulch over all the landscaped areas with pitchforks. Spreading a little mulch isn't terribly taxing, but we didn't spread a little. When full, our dump truck held a load ten feet long, six feet wide, and five feet deep. We'd get a load, spread it all, then get another load. All day. All summer.

I didn't realize it at the time, but pushing an old mower through wet grass at the end of a long day, stopping every few steps to pull clumps out of a clogged exhaust, had benefits beyond the bucks. Hard work is an incomparable instructor. It helped me understand gratitude, integrity, and accountability. I gained an appreciation for others' work and valued my meager income. I developed integrity when I did a good job, even when others weren't watching. I learned that responsibility builds resolve and effort brings the satisfaction of accomplishment.

> Being forced to work, and forced to do your best,
> will breed in you temperance and self-control,
> diligence and strength of will, cheerfulness and content,
> and a hundred virtues which the idle will never know.
> —Charles Kingsley

* * * * *

It's tempting to think successful people have advantages ordinary people don't and that they haven't had to work hard to be successful. That's universally wrong. The most successful people in history—like Thomas Edison, Henry Ford, and Teddy Roosevelt—earned their success through effort. Many of them were born into modest circumstances. Some might have had better-than-average skills or unique traits that made them stand out early on, but only through consistent effort, as part of boundless Unconditional Endeavor, did they achieve success.

We can be fooled. When we suddenly become aware of others' recent accomplishments, it can seem like their rise was meteoric. On the contrary, overnight successes happen when hardworking, skilled people find opportunities and discover their abilities match what others need or want. No one achieves success immediately and without working for it.

> If you knew how much work went into it, you wouldn't call it genius.
> —Michelangelo

Just talking about effort doesn't count. Action requires energy. Sometimes, the hardest part is starting. We must remind ourselves that our efforts need not be massive; they must only be continuous, but they must commence. As Lao Tzu said, "A journey of a thousand miles begins with a single step."

Sustained hard work can be grueling, especially for long, complex projects. When we feel discouraged, we should reflect on how far we've come rather than fixating on what's left. Every ounce of effort is a testament to our character and a catalyst for growth. Each action builds on the last, and the cumulative impact of consistent, purposeful effort enables us to reach our goals and discover how much we're capable of.

Focus

Throughout history, technologies have been developed to simplify our lives. They've reduced or eliminated the time we spend on daily survival tasks, household chores, and many professional jobs. However, when technologies free our time, we fill it with other activities. We create new tasks and invent diversions. Particularly in the first world, as technologies have taken over more of our tasks, we've dramatically increased the variety and number of distractions. As distractions mount, cultivating and maintaining focus has become more valuable and difficult.

The first step is prioritizing tasks and concentrating on the most important ones. We use selective attention to dedicate ourselves to a single task and avoid daydreams or task switching. We stop nonessential activities and try to minimize, filter, or ignore distractions. This focus on focus can immediately improve productivity and performance.

In its most potent form, focus means fixation, total absorption. In 1990, psychologist Mihaly Csikszentmihalyi coined the term *flow* in his book *Flow: The Psychology of Optimal Experience*. Flow is characterized by deep focus and intense effort. He says we find true happiness—and are most creative and productive—when in a flow state.

> Flow is being completely involved in an activity for its own sake.
> The ego falls away. Time flies. Every action, movement, and thought
> follows inevitably from the previous one, like playing jazz.
> —Mihaly Csikszentmihalyi[87]

Csikszentmihalyi explains that we can experience flow by controlling our attention and strengthening our resolve against diversions. We must immerse ourselves in tasks that are rewarding on their own—without external incentives like money or fame—and stretch us slightly beyond previous achievements. Flow can be achieved by losing self-consciousness, selfishness, and our sense of time. We feel in the groove and want to keep it going.[88]

Unfortunately, we've trained our brains to crave distractions, so we must rewire them to resist. The key is to create routines that minimize the willpower needed to transition into and maintain focus. One method is to establish a flow space. We make it quiet if we focus best in silent situations or noisy if preferred. We strictly structure our environment by turning off, putting away, and leaving behind anything not required for the task and blocking all but emergency notifications. We can't multitask. The objective is to construct a fortress that repels distractions and welcomes sustained attention.[89] Another method is mindfulness—mental engagement in the present. By removing mental clutter, we free cognitive resources for focus. We ignore our surroundings but monitor our thoughts to intercept intrusions and ward off wandering.[90] In addition to creating a conducive space and being mindful, we must allocate time to focus and commit to it. Consistency is critical.[91]

> If you are in an extremely productive or creative phase,
> you don't let anything interrupt.
> —Stephen R. Covey[92]

*　*　*　*　*

My success with focus is mixed. I'm often distracted at work by the buzz of emails and instant messages. The endorphin rush from completing tasks, even trivial ones, frequently pulls me into this swarm. When I succeed, it's usually because I employ techniques that work for me—closing apps, ignoring the phone, and, if necessary, unplugging from the network. Sadly, the delusion of self-importance—that someone needs me—sidetracks me too often. My experience writing this book has been better. I've found flow spaces, created environments, and dedicated times when I can avoid distractions. With practice, I've trained myself to get into flow quickly. My passion for the work helps (as does my understanding family). As

Csikszentmihalyi suggests, the combined sense of enjoyment, development, and accomplishment that flow produces is deeply satisfying.

*   *   *   *   *

Although flow is fulfilling, it can be intense. When deep in flow, we might lose our sense of time or forget to eat or sleep. Flow is enjoyable, but balance is necessary. Setting aside blocks of time for intense focus with regular breaks helps. Healthy habits like sufficient sleep, nourishment, and physical activity support focus and personal well-being.[93]

Focus is vital because our time and energy are finite. Reaching our potential requires that we learn to fully engage in important endeavors. Focus isn't just saying yes to the right things; we must choose our highest priorities and say no to everything else. We set boundaries and fiercely protect them. We find a flow space, turn off notifications, and immerse ourselves, even if we can initially manage only short stretches. Finally, we must remember that well-being is more valuable than productivity, and life balance is a sign of strength, not weakness.

Excellence

As I explained earlier, excellence isn't about meeting expectations or being superior to others, nor is it about ability or accomplishment. It's living to our full potential each day.[94]

Doing our best requires investing in the present rather than dwelling on the past or wishing for the future. Each moment is an opportunity to excel. We owe it to everyone we interact with (and, more importantly, to ourselves) to give our all. Mundane chores make it easy to zone out, and it's tempting to slack off when working alone, but doing our best when nobody's looking enables success at anything.[95] Excellence also goes beyond doing our best in the moment. It's putting ourselves in position to perform at our peak. We can't show up expecting that giving one hundred percent on the spot is enough. Meaningful endeavors need preparation, and doing our best applies as much beforehand as to the effort itself.[96]

*   *   *   *   *

Michelangelo is widely considered the greatest sculptor in history. His pursuit of excellence transcended artistic skill. He approached each sculpture as a dialogue with the stone, studying its intrinsic qualities before making a single chisel mark. His preparatory drawings and models revealed extraordinary commitment to understanding form, anatomy, and potential—transforming preparation from a technical process into a practice of artistic revelation.[97] He showed how excellence requires our best both as we execute and as we prepare for endeavors.

* * * * *

Ganbaru is a Japanese word that translates as "doing one's best," but in Japanese culture, it means more. It's a mindset of committing fully to complete a task. It's maintaining determination and dignity in difficult situations. What makes *ganbaru* noteworthy is that it emphasizes operations over outcomes. Even if we fail, having *ganbatta* (the past tense) is worthy of respect. The full meaning of *ganbaru* contains elements of accountability (not letting others down) and perseverance (not giving up). *Ganbaru* is embedded in Japanese education, workplace culture, and sports. Employees who show *ganbaru* spirit through their dedication are highly valued. Students are praised more for their ganbaru attitude than for their natural talent. One critique of *ganbaru* is that, when taken to extremes, it can create undue pressure and lead to overwork and stress. But any virtue can be carried to unhealthy excesses.[98]

Ganbaru aligns with excellence as I believe it's intended. It's not about results. Despite giving our best, we sometimes don't achieve our desired outcomes. A critical part of excellence is knowing we did our best in successes and failures. When we do our best, we have no regrets. We can adjust our approach and try again with confidence that we can and will do our best. Doing our best with what we have for as long as possible eventually leads to success.[99]

Excellence is a continuous process. When we do our best, our best gets better. We can do more with less. We naturally advance toward our goals.[100] Whether an endeavor is mundane or momentous, doing our best is fulfilling, makes us happy and helps us become our best selves.

> Whatever you do, do it well.
> —Walt Disney

Individuality

Individuality—in the forms of creativity, originality, and innovation—is critical to the success of our endeavors. If our attitude turns negative and our focus blurs, creativity is the spark that invigorates our success. If preparation is poor and excellence isn't enough, originality helps us achieve our goals. When effort is blocked, innovation provides the impulse to break through.

In the discussion of focus, I introduced Csikszentmihalyi's flow concept as a state that combines deep focus with intense effort to heighten creativity. In his 1996 book *Creativity: Flow and the Psychology of Discovery and Invention*, he expands on this idea, explaining that creativity cultivates fulfilling moments. He also advocates for creativity as a societal necessity.

> Creativity is a central source of meaning in our lives . . .
> Most of the things that are interesting, important, and human
> are the results of creativity . . .
> Creativity is so fascinating [because] when we are involved in it,
> we feel that we are living more fully than during the rest of life.
> —Mihaly Csikszentmihalyi[101]

Individuality helps us solve problems. We can get stuck in methods that lead to the same solutions; creativity breaks our patterns and uncovers new ideas. Viewing problems from fresh angles fosters learning and growth. We're productive when we're innovative, finding efficient and effective ways of doing things. Originality provides an outlet to express our emotions. Research has linked creativity to a reduced risk of anxiety, improved cognitive function, and increased happiness. Ultimately, individuality helps us find meaning and fulfillment.[102]

Embracing our individuality can be uncomfortable if we've been conditioned to conform. We must remember that we have unique strengths and perspectives, and withholding them deprives our teams and ourselves of all the benefits we can offer. Our differences are often our greatest assets.

* * * * *

Renowned architect, inventor, and futurist R. Buckminster Fuller exemplified individuality through unconventional thinking and innovative designs. He pioneered the geodesic dome, a revolutionary, lightweight structure that maximizes strength and space with minimal materials. He developed eco-friendly designs like the Dymaxion House that showcased a forward-thinking approach to sustainability and efficiency. His individuality extended to a personal philosophy of "comprehensive anticipatory design science," seeking to solve global problems through technology while respecting the planet's finite resources. Fuller brought originality to various fields, from mathematics to cartography. Insatiable curiosity and unorthodox perspective propelled him to push the boundaries of possibility, cementing his status as one of the twentieth century's most innovative and influential thinkers.[103]

> Never forget that you are one of a kind. Never forget that if there weren't any need for you in all your uniqueness to be on this earth, you wouldn't be here in the first place. And never forget, no matter how overwhelming life's challenges and problems seem to be, that one person can make a difference in the world. In fact, it is always because of one person that all the changes that matter in the world come about. So be that one person.
>
> —R. Buckminster Fuller

Perseverance

Overcoming slipups and bouncing back from disasters involves dedication and determination. It requires looking past adversity toward our goals and recognizing that perseverance can get us there.[104]

The Stoics, ancient Greek and Roman philosophers, emphasized the value of perseverance. They taught that enduring hardships through commitment to our principles is essential for a fulfilling life.[105] Obstacles should be embraced for learning and growth.

Perseverance means not giving up, no matter how hard things get or how often we fail. Winston Churchill powerfully preached about perseverance to inspire his countrymen through World War II, including one of his most famous statements early in the war:

> This is the lesson: never give in, never give in, never, never, never, never—in nothing, great or small, large or petty—never give in except to convictions of honour and good sense. Never yield to force; never yield to the apparently overwhelming might of the enemy.

Perseverance demands patience. In his highly successful book *Atomic Habits*, James Clear explains that meaningful change happens through small, consistent improvements over time.[106] The process may be slow, but persistence is essential. Small successes stimulate areas of the brain associated with rewards and motivation, boosting confidence and willingness to take on challenges.[107] Perseverance isn't one long climb; it's many short climbs, one after the other, each more challenging. The most successful people hang on after others have let go.

> Winners and losers have the same goals. . . .
> Every Olympian wants to win a gold medal. . . .
> The goal cannot be what differentiates the winners from the losers. . . .
> It was only when they implemented a system of continuous small improvements that they achieved a different outcome.
> —James Clear[108]

Fear of failure can be a major obstacle to perseverance. If our endeavor is conditional, we react to failure with disappointment, shame, and insecurity that overwhelm us and prevent us from trying again. It can paralyze us.

However, fear of failure doesn't have to be debilitating. It can be motivating. Superstar Michael Jordan said fear of failure drove him throughout his basketball career. It pushed him to work harder than anyone else. He practiced relentlessly to ensure he wouldn't fail.[109] Bestselling author J. K. Rowling explained that her fear of remaining a single mother on welfare compelled her to keep writing, despite multiple rejections, until she found success with the *Harry Potter* books.[110] Perseverance sees failure as a stepping stone instead of a stop sign.

Failure isn't the opposite of success; it's a prerequisite. Only by feeling failure can we achieve great things. Failure is essential to the pursuit of Unconditional Endeavor, as we must fail to persevere, and we must persevere to grow.[111] Walt Disney said, "You may not realize it when it happens, but a kick in the teeth may be the best thing in the world for you." If we can endure the short-term pain of failure and push past it, we can grasp the long-term benefits of perseverance: learning, improvement, and self-confidence.[112]

Our challenges are unique, but our conditional responses are the same: doubt, frustration, helplessness. To overcome obstacles, we must do what we think we can't. Perseverance can also mean summoning the courage to do what we fear. If we face our fears, we conquer them, but we don't necessarily eliminate them. Courage is mastery of fear, not absence of it.

* * * * *

Born into poverty, Abraham Lincoln's early years didn't offer many prospects. He rose above his origins only to experience great losses, rejections, and failures. Many of those closest to him—his mother, sister, close female friend, and son—died. He had two failed courtships and suffered a nervous breakdown; he could have given up on relationships. He failed twice running businesses and was turned down for several others; he could have given up on work. He lost or forfeited eight elections; he could have given up on politics. He could have quit many times. Yet, because of his perseverance, he became one of the greatest presidents in American history.[113]

* * * * *

My great concern is not whether you have failed,
but whether you are content with your failure.
—Abraham Lincoln

Practice

In his 2008 book *Outliers: The Story of Success*, Malcolm Gladwell advanced the idea that becoming an expert takes ten thousand hours of practice. But he didn't intend ten thousand hours to be a magic number for achieving mastery. He meant that becoming an expert takes years of dedication, including many hours of practice. He used Bill Gates as an example. Gates's Seattle high school was an early adopter of computers, allowing independent access. This enabled Gates to practice for thousands of hours, becoming more proficient than his peers.[114]

Deliberate practice, coined by psychologist Anders Ericsson in the early 1990s, refers to purposeful, systematic practice focused on improving performance.[115] As Gladwell explains, although the media and society frequently praise talent as the key to expertise, research suggests otherwise. Rather, the accumulation of deliberate practice differentiates great from good and world champions from professionals. Time spent in deliberate practice dominates other factors in determining success in most fields.[116]

*   *   *   *   *

Benjamin Franklin, a paragon of self-improvement, developed his own system to practice virtuous living. He identified thirteen core virtues, including temperance, silence, and humility, and focused on one each week, tracking his progress in a notebook. By cycling through them repeatedly, Franklin honed his character. His meticulous method and self-reflection transformed practice from a passive exercise into an active pursuit of virtue and showed that even personal principles can be mastered through deliberate practice.[117]

> Practice is the best of all instructors.
> —Publilius Syrus

*   *   *   *   *

By practicing an endeavor, we understand it better, and our nerves and muscles learn. We're all familiar with muscle memory, where physical activities like riding a bike quickly come back to us even after decades of dormancy. Likewise, practice stimulates the brain to produce myelin, which acts like structural support beams around neurons, strengthening them and making repeated actions easier.[118]

Although we improve when we practice, our performance plateaus if we repeatedly practice the same things the same ways. To continue improving, we must stretch our limits. Only by pushing ourselves can we reach our full potential.[119]

Practice isn't always invigorating. We'll be tired sometimes. It's okay to get frustrated. We must have self-compassion. The key is approaching practice with curiosity about what else we can learn. Every repetition is an investment in ourselves, growing the value we bring to our chosen endeavors through deliberate practice.

Growth

Growth is an ongoing process of self-discovery and self-improvement. It acknowledges there's always something to learn, no matter our age or accomplishments, and commits to strive constantly for a more fulfilling, impactful life.

Combining prior work and groundbreaking research, Carol Dweck published the 2006 bestseller *Mindset: The New Psychology of Success*. She says our mindset is our characteristic mental attitude, and she differentiates between a fixed mindset and a growth mindset. If we have a fixed mindset, we believe personal qualities are innate and unchangeable. We don't expect to improve our skills, so we give up when faced with barriers.[120]

With a growth mindset, we believe intelligence and abilities can be developed through learning and hard work. We're confident in reaching our goals. We're willing to step outside our comfort zone. We don't fear obstacles; we run toward them. We take on challenges to grow, and we grow to take on more significant challenges. The journey is as much about learning as reaching goals. A growth mindset changes "I can't" to "I can't yet" and eventually to "I can."

> The passion for stretching yourself and sticking to it,
> even (or especially) when it's not going well,
> is the hallmark of the growth mindset.
> —Carol Dweck[121]

Setbacks are always possible, regardless of experience, expertise, or authority. We may embrace every aspect of Unconditional Endeavor—from purpose to perseverance—but success isn't guaranteed.[122] The growth mindset keeps us from being discouraged by difficulties. We welcome the chance to analyze our mistakes and adjust our strategies to keep growing. We reflect, replan, reenergize, and move on.

> Those with the growth mindset found setbacks motivating.
> They're informative. They're a wake-up call.
> —Carol Dweck[123]

The key to growth is seeing defeat differently. If we don't call something a disappointment, it isn't one. The world may label missing a goal as a failure, but we can choose labels like *lesson*, *redirection*, and *inspiration* instead. With a growth mindset, adversity leads to achievement.

> If you aren't making any mistakes, it's a sure sign you're playing it too safe.
> —John C. Maxwell

*   *   *   *   *

Mahatma Gandhi's life exemplified the growth mindset. As a young lawyer, he was shy and lacked confidence. However, through his experiences in South Africa and India, he grew into a transformative leader. He learned from his failures and adapted his strategies. By embracing challenges as opportunities for learning, he continuously evolved his philosophy of nonviolence and his leadership. Gandhi's growth mindset not only fueled personal growth but enabled him to lead India's independence movement.[124]

*   *   *   *   *

When our endeavors are conditional, we do less than our best. We look for short-term results and quit when they don't happen. We let obstacles become failures and slide down the spectrum to inaction.

Unconditional Endeavor saves us from self-doubt, fear of failure, apathy, and withdrawal. It delivers us from conditionality and gives us the confidence to confront any endeavor. When we encounter obstacles, we learn and grow from them, becoming stronger and better versions of ourselves.

How to Live It

UNCONDITIONAL ENDEAVOR SEPARATES us from the Spectrum of Conditional Endeavor. It enables us to overcome obstacles, maintain fortitude through failures, and keep from questioning our capabilities or courage. This section provides practical advice for pursuing Unconditional Endeavor in key areas of life: personal, relational, as a parent, at work, and as a leader.

Endeavor is last on the list of Unconditionals because it animates the other four and depends on them. We must endeavor from a foundation of love, gratitude, integrity, and accountability. Like driving at high speed with a blind spot, pursuing endeavors without one of these values leaves us vulnerable. If we venture into areas where we lack confidence in The Unconditionals, we risk crashing into trouble, causing our endeavor (and possibly our life) to career out of control. However, if we strive for Unconditional Endeavor built on the other four values, we'll be on the road to self-actualization.

Personal

For personal endeavors, we spend the most time thinking about purpose for long-term, big-picture purposes—our big dreams. Sometimes, those big dreams can seem unachievable. We must break them into smaller, short-term goals, defining them clearly and in detail to make them actionable. Then we execute the endeavor process toward each goal with our big dream in mind.

We need a positive attitude for personal endeavors. If we're struggling to stay positive, we'll have trouble with one or more of the other endeavor elements, like finding the energy for effort or doing our best. We should find and fix the root cause so we can adjust our attitude and approach endeavors with positivity and motivation.

Preparation starts with understanding the task. Whether we invent the task or it's given to us, We must understand what success looks like. If we're working for someone else, we try to put ourselves in our customer's shoes. Understanding their purpose helps us align with their goals. If we're working on our own tasks, we define success. Once we understand the task, we need to acquire the resources for it. For personal endeavors, that means knowledge and skill.

* * * * *

In the last section, I discussed working for a local construction company in high school. My last summer before college, I got a job in the construction big leagues, with the company that built all the major roads for the state. They had *real* dump trucks and every large piece of equipment imaginable. Of course, I didn't get to operate any of them. I wasn't qualified, and as a short-timer, I wasn't worth training. I spent most of the summer as a traffic control flagger, wearing an orange vest and helmet. Such was my skill level that I wasn't assigned to the main thoroughfare—I was put on the side roads, where only a couple of cars an hour came by. Picture it: an ambitious, prospective rocket scientist, standing on a lonely side street, desperately waiting for a car to arrive so he can hold up his orange flag to stop it from driving onto the main road. It was great motivation for college.

My pre-career jobs taught me more than the value of physical labor. Humility is paramount. Respect for self and others must be unconditional and independent of vocation. There are no inferior jobs, only inferior effort. All work is hard at times; showing up and doing the job requires commitment. The best way to get a better job is to do well in our current one.

Do not despise the bottom rungs in the ascent to greatness.
—Publilius Syrus

* * * * *

There's no substitute for hard work. True achievement can't be attained by shortcuts. Hard work leads to meaningful results when driven by commitment to the process rather than obsession with the outcome. Our motivation must come from within—not from external validation but because hard work aligns with our core values. We can trust the results will follow when we consistently put in the effort.

To manage endeavors effectively, we prioritize tasks based on urgency (i.e., deadlines) and importance (i.e., long-term value). Then, we focus on those tasks by limiting distractions, setting boundaries, and striving for immersive concentration.

> Most of us spend too much time on what is urgent
> and not enough time on what is important.
> —Stephen R. Covey

Excellence requires relentless commitment. It's meticulous, always looking to improve. We can't let others define excellence for us; if we do our best, we don't need to judge ourselves because there are no regrets. Though we may not see the results, excellence always pays off. Every time we do a job, we make an impression; excellence gets noticed. We should enjoy the satisfaction that comes from doing little things well. If we do the little things well, the big ones get easier. Insignificant acts often lead to significant accomplishments. From arts to business and academics to sports, excellence requires that we do our best and strive to get better. Consistently performing with excellence is critical to reaching our goals. More importantly, it's vital to personal growth. Always doing our best enhances our well-being, relationships, and fulfillment.

Individuality is intrinsic in personal endeavors, so we must be creative, open-minded, and flexible. We should take advantage of opportunities to be different. Creativity unlocks vital parts of ourselves that might otherwise remain hidden. Individuality also helps us adapt to changing circumstances. As the saying goes, there's nothing more certain than change, so we must be able to evaluate situations and adjust our tactics or change our goals to fit the new reality.

* * * * *

I previously acknowledged that my adolescent dream of becoming an astronaut was incomplete, missing the critical characteristics of purpose. My purpose was compelling—dreaming of traveling among the stars surely qualifies. It was consistent, as I held on to the dream through high school and early college. But it wasn't clear. I hadn't taken the time to fully imagine myself as an astronaut, to immerse myself in that concept. I didn't fully appreciate what was required and assess the possible paths to achieve the goal. I wanted it, but not enough. I lacked sufficient passion for my purpose.

As a practicing aerospace engineer in 2016, I attended the Wernher von Braun Memorial Dinner at the US Space & Rocket Center in Huntsville, Alabama. An award recipient that night was Mike Massimino, a former NASA astronaut. (He had spoken at the banquet the previous year. Massimino is a delightful speaker with an infectiously upbeat personality and engaging stories from his career.) As a remembrance, the dinner's presenting sponsor generously provided all attendees with signed copies of Massimino's newly released book, *Spaceman: An Astronaut's Unlikely Journey to Unlock the Secrets of the Universe*. Soon afterward, I read the book. Interestingly, there were similarities between his life story and mine. He had dreamed of flying in space too. In fact, he had submitted applications to the astronaut office at NASA Johnson around the same time I was calling the astronaut doctor from Langley. Before being selected for the astronaut corps, he had applied and been rejected multiple times due to poor eyesight, the same affliction I had.[125]

That's where his story diverged from mine. While I had a vague dream of becoming an astronaut, Massimino's purpose was clear. He made a plan with a vivid goal and doggedly pursued it. He took a job in Houston where he worked closely with current astronauts, befriended them and those associated with the office, and spent time understanding the selection process. Most importantly—what differentiated his approach from mine—he investigated methods to improve his eyesight and trained his eyes to improve. Massimino had a clear, compelling, and consistent purpose, took on challenges, got out of his comfort zone, had courage, and accepted risks. He understood the power of purpose and used it to accomplish an amazing endeavor.[126]

> Vision is the art of seeing things invisible to others.
> —Jonathan Swift

* * * * *

A growth mindset is critical to personal endeavors. We will fail sometimes. We must use failures as chances to grow and learn. We should always be curious and seek opportunities to build knowledge. We acknowledge when we fall short but also celebrate our achievements. We regularly reflect on our progress, trying to turn successful approaches into habits and adjusting our strategies when necessary. Personal endeavors should lead to personal growth. The more we embrace this mindset, the more we'll grow, and the more fulfilled we'll become.

Thinking about how to infuse our tasks with purpose, positivity, and all the other elements can be overwhelming; we may not know where to start. Remember that Unconditional Endeavor is an ideal—no one does everything right. We must go easy on ourselves, appreciating what we do well and acknowledging there are always areas to improve. With healthy self-compassion, we can identify one area for improvement—like greater optimism or deeper practice—concentrate on that area, and celebrate incremental progress as it happens. Over time, we can cultivate a new skill and a habit of improvement that enriches our endeavors.

Relational

It would be callous to say human relationships are endeavors. Endeavors have purposes, and relationships shouldn't be reduced to objectives. Relationships are about forging connections and fostering understanding. While relationships can involve shared purposes when we're engaged in endeavors together, they don't require joint endeavors to exist and thrive. The vitality of relationships stems from the emotional bonds that connect us, even in superficial, transactional interactions.

That said, while relationships aren't endeavors per se, the two are deeply intertwined. Endeavors often require the coordinated efforts of multiple people. As with individual pursuits, team endeavors need all the elements of Unconditional Endeavor to succeed. Moreover, the quality and dynamics of the relationships among team members can significantly impact an endeavor's trajectory and outcome.

The most essential element for relational endeavors is communication. Communication helps us understand each other's perspectives and express our thoughts, needs, and boundaries with clarity and empathy. It ensures all participants are aligned. When communication is honest, it builds trust that sustains relationship stability and longevity. It equips us to resolve conflicts constructively and adapt to changes gracefully.

Collaboration, the second most critical aspect of relational endeavors, is about harnessing collective ideas, skills, and efforts to achieve an outcome that no individual could accomplish alone. By pooling resources and leveraging diverse strengths, our teams deliver results that surpass the sum of their parts. They also foster strong interpersonal bonds. Members of high-functioning teams encourage each other to bring our best in an environment of trust and mutual support.[127] Effective collaboration values each member's abilities. It creates a sense of belonging by helping us understand where we fit and how our skills contribute to the collective mission. We involve all members in decision-making and tackle challenges together.

Successful teams have optimistic cultures. Members possess the emotional intelligence to navigate interpersonal dynamics skillfully. We welcome open dialogue to confront conflicts quickly and constructively. We regularly review results to improve individual and team performance and prioritize continuous learning. We have a shared understanding that nobody reaches their goals unless everybody does.

*   *   *   *   *

As a child in Kenya, Jacqueline Nyetipei Kiplimo dreamed of becoming a world champion runner. Early on, she realized she had the talent and determination to compete at the highest level. Like all elite athletes, she had to train full-time, so she couldn't support her family with a regular job. Instead, she hoped to win races and bring home prize money.[128]

In 2010, she traveled to China for the Zhengkai marathon, eyeing the $10,000 first-place prize. She was well prepared and had posted some of the field's best times leading up to the race, so she knew she had a solid chance to win.[129]

Kiplimo started strong and led the women's division at the twenty-kilometer mark. As she slowed to grab a bottle at the water station, she noticed a male runner struggling. The man was running at a good pace, but due to a congenital disability that left him without hands, he had trouble drinking from the slippery plastic bottles. The race rules prevented officials or fans from assisting him, or he would be disqualified. She knew he needed help. Without water, he wouldn't be able to finish.[130]

She grabbed a bottle and helped the man drink. The two continued together, with Kiplimo adjusting to his slower tempo so she could occasionally help him sip. Many female runners caught and passed her, but she stayed with the man, side by side, for almost twenty kilometers, nearly half the race.[131]

With four kilometers left, she knew the man was sufficiently hydrated to finish, so she kicked into a higher gear. With long, swift strides, she weaved through groups of competitors, passing her opponents one by one. She crossed the finish line with incredible momentum, just behind her last competitor, finishing second.[132]

Kiplimo fell short of her original goal. However, during the race, her goals changed to meet the situation, and she more than met those goals: to run the best race she could and be the best person possible. She did win a smaller cash prize for second place. When asked about missing out on the larger purse, she said, "Money isn't everything." Neither is winning.[133]

You're not obligated to win.
You're obligated to keep trying to do the best you can every day.
—Marian Wright Edelman

* * * * *

Relational endeavors are fundamentally about sharing. No matter what each person brings or how much each contributes, all share the experience. The more deeply we connect, communicate, and understand each other, the more fulfilling each experience becomes. Every endeavor presents an opportunity to be open, authentic, and attentive, to strive to be the best teammate, partner, and friend we can be.

As a Parent

Some say the most important thing for parents to teach their kids is a strong work ethic. Others believe that teaching excellence or perseverance is paramount. Still others prioritize helping them appreciate their uniqueness. I believe all of these are equally essential, and parents' duties include trying to teach all elements of endeavor to their children.

We guide our children to set personal goals to teach the power of purpose, encouraging them to aim high and dream big while remaining realistic. We demonstrate how to break big goals into smaller steps. They must also see us set and strive for our own goals. Showing we can reach our goals inspires them and proves it's possible.

Optimism is hard to share in teachable moments when children feel sour. No matter how much sugar we try to pour on, they won't suddenly become sweet. We can model positivity, but that doesn't always work. The best starting point is gratitude; when we teach gratitude, a positive outlook usually follows.

> If you were allowed one wish for your child, seriously consider wishing him or her optimism. Optimists are normally cheerful and happy, and therefore popular; they are resilient in adapting to failures and hardships, their chances of clinical depression are reduced, their immune system is stronger, they take better care of their health, they feel healthier than others and are in fact likely to live longer.
>
> —Daniel Kahneman

Kids often aren't equipped to absorb lessons about preparation. We can help them learn to organize their tasks and manage their time accordingly.

If they can handle their homework, activities, chores, social life, and free time by the time they leave home, we've done our job well.

Everyone understands at a young age that effort is critical to getting things done. However, children naturally avoid work (a trait that's hard to shake in adulthood), so parents must convince them that effort's benefits outweigh their enjoyment of evading it. We must teach the value of effort itself, not just the results. Positive reinforcement should focus on the effort rather than the outcome. To support that message, we can share stories of people, including ourselves, who achieved success through hard work and dedication.

*　　*　　*　　*　　*

Theodore Roosevelt's evolution from a frail, asthmatic child to a vigorous, indomitable leader exemplifies the power of effort. Determined to overcome his physical limitations, young Teedie committed to a rigorous exercise regimen, strengthening his body and spirit. This same tireless tenacity characterized his public service. As president, he poured immense effort into tackling the nation's challenges, from conservation to corporate regulation. His legacy as one of America's most respected leaders was built not on chance or circumstance but a lifetime of strenuous, purposeful work. His story powerfully demonstrates that current conditions don't dictate our future if we're willing to put in the effort.[134]

*　　*　　*　　*　　*

Focus is the hardest element of endeavor for children to master. Their brains aren't built for it, and the world's distractions make it tougher. Typically, the best we can hope is that they learn to prioritize what's important and set healthy boundaries between tasks, friends, family, and time for themselves.

We want our children to always strive for excellence, but childhood is about personal growth, not family achievement, and excellence isn't about success but about doing our best. When we play games with our kids, we should focus on having fun, being together, and sharing lessons about following rules, fairness, and strategy. We involve them in competitive activities to learn about winning and losing but more critically about teamwork, sportsmanship, discipline, goal-setting, and handling pressure. We cheer for their teams to win and want them to perform well, but we should care more about their mental, physical, and emotional growth. Parents may sometimes push, because we all need help learning to do our best; but we only nudge with loving encouragement, never bullying. The goal is to help them learn to expect the best of themselves.

Teaching kids to count is fine, but teaching them what counts is best.
—Bob Talbert

* * * * *

The balance between encouragement and understanding is beautifully illustrated in the inspiring relationship between Anne Sullivan and Helen Keller. Sullivan refused to accept that Keller's disabilities limited her potential. She helped Keller achieve what many thought impossible through patient but demanding instruction. She demonstrated how maintaining high expectations while providing support enables children to exceed perceived limitations. Her methods proved that combining confidence in a child's potential with compassionate guidance can unlock extraordinary capabilities.[135]

* * * * *

Our children spend more time thinking about individuality than any other element of endeavor. Developing a healthy sense of self (and self-love) is crucial, and parents must do all they can to support this process. First, we celebrate their uniqueness by accepting and affirming their abilities and interests in endeavors and in general. We encourage them to try new things to learn what they like. We want them, not us, to decide. This doesn't mean we let them do only things they enjoy, but we nurture their interests. Next, we help them understand their personality by letting them express it. When they're young, we allow trivial choices, like whether they want fries or fruit with their burger. When they understand what individuality means, we let them choose more important things, like extracurricular activities. Supported by Unconditional Accountability, they gradually grow to appreciate who they are by making their own decisions. We may not agree with all aspects of it, but other than keeping them from harm and guiding them toward values essential to their well-being, we should support their individuality.

Many kids go through a phase of not wanting to be different, and we need to gently but consistently share the value of originality to help them establish a strong self-image. One way is to discuss the unique and valuable qualities of others. Another is to share our own originality. Being authentic and highlighting our quirks can amuse our kids and help them understand that weirdness is normal. The more we demonstrate comfort with ourselves, the greater chance our children have of becoming comfortable with themselves.

> You are the only person who is exactly like you,
> so in a way you've already won in this world.
> Because you're the only one who can be you.
> —Fred Rogers, "Mister Rogers"

*　*　*　*　*

Young Winston Churchill struggled in traditional academics. Raised in an aristocratic family, he was expected to study the classics and attend a prominent university. But he fared poorly at Harrow School. Instead of university, he decided on another route, but he twice failed the entrance examination for the Royal Military College at Sandhurst. However, when finally admitted, he discovered the curriculum aligned with his interests in military history and strategy, and he flourished, graduating near the top of his class and developing skills that later carried Britain through its darkest hours of World War II. His experience demonstrates that a child's unique strengths may emerge in unexpected places when given the right opportunities.[136,137]

*　*　*　*　*

Even if our kids learn to work hard, if they repeatedly run into barriers, they might feel defeated and give up. We must teach them to overcome obstacles. We can tell them about the positive aspects of adversity—the strength it builds and the lessons learned. We can share stories of successful people who broke down barriers. But ultimately, they must learn it for themselves, and we must provide emotional support. We let them know it's okay to struggle—we describe times we've struggled—and that we're always there to help and encourage them.

Few traits are as valuable as a growth mindset. To instill it in our kids, we emphasize that abilities aren't all innate but can be learned and developed through effort and practice. We reinforce that mistakes are natural and expected. We share the joy that comes from gaining knowledge through failure. When appropriate, we provide nurturing, constructive feedback with specific strategies to help them understand how to improve. We remind them that by following the proper process of endeavor, they may or may not reach every goal, but they'll learn, improve, and grow, and those are the accomplishments we should celebrate most.

Open dialogue and sharing feelings and dreams are critical in a parent-child relationship, especially when the parent or child is engaged in endeavors. Parents sometimes mistake one-way wisdom for communication, thinking well-meaning monologues can replace dialogue. However, listening is imperative for effective parenting. We must show genuine interest and fully attend to our children's thoughts, concerns, and experiences to help them endeavor unconditionally.

A child seldom needs a good talking to as much as a good listening to.
—Robert Brault

On the other hand, children learn more by observing than listening. Our actions teach more than our words. (That's good news for some of us—for others, not so much.) Luckily, they can also learn to overcome bad examples. Nonetheless, we should strive to set them on the right path, and guiding them through endeavors can powerfully impact their learning.

The weight of all these parenting guidelines can feel suffocating. The therapeutic truth is that no one gets them all right, and no one needs to. Our children don't need perfection—they need authenticity. We must be honest about our struggles and try to demonstrate resilience in the face of challenges. Our willingness to be vulnerable and learn from mistakes will teach them far more than a facade of constant success. Our goal should be, by our example, to instill in them the belief that by striving for Unconditional Endeavor, they can reach their highest potential.

*   *   *   *   *

Thomas Edison demonstrates the growth mindset we should cultivate in our children. The best-known example is his invention of the light bulb. After many attempts at finding a solution, he said, "I have not failed. I've just found 10,000 ways that won't work."[138] He loved learning from experimentation and believed every outcome offered valuable lessons. He saw each setback not as a problem but as progress toward success. This perspective provides an inspiring model for helping children develop the resilience and curiosity that drive lifelong growth.

> If parents want to give their children a gift, the best thing they can do is to teach their children to love challenges, be intrigued by mistakes, enjoy effort, seek new strategies, and keep on learning. That way, their children don't have to be slaves of praise. They will have a lifelong way to build and repair their own confidence.
>
> —Carol Dweck

At Work

We're usually task-oriented at work, acting as if our professional success depends solely on getting things done. However, our success rarely depends only on our actions. It's largely based on our ability to collaborate. It comes down to teamwork.

A professional organization is a community. Nearly every person's job is interconnected with and dependent on others. We rely on our coworkers to achieve team goals. We're still interdependent in single-person organizations and when we interact across companies. We form a team because we depend on others, and they rely on us. To some extent, the success of one member is tied to the performance of the entire team. A bunch of disconnected individuals doing their own thing doesn't make a team and won't usually do as much or as well as a high-performance team.[139] If we can't work with others, we'll likely fail.

* * * * *

The 1970 Apollo 13 mission was the ultimate testament to collaborative problem-solving, where teamwork became a matter of life and death. When an oxygen tank exploded 200,000 miles from Earth, turning a moon landing into a fight for survival, astronauts, ground control, and spacecraft engineers displayed extraordinary collaboration under extreme pressure. Working with limited resources, they solved seemingly impossible challenges—even ingeniously adapting a square filter to fit a round hole using only onboard materials. They worked seamlessly together, transforming a potential disaster into a remarkable rescue. By bringing the astronauts home safely, they proved collaboration can overcome almost impossible obstacles and save lives.[140]

* * * * *

Work endeavors are both active and interactive, so clear communication across all levels of an organization is crucial. Tasks are distributed based on individual strengths and expertise. Team members work to build and maintain trust that all colleagues will complete their assigned tasks. By communicating efficiently about project objectives, timelines, and tasks, we coordinate efforts, share ideas, and provide critical feedback. Good communication prevents catastrophes and builds camaraderie, driving team success.

Workplace collaboration is so critical that some companies specifically watch out for individuals who seem overly competitive during the hiring process. Such prospective employees speak in *me* rather than *we* terms and emphasize their interests and achievements over others'. When these companies encounter applicants who seem likely to prioritize their goals over a shared purpose, they typically look elsewhere.

I've noted several times that purpose must be clear, compelling, and consistent. For teams, it must also be collective and collaborative. The critical first step is clarity; clarity of purpose is unifying, while confusion is crippling. Then, all team members must prioritize the shared purpose over individual agendas. That shared purpose fuels each member's productivity. Ideally, when the shared purpose is accomplished, all team members experience meaningful personal growth, and many achieve individual goals.

> Alone we can do so little; together we can do so much.
> —Helen Keller

Optimism is important at home, but it's even more powerful at work. One negative colleague drains energy from the workplace, making work feel like an uphill battle. Conversely, a positive outlook quickly spreads, boosting motivation. Optimism enhances performance and improves employee retention rates by stimulating sociability, hope, and feelings of being valued.

A common saying in the rocket launching world is, "To get to orbit, there are a million things that have to go right, and nothing can go wrong." Work endeavors are generally complex, so they require much more planning. One thing employees fresh out of college quickly learn in their first real-world jobs is that professional endeavors plan much farther in advance than personal ones. In the aerospace industry, for example, planning for endeavors that won't occur until halfway through a new employee's career isn't uncommon, and we sometimes plan for events we know will happen after our retirement. Planning is critical to reducing risk, and organizations invest enormous energy into minimizing risks for workplace endeavors.

> A man who does not think and plan long ahead
> will find trouble right at his door.
> —Confucius

* * * * *

When Henry Ford envisioned making automobiles affordable for average Americans, he knew he needed a revolutionary production method that required meticulous preparation. Throughout 1912–1913, his team studied every aspect of automobile assembly. They observed workers, timed their movements, and analyzed parts flow. The planning was exhaustive: they built a crude prototype assembly line with string and pieces of wood, tested it with toy cars, and then ran small-scale experiments moving actual car parts. Only after months of testing did they implement the first assembly line for the Model T's magneto. The process required intense coordination between factory retrofitting, worker training, and part supply teams. Their small experiment grew into a revolution that transformed the entire industrial world.[141]

✻ ✻ ✻ ✻ ✻

We must be able to bring our individuality to work. If we can't, we should find another job; it's that important. All team members should be encouraged to bring their own experiences, ambitions, and specialties to the job for the betterment of the organization. Companies should allow employees to be themselves—within the bounds of company policies and industry norms.

Workplace individuality has many benefits. First, accepting colleagues as their authentic selves makes them feel valued as part of the team. Next, diversity in skills and backgrounds greatly enhances creative problem-solving, brings a richer range of ideas, and leads to more original solutions. The fact that a team has a shared purpose shouldn't suppress different opinions or new perspectives. Sometimes, especially in large organizations with many strict processes to follow, it's healthy to challenge the status quo. Innovation also helps us adapt to new market conditions. Thinking outside the box is most effective when we hear all viewpoints.

A diverse mix of voices leads to
better discussions, decisions, and outcomes for everyone.
—Sundar Pichai

✻ ✻ ✻ ✻ ✻

Thomas Edison redesigned how innovation happens when he established his research laboratory in Menlo Park, New Jersey. Previously, inventors typically worked alone or in small partnerships. He created the world's first industrial research and development (R&D) facility, bringing together skilled craftsmen, physicists, and mathematicians. His team included Charles Batchelor, a mechanic from Britain who became his chief assistant; John Kruesi, a Swiss-born machinist who built many of his early designs; and Ludwig Boehm, a German glassblower whose expertise was crucial for light bulb development. His collaborative approach led to over 400 patents from the Menlo Park lab alone. Modern corporate R&D labs trace their origins to Edison's model of combining diverse technical skills under one roof.[142]

* * * * *

We should strive for a growth mindset on the job. In doing so, we seek professional development and training. We challenge ourselves by taking on new and complex assignments. We celebrate collective milestones, emphasizing teamwork and effort more than achievements.

Following these methods, we can cultivate a culture of Unconditional Endeavor at work. We can't expect ourselves to do everything right, but by bringing our full effort, expertise, and individuality to every project, we can model being our best. Taking that approach, along with embodying the team's shared values and purpose, will amplify our professional growth and personal fulfillment and inspire others to be their best.

As a Leader

Leymah Gbowee was born in central Liberia. At seventeen, she lived in Monrovia with her family when civil war erupted, throwing the country into chaos. She learned about a program to train social workers to counsel those traumatized by war. After three months of training, she became aware of the abuse she suffered from the father of her two young children. Seeking peace, Gbowee and her family lived as refugees in Ghana, nearly starving. They returned to war-torn Liberia, where her parents and relatives still resided. In 1998, to gain admission to a degree program in social work, Gbowee volunteered with the Trauma Healing and Reconciliation Program (THRP), launching her journey into peace activism. She studied while continuing to work rehabilitating ex-child soldiers. Surrounded by war, she realized that "if any changes were to be made in society, it had to be by the mothers."[143]

Don't wait for a Gandhi, don't wait for a King, don't wait for a Mandela.
You are your own Mandela, you are your own Gandhi, you are your own King.
—Leymah Gbowee

At THRP, she met the executive director of the West Africa Network for Peacebuilding (WANEP), Africa's first regional peace organization. In late 1999, WANEP began involving women, and Gbowee met Thelma Ekiyor, a well-educated Nigerian lawyer, at a conference in Ghana. Within a year, Ekiyor and Gbowee secured funding and organized the first meeting of the Women in Peacebuilding Network (WIPNET) in Accra, Ghana. There, Gbowee shared her painful life story for the first time, including sleeping on a hospital floor with her newborn for a week because she had no money to pay the bill and nobody to help her. Ekiyor and Gbowee soon launched WIPNET in Liberia, with Gbowee as coordinator.[144]

In 2002, while working in trauma healing and leading WIPNET without pay, Gbowee dreamed that God told her, "Gather the women and pray for peace!" She recruited women from across religious and ethnic lines, and they began going to mosques, markets, and churches, distributing flyers proclaiming, We are tired of our children being killed! We are tired of being abused! Women, wake up—you have a voice in the peace process! They handed out simple drawings explaining their purpose to the illiterate. Gbowee led the women to gather in the Liberian capital of Monrovia for months, praying for peace using Muslim and Christian prayers and holding nonviolent demonstrations and sit-ins in defiance of President Taylor's orders.[145]

In 2003, the women took over a soccer field along a route they knew President Taylor traveled twice daily. They wore white hair ties and T-shirts with the peace symbol and WIPNET logo. Taylor finally granted them a hearing. More than two thousand women gathered outside his mansion. With Gbowee as spokeswoman, the women secured his promise to attend peace talks in Ghana. Gbowee led a delegation of women to Ghana to pressure the factions. Initially, they sat outside the hotels where talks were held. As negotiations dragged on without progress amid continued Liberian violence, Gbowee led hundreds of them inside the hotel. They sat blocking the meeting room doors, arms interlocked, vowing to stay until an agreement was reached. They held signs saying, Butchers and murderers of the Liberian people—STOP! When the men tried to leave, the women threatened to rip off their clothes (In Africa, seeing married or older women naked is thought to bring curses on men). The women remained outside the negotiating room over the following days, their presence helping calm the atmosphere. After several more weeks, the war ended with the signing of the Accra Comprehensive Peace Agreement.[146]

Besides helping end fourteen years of war, Gbowee's movement contributed to the election of Ellen Johnson Sirleaf as Liberia's president, Africa's first elected female head of state. Gbowee and Sirleaf won the 2011 Nobel Peace Prize "for their non-violent struggle for the safety of women and women's rights to full participation in peace-building work."[147]

> The size of your dreams
> must always exceed your current capacity to achieve them.
> If your dreams do not scare you, they are not big enough.
> —Ellen Johnson Sirleaf

Gbowee embodied The Unconditionals in promoting peace, reconciliation, and women's rights during Liberia's civil war. Her efforts helped end violence and enable a more inclusive and just postconflict society.[148]

*　　*　　*　　*　　*

The following paragraphs describe the qualities, abilities, and values of great leaders of team endeavors. As in the other "As a Leader" sections, I express them in the first person—*we* are leaders who guide our teams, and these are the principles we need to lead well. We must keep in mind that no leader can demonstrate all the principles at once; these are simply suggestions to consider as good practices. As leaders, one of our lifelong endeavors should be incorporating as many of them as possible into our leadership toolbox.

Leaders communicate the organization's values and mission and effectively translate them into the team's objectives. We speak clearly to foster an open environment and candidly without being blunt.[149,150] It's vital that we listen to our colleagues' opinions, needs, and concerns and provide feedback and advice when welcomed. Their trust in our leadership is built through authenticity and transparency.

*   *   *   *   *

Leymah Gbowee's strength as a leader started with communication, which came from her ability to reach across divides. She created powerful messages that resonated with audiences—from sharing simple sketches with illiterate women to showing stark signs and staging sit-ins for peace negotiators. She built consensus through accessible information that transcended social and educational barriers. Her approach earned others' trust and catalyzed positive change.[151]

*   *   *   *   *

Collaborative leaders make people around them better by prioritizing their success. To do so, we hire high-quality team members, invest in their development, and provide them with all possible resources, tools, skills, and guidance.[152] We understand the strengths and weaknesses of our team members and assign tasks wisely. By empowering them with autonomy, we unleash previously unseen capabilities, encourage initiative and creativity, and cultivate growth. We can be a resource for coaching without micromanaging. Leaders with humility think of themselves less and colleagues more, advocating for what team members need. Strong leaders also manage conflicts, crises, and challenges with composure and address issues promptly, constructively, and fairly, using appropriate dialogue to reach resolutions.

> The leaders who work most effectively, it seems to me, never say "I." And that's not because they have trained themselves not to say "I." They don't think "I." They think "we;" they think "team." They understand their job to be to make the team function.
>
> —Peter Drucker

Visionary leaders always think ahead about where the team is going and should go, keeping the bigger picture in mind while making data-driven decisions. We ensure the purpose aligns with team strategy and connects to individual tasks. No matter the endeavor's complexity, we use shared purpose to set goals everyone can confidently work toward.[153] Our vision convinces colleagues to join the team because they want to contribute to something bigger than themselves. Leaders build rapport to understand team members' motivators to develop impactful incentives. Purposeful inspiration makes endeavors feel less like work and more like missions.

* * * * *

Gbowee exemplified the qualities of a visionary leader, rallying diverse religious and ethnic groups around a compelling collective purpose. After receiving divine inspiration to "gather the women and pray for peace," she united Christian and Muslim women in a nonviolent movement. Her clear purpose—ending Liberia's civil war—related so broadly that thousands of women joined, proving that a shared mission can overcome deep-seated societal divisions. She demonstrated the power of leadership to motivate, unify, and drive transformative change.[154]

* * * * *

Optimistic leaders set the tone for the team and influence how outsiders perceive it. We maintain a positive attitude during hardships, which motivates members to do the same and keeps the team focused on solutions. We aim for realistic optimism, staying grounded while working toward the team's highest potential.

Effective preparation means balancing short-term goals with long-term strategies. It requires watching trends and listening to customers to anticipate changes and risks. Leaders must understand project planning, prioritize tasks, and efficiently allocate resources. We evaluate options and optimize the use of tools and technology to excel at change and risk management.

Strong leaders highly value effort. We work hard and enjoy getting our hands dirty, but we also know how to use our time effectively and efficiently. As leaders, we must have a bias toward action—we talk about what needs to happen, then do it.[155]

Decisive leaders dare to take calculated risks with imperfect information. We gather data, consider suggestions from the team, and make decisions confidently. We're flexible with compromises in win-win scenarios while staying steadfast in our values.[156]

Open-minded leaders welcome individuality, listening to new ideas and implementing novel approaches to improve performance. We encourage our team to constantly innovate.

> Would you like me to give you a formula for success? It's quite simple. Double your rate of failure. You are thinking of failure as the enemy of success. But it isn't at all. You can be discouraged by failure or you can learn from it, so go ahead and make mistakes. Make all you can. . . . That's where you will find success.
>
> —Thomas J. Watson Jr.

Persevering leaders know and show that barriers are normal and manageable. When we encounter obstacles, we assess ourselves and the team, make adjustments, and push the team to bring its best to overcome challenges. We provide stability during changes and challenges so the team can thrive. Leadership is seeing opportunity in every difficulty rather than difficulty in every opportunity.

* * * * *

Gbowee exemplified the power of perseverance over seemingly impossible odds. She organized peaceful protests in the face of opposition from warlords and government officials. Even when President Taylor ordered them to stop, She led the women to continue demonstrating. Her conviction culminated in the women's occupation of the peace talks venue, where their interlocked arms became a powerful symbol of collective resolve. Her determination, despite threats and setbacks, illustrates how perseverance enables leaders to rally their teams to overcome obstacles and achieve ambitious goals.[157]

* * * * *

As growth-minded leaders, we never see ourselves or our team as a finished product. We'll always keep learning from difficulties and defeats; we build a team culture of continuous learning. A growth mindset keeps us seeking new experiences. We know we don't have all the answers, but we know how to find them. We must be coachable, open to criticism from anyone, and humble enough to listen and accept it graciously.[158]

As leaders, we must be present. Present leaders are self-aware and conscious of the messages their actions, words, and nonverbal communications send. We're attentive to and value our team members' ideas and actions. We must quickly and appropriately react to issues with tact, diplomacy, and poise.[159]

Our most significant responsibility as a leader is to foster an environment in which pursuit of Unconditional Endeavor is the norm. We can do that by modeling the mindset and behaviors we wish to see in our teams. We must accept that we'll fail often, but we acknowledge those mistakes and continue striving for the ideal every day.

* * * * *

Gbowee's path illustrates the power of embracing a growth mindset as a leader. Beginning as a trauma counselor working with ex-child soldiers, she grew to coordinate WIPNET, then led a nationwide peace movement. After helping end Liberia's civil war, she broadened her focus to international advocacy for democracy, human rights, and social justice. Each success became a stepping stone to greater impact. By taking on new challenges and expanding her sphere of influence, Gbowee exemplified how a commitment to growth enables leaders to evolve their purpose and make increasingly meaningful contributions over time.[160]

> Leadership is standing with your people.
> People say you have to live to fight another day,
> but sometimes you have to show you are a true leader.
> —Leymah Gbowee

Gbowee demonstrated all elements of endeavor. (Recall the acrostic: **P**aper **A**irplanes **P**ushed **E**astward **F**ly **E**legantly **I**nto **P**eaceful **P**lum **G**roves.) Peace was her driving purpose. Despite difficulties, she stayed optimistic about the grassroots power to effect change. Her experiences as a homeless mother, social worker, and trauma counselor helped her understand war's psychological and emotional toll and prepared her to organize and mobilize women. She invested immense effort in nonviolent protests and peace initiatives.[161] The movement's impact on ending the war and electing Liberia's first female president exemplified excellence. She used individuality in developing ways to connect and enlist diverse women across a war-torn society. Confronting personal risks from warlords and officials, she persevered. Her impact grew with effort and practice, from social work to organizing protests, and directly influencing peace talks. Exhibiting ongoing personal and professional growth, she expanded her work to advocate for international women's rights, human rights, and social justice.[162]

Chapter Summary

Unconditional Endeavor is the synergy of The Unconditionals, bringing love, gratitude, integrity, and accountability to life through purposeful action. By understanding its elements, we can approach every endeavor with a clear purpose, an optimistic attitude, diligent preparation, wholehearted effort, unwavering focus, excellence, individuality, and perseverance to push to completion. We can use deliberate practice to enhance our skills and improve in future endeavors. Most importantly, we can cultivate a growth mindset that empowers us to cherish challenges and maintain fortitude through failures.

Too often, we let conditionality hold us back. We make excuses like "I'm not ready" or "It's too hard" and slip down the Spectrum of Conditional Endeavor toward inaction. Our endeavors are aimless, hopeless, ill-equipped, lethargic, distracted, inept, bland, defeated, and stagnant. We can break free from those limitations by aiming for Unconditional Endeavor. It requires changing our way of thinking and living. We stop confronting endeavors conditionally and instead tackle them based on our principles. Our goal isn't just achieving success; it's finding fulfillment in the endeavor. Devoting ourselves to Unconditional Endeavor keeps us on the path to realizing our potential.

When we seek Unconditional Endeavor, it becomes a defining characteristic. Others view us differently, and we see ourselves changed, better than before. It gives a new vantage point from which we can see our best future. With Unconditional Love, Unconditional Gratitude, Unconditional Integrity, and Unconditional Accountability, it offers the promise of prosperity—not in finances or fame but in personal transformation. Unconditional Endeavor is a superpower that can be ours if we're willing to work for it.

Encouragement and Questions for the Reader

It's easy to feel discouraged by the challenge of Unconditional Endeavor. Substantial improvement that you can see in yourself can seem unachievable. Recognize that personal growth is a lifelong endeavor unto itself. There will be times when your purpose is unclear, your effort is lackluster, or your attitude stinks. Grant yourself grace. Accept that perfection isn't possible—for anyone—and move on. Failures are opportunities. Unconditional is an objective that helps you improve as you pursue it. Every decision to show up, work, persist, and learn builds you up. Every step beyond your comfort zone makes you stronger. Striving for Unconditional Endeavor is the most important action you can take.

The following are questions to ask yourself. As you seek to cultivate meaningful endeavors, use them to help you choose one area where you can strive for unconditionality.

- Do you pursue endeavors that align with your values and life purpose? How can you connect your daily actions, big and small, to your core principles and mission?
- Do you control your attitude or let circumstances control it? What can you do daily to remind yourself that attitude is a choice?
- Do you prepare effectively for important endeavors in your personal or professional life? What steps can you take to prepare logistically and mentally?
- Do you consistently give vigorous effort to all endeavors? Where are you holding back? How can you apply yourself completely?
- Do you focus on endeavors with intentionality, resisting distractions? How can you improve your ability to enter a state of flow?
- Do you strive for excellence by always doing your best? How can you consistently go beyond good enough to deliver your best?
- Do you bring your unique gifts to endeavors, approaching them with creativity? How can you lean into your individuality?
- When facing obstacles, do you get discouraged or quit? How can you reframe obstacles as opportunities to learn and grow?
- What valuable skill could you improve upon if you committed to regular, deliberate practice? What's stopping you?
- Are you stretching beyond your comfort zone and taking on challenges that force growth? How can you embrace a growth mindset in all areas of life?
- What's one daily practice you can start today in pursuit of Unconditional Endeavor as a lifelong commitment and source of fulfillment?

Every day you may make progress. Every step may be fruitful. Yet there will stretch out before you an ever-lengthening, ever-ascending, ever-improving path. You know you will never get to the end of the journey. But this, so far from discouraging, only adds to the joy and glory of the climb.

—Winston Churchill

EPILOGUE

> Success is . . .
> knowing you made the effort to become the best you are capable of becoming.
> —John Wooden

IN THE INTRODUCTION, I used the metaphor of a house to explain the organization of the book. I described the land the house rests on, its foundation, structure, walls, and roof to respectively represent the book's fundamental premises, its central principles, what the principles are and why they matter, where we go wrong, answers from timeless wisdom, and how to live the principles. The graphic below is a visualization of this metaphorical home.

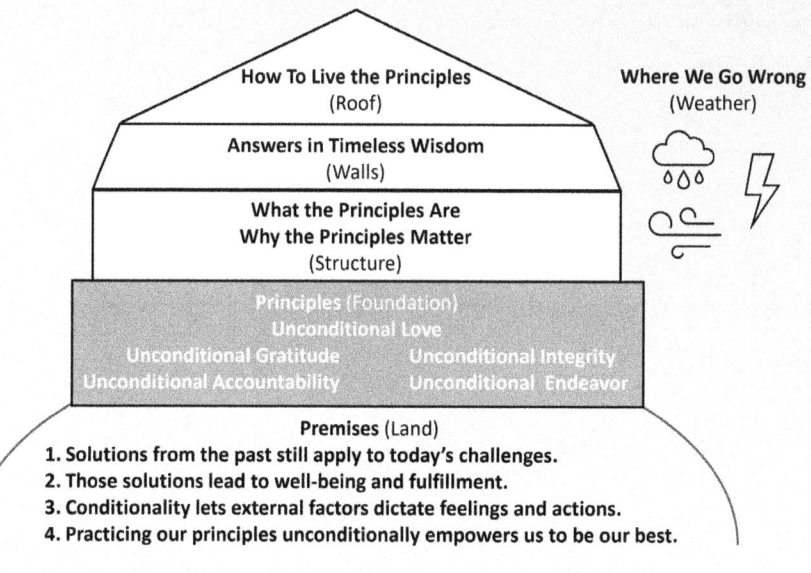

The organization of the book as a metaphorical house

Built atop the four premises, the book focuses on five principles. Why these five? They shape our convictions, character, connections, and conduct.

- Love is the heart of all good values.
- Gratitude fortifies our inner thoughts.
- Integrity is our identity.
- Accountability creates supportive connections.
- Endeavor turns action into personal growth.

Each value is essential, but they're most powerful when practiced together and centered on love. They operate in harmony, supporting and reinforcing each other, creating something much greater than the sum of their parts.

These five values may be justified, but why not others? I believe the five Unconditionals are the foundational elements of being human. They separate successful, fulfilled people from the unsuccessful and unfulfilled. When we learn, model, and share them, we nourish relationships, understand what's needed to make the best of situations, convert intentions into actions, and harness resources to reach our goals. They help us positively influence the people and world around us. We can build on The Unconditionals to incorporate other principles.

Beyond gratitude, practices that promote mental strength are:

- Cultivate self-awareness.
- Focus on what we can control.
- Maintain balance throughout your life.

Beyond integrity, ideas that impact how we look at the world are:

- Appreciate change.
- Accept that life is short, but plan for the long run.
- Don't care what others think.

Beyond accountability, ways to create connections are:

- Family.
- Friendship.
- Realize every person is equal and every person is different.
- Cherish community.
- Serve others.

Beyond endeavor, approaches to accomplish actions that matter are:

- Nurture a love of learning.
- Leave a legacy.

Although pursuing The Unconditionals brings accomplishment, contentment, and fulfillment, I recognize that's not enough. Most of us also seek meaning that surpasses ourselves and transcends this world. We may find it in a relationship with or sense of oneness with God. I don't rank The Unconditionals above that kind of meaning, but while we're alive on Earth, they're vital to becoming our best.

Throughout the book, I've described five spectra that represent our conditional responses to situations and people, trapping us in negative patterns of thought and behavior:

- Spectrum of Conditional Love: We feel and act based on who others are or how they treat us.
- Spectrum of Conditional Gratitude: We feel and act based on what we have.
- Spectrum of Conditional Integrity: We behave based on how we evaluate costs and benefits in our circumstances.
- Spectrum of Conditional Accountability: We act based on whether we perceive the outcomes as favorable.
- Spectrum of Conditional Endeavor: We wait to see if circumstances are favorable before deciding whether to act and how much effort to give.

These spectra explain how we allow external factors to dictate our feelings and actions.

Conditionality is like a drug. It creates dependencies. We think it gives us an easy way out, relieves us of hard decisions, and allows us to behave however we please. We believe it provides freedom, but reliance on external things imprisons us; it traps us in conditionality.

When we let externalities determine our responses, we relinquish control of our ideas and impacts, but even more dangerous, we surrender to irrationality. Our unthinking nature is powerless to stop our slide down the spectra, and we end up entangled in hate, ingratitude, disintegrity, unaccountability, and inaction.

However, by recognizing our conditional tendencies, we can break free from them. Unconditionality helps us reclaim our power, stay true to our principles, and experience freedom.

Unconditional isn't about who anyone or anything else is; it's about who we are. It liberates us from the struggle of evaluating others' actions, comparative thinking, or basing our behavior on circumstances. It frees us to treat everyone equally in all situations, making our lives simpler and more consistent. Unconditional offers personal transformation. Others will see us—and we'll see ourselves—as better than ever. When we strive to be Unconditional, we become electrified, illuminating everything around us. The Unconditionals enable us to

Live without Limits and Ignite Our Superpower.

*　*　*　*　*

Conditional rejects some because they're them.
Unconditional welcomes all because they're us.

Conditional makes our world smaller.
Unconditional makes our world larger.

Conditional is about except.

                Unconditional is about accept.

Conditional fears others.

                Unconditional frees us.

Conditional is selfish.

                Unconditional is selfless.

Conditional is want.

                Unconditional is wealth.

Conditional sees holes.

                Unconditional sees a whole.

Conditional is about when and until.

                Unconditional is about now and forever.

Conditional is about difference.

                Unconditional is always the same.

Conditional flees failures.

                Unconditional welcomes failures.

Conditional is exhausting.

                Unconditional is exhilarating.

Conditional seeks control.

                Unconditional lives liberated.

Conditionality is never enough.

                Unconditional is enough.

ACKNOWLEDGMENTS

FIRST, THANK YOU to my patient, thorough, and compassionate early reviewers: my wife, my dad, my sister, Tristan Macke, Keith Heitzman, and John Lemons.

Next, thank you to the Bublish team for helping carry the ball across the goal line.

Finally, thank you to my family for their unwavering support and encouragement. Thank you to my children for their understanding, even when they didn't understand. Most of all, thank you to my wife, Beth, for endless tolerance, graciousness, and perspective, and for being the best example of—and the main object of my—Unconditional Love.

All Quotes

Sorted Alphabetically by Attributed Author

Achor, Shawn   **1978–**

American author and speaker; author of *The Happiness Advantage*; founder of GoodThink, Inc.

"Countless studies have shown that consistently grateful people are more energetic, emotionally intelligent, forgiving, and less likely to be depressed, anxious, or lonely."

"I often ask managers to write an e-mail of praise or thanks to a friend, family member, or colleague each morning before they start their day's work—not just because it contributes to their own happiness, but because it very literally cements a relationship."

Anouilh, Jean   **1910–1987**

Born Jean Marie Lucien Pierre Anouilh; French dramatist and screenwriter.

"Our entire life. . . consists ultimately in accepting ourselves as we are."

Aquinas, Saint Thomas   **1225–1274**

Italian-Dominican friar, philosopher, and theologian.

"Justice is a certain rectitude of mind whereby a man does what he ought to do in the circumstances confronting him."

Ariely, Dan   1967–

Israeli-American professor and author; James B. Duke professor of psychology and behavioral economics at Duke University; cofounder of several companies implementing insights from behavioral science.

"Our behavior is driven by two opposing motivations. On one hand, we want to view ourselves as honest, honorable people. We want to be able to look at ourselves in the mirror and feel good about ourselves. . . . On the other hand, we want to benefit from cheating and get as much money as possible. . . . Clearly these two motivations are in conflict. . . . This is where our amazing cognitive flexibility comes into play. Thanks to this human skill, as long as we cheat by only a little bit, we can benefit from cheating and still view ourselves as marvelous human beings. This balancing act is the process of rationalization."

"The question is: where is the line?"

"We have an incredible ability to distance ourselves in all kinds of ways from the knowledge that we are breaking the rules, especially when our actions are a few steps removed from causing direct harm to someone else."

Aristotle   384–322 BC

Greek philosopher and polymath; writings cover natural sciences, philosophy, linguistics, economics, politics, psychology, and the arts; founded the Aristotelian philosophical tradition, which set the groundwork for the development of modern science.

"All virtue is summed up in dealing justly."

"Excellence is an art won by training and habituation. We do not act rightly because we have virtue or excellence, but we rather have those because we have acted rightly. We are what we repeatedly do. Excellence, then, is not an act but a habit."

"Love is the cause of unity in all things."

"Moral excellence comes about as a result of habit. We become just by doing just acts, temperate by doing temperate acts, brave by doing brave acts."

"What it lies in our power to do, it lies in our power not to do."

Arouet, François-Marie, "Voltaire"   1694–1778

Better known by pen name; French Enlightenment writer, philosopher, satirist, and historian.

"Appreciation is a wonderful thing: It makes what is excellent in others belong to us as well."

Augustine, Saint   354–430

Also known as Augustine of Hippo; theologian and philosopher; writings influenced development of Western philosophy and Western Christianity; works include *The City of God*, *On Christian Doctrine*, and *Confessions*.

"What does love look like? It has the hands to help others. It has the feet to hasten to the poor and needy. It has eyes to see misery and want. It has the ears to hear the sighs and sorrows of men. That is what love looks like."

Aurelius, Marcus   121–180

Born Marcus Aurelius Antoninus; Roman emperor from 161–180; Stoic philosopher; last emperor of the Pax Romana, an age of relative peace, calm, and stability for the Roman Empire lasting from 27 BC to 180 AD.

"All you need are these: certainty of judgment. . .; action for the common good in the present moment; and an attitude of gratitude in the present moment for anything that comes your way."

"If it is not right, do not do it; if it is not true, do not say it."

"The happiness of your life depends upon the quality of your thoughts."

"Waste no more time arguing about what a good man should be. Be one."

Beyle, Marie-Henri, "Stendal"   1783–1842

Better known by pen name; nineteenth-century French writer; author of *The Red and the Black* and *The Charterhouse of Parma*; considered one of foremost practitioners of realism.

"One can acquire everything in solitude—except character."

Bojaxhiu, Mary Teresa, "Mother Teresa"   1910–1997

Born Anjezë Gonxhe Bojaxhiu; Albanian-Indian Catholic nun; founder of Missionaries of Charity; canonized by Catholic Church as Saint Teresa of Calcutta.

"Let no one ever come to you without leaving better."

"Not all of us can do great things. But we can do small things with great love."

"The best way to show my gratitude is to accept everything, even my problems, with joy."

Brault, Robert   1948–

American writer; contributor to magazines and newspapers for over fifty years; author of *Round Up The Usual Subjects*, *Short Thoughts For The Long Haul*, *A Few For The Road*, etc.

"A child seldom needs a good talking to as much as a good listening to."

"A parent's love is whole, no matter how many times divided."

Buddha   6th or 5th century BC

Born as Siddhartha Gautama; wandering ascetic and religious teacher who lived in South Asia; founded Buddhism.

"Three things cannot be long hidden: the sun, the moon, and the truth."

Burdette, Robert Jones   1844–1914

American humorist, and clergyman.

"Don't go around saying the world owes you a living. The world owes you nothing. It was here first."

Carver, George Washington   1864–1943

American agricultural scientist and inventor; promoted alternative crops to cotton and methods to prevent soil depletion.

"Ninety-nine percent of all failures come from people who have a habit of making excuses."

Chesterton, G. K. 1874–1936

English writer, philosopher, Christian apologist, and literary and art critic.

"The doctrine I should always have liked to teach. . . . is the idea of taking things with gratitude, and not taking things for granted."

"We men and women are all in the same boat, upon a stormy sea. We owe to each other a terrible and tragic loyalty."

Churchill, Winston 1874–1965

British statesman, soldier, and writer; twice served as prime minister of the United Kingdom; apart from two years between 1922 and 1924, member of British Parliament from 1900 to 1964 and represented a total of five constituencies.

"Every day you may make progress. Every step may be fruitful. Yet there will stretch out before you an ever-lengthening, ever-ascending, ever-improving path. You know you will never get to the end of the journey. But this, so far from discouraging, only adds to the joy and glory of the climb."

"Life is a test and this world a place of trial. Always the problems or it may be the same problem will be presented to every generation in different forms. The problems of victory may be even more baffling than those of defeat. However much the conditions change, the supreme question is how we live and grow and bloom and die, and how far each life conforms to standards which are not wholly related to time and space."

"This is the lesson: never give in, never give in, never, never, never, never—in nothing, great or small, large or petty—never give in except to convictions of honor and good sense. Never yield to force; never yield to the apparently overwhelming might of the enemy."

"Everyone remembers the remark of the old man at the point of death: that his life had been full of troubles most of which had never happened."

Cicero, Marcus Tullius 106–43 BC

Roman statesman, lawyer, scholar, philosopher, writer, and academic skeptic; extensive writings include treatises on rhetoric, philosophy, and politics.

"Gratitude is not only the greatest of virtues but the parent of all others."

Clear, James   1986–

American writer; author of *Atomic Habits*.

"Winners and losers have the same goals. . . . Every Olympian wants to win a gold medal. . . . The goal cannot be what differentiates the winners from the losers. . . . It was only when they implemented a system of continuous small improvements that they achieved a different outcome."

Confucius   551–479 BC

Chinese philosopher; traditionally considered the paragon of Chinese sages; teachings and philosophy underpin East Asian culture and society and remain influential across China and East Asia; philosophical teachings called Confucianism.

"A man who does not think and plan long ahead will find trouble right at his door."

"A superior man is modest in his speech but exceeds in his actions."

"I was complaining that I had no shoes till I met a man who had no feet."

"It is better to light one small candle of gratitude than to curse the darkness."

"Success depends upon previous preparation, and without such preparation, there is sure to be failure."

Covey, Stephen R.   1932–2012

American educator, author, businessman, and speaker; author of many books, including *The 7 Habits of Highly Effective People*, *First Things First*, *Principle-Centered Leadership*, *The 7 Habits of Highly Effective Families*, and *The 8ᵗʰ Habit*.

"All things are created twice. There's a mental or first creation, and a physical or second creation to all things. Take the construction of a home, for example. You create it in every detail before you ever hammer the first nail into place. . . . Then you reduce it to blueprint and develop construction plans. . . . You have to make sure that the blueprint, the first creation, is really what you want, that you've thought everything through. Then you put it into bricks and mortar. . . . You begin with the end in mind."

"Be loyal to those who are not present. In doing so, you build the trust of those who are present."

"Building character and quality of life is a function of aligning our beliefs and behaviors with universal principles. These principles are impersonal, external, factual, objective, and self-evident. They operate regardless of our awareness of them or our obedience or disobedience to them."

"Caring about the individual works because it's a paradigm focused on people, not things; it's focused on relationships, not schedules; it's focused on effectiveness, not efficiency; it's focused on personal leadership, not resource management."

"Clear back to ancient times, thoughtful people have made lists of useful principles."

"I am not a product of my circumstances. I am a product of my decisions."

"If you are in an extremely productive or creative phase, you don't let anything interrupt."

"Inner character is far more significant a factor in success than talent or intelligence or circumstances."

"Most of us spend too much time on what is urgent and not enough time on what is important."

"The deepest hunger of the human soul is to be recognized, valued, appreciated, and understood."

"We are not a product of our circumstances; we are a product of our decisions."

"We may honestly admit to ourselves that we are at least partly to blame for the problem."

"When you take proactive responsibility for your problems, you empower yourself to create the solutions."

Csikszentmihalyi, Mihaly   1934–2021

Hungarian-American psychologist; author of *Flow: The Psychology of Optimal Experience* and *Creativity: Flow and the Psychology of Discovery and Invention*; head of the psychology department at the University of Chicago.

"Creativity is a central source of meaning in our lives. . . Most of the things that are interesting, important, and human are the results of creativity. . . Creativity is so fascinating [because] when we are involved in it, we feel that we are living more fully than during the rest of life."

"Flow is being completely involved in an activity for its own sake. The ego falls away. Time flies. Every action, movement, and thought follows inevitably from the previous one, like playing jazz."

"Purpose provides activation energy for living."

"Unless a person knows how to give order to his or her thoughts, attention will be attracted to whatever is most problematic at the moment."

Cunningham, Glenn   1909–1988

American middle-distance runner; considered the greatest American miler of all time.

"I think it was at that very moment that I made one of the biggest decisions of my life. I'm NOT going to be an invalid! I remember saying over and over, 'I will walk! I will walk!'"

"In running, it is man against himself, the cruelest of opponents. The other runners are not the real enemies. His adversary lies within him, in his ability with brain and heart to master himself and his emotions."

Disney, Walt   1901–1966

American animator, film producer, and entrepreneur; pioneer of the American animation industry and one of the most successful people in entertainment history.

"All our dreams can come true, if we have the courage to pursue them."

Drouet, Juliette   1806–1883

Born Julienne Josephine Gauvain; French actress; abandoned career on stage after becoming the mistress of writer Victor Hugo.

"I love you because I love you, because it would be impossible not to love you. I love you without question, without calculation, without reason good or bad, faithfully, with all my heart and soul, and every faculty."

Drucker, Peter   1909–2005

Austrian-American management consultant, educator, and author; contributor to philosophical and practical foundations of modern management theory.

"The leaders who work most effectively, it seems to me, never say 'I.' And that's not because they have trained themselves not to say 'I.' They don't think 'I.' They think 'we'; they think 'team.' They understand their job to be to make the team function."

Durant, Will   1885–1981

American historian and philosopher; with his wife, author of eleven-volume work, *The Story of Civilization*, written over forty years, detailing the history of Eastern and Western civilizations; also author of *The Story of Philosophy*.

"If a man is fortunate he will, before he dies, gather up as much as he can of his civilized heritage and transmit it to his children. And to his final breath he will be grateful for this inexhaustible legacy, knowing that it is our nourishing mother and our lasting life."

Dweck, Carol   1946–

American psychologist; Lewis and Virginia Eaton professor of psychology at Stanford University; known for work on motivation and mindset.

"If parents want to give their children a gift, the best thing they can do is to teach their children to love challenges, be intrigued by mistakes, enjoy effort, seek new strategies, and keep on learning. That way, their children don't have to be slaves of praise."

"The passion for stretching yourself and sticking to it, even (or especially) when it's not going well, is the hallmark of the growth mindset."

"Those with the growth mindset found setbacks motivating. They're informative. They're a wake-up call."

Edelman, Marian Wright   1939–

American activist for civil and children's rights; founder/president of Children's Defense Fund.

"You're not obligated to win. You're obligated to keep trying to do the best you can every day."

Edison, Thomas   1847–1931

American inventor and businessman; researcher in electric power generation, mass communication, sound recording, and motion pictures;

inventions include the phonograph, the motion picture camera, and early versions of the electric light bulb.

"If we all did the things we are really capable of doing, we would literally astound ourselves."

"I have not failed. I've just found 10,000 ways that won't work."

"Many of life's failures are people who did not realize how close they were to success when they gave up."

"Nothing is impossible. We merely don't know how to do it yet."

"Our greatest weakness lies in giving up. The most certain way to succeed is always to try just one more time."

Einstein, Albert   1879–1955

German-born theoretical physicist; widely held as one of the most influential scientists of all time; developer of the theory of relativity and made important contributions to quantum mechanics; received Nobel Prize in Physics.

"Try not to become a man of success but rather to become a man of value."

"We have to do the best we can. This is our sacred human responsibility."

Emerson, Ralph Waldo   1803–1882

American essayist, lecturer, philosopher, abolitionist, and poet; leader of the Transcendentalist movement of the mid-nineteenth century; champion of individualism and critical thinking.

"Nothing so marks a man as imaginative expressions. A figurative statement arrests attention and is remembered and repeated."

"Self-trust is the first secret of success."

"What lies behind us and what lies before us are tiny matters compared to what lies within us."

Ewing, Sam   1920–2001

American businessman, author, and humorist.

"Hard work spotlights the character of people: some turn up their sleeves, some turn up their noses, and some don't turn up at all."

Faulkner, William   1897–1962

American writer, winner of the Nobel Prize for Literature; often considered the greatest writer of literature of the American South.

"Don't bother just to be better than your contemporaries or predecessors. Try to be better than yourself."

Ford, Henry   1863–1947

American industrialist and business magnate; founder of the Ford Motor Company; pioneer in making automobiles affordable for middle-class Americans; revolutionized American industry; one of the richest and best-known people in the world in his time.

"I will build a car for the great multitude. It will be large enough for the family but small enough for the individual to run and care for. It will be constructed of the best materials, by the best men to be hired, after the simplest designs that modern engineering can devise. But it will be so low in price that no man making a good salary will be unable to own one."

"Whether you think you can, or you think you can't—you're right."

Frankl, Viktor   1905–1997

Austrian psychiatrist and Holocaust survivor; founder of logotherapy, school of psychotherapy that describes search for meaning as central human motivational force; author of *Man's Search for Meaning*.

"Everything can be taken from a man but one thing: the last of human freedoms--to choose one's attitude in any given set of circumstances, to choose one's own way."

Franklin, Benjamin   1706–1790

American polymath, writer, scientist, inventor, statesman, diplomat, printer, publisher, and political philosopher; among most influential intellectuals of his time; one of the Founding Fathers of the United States.

"By failing to prepare, you are preparing to fail."

Fromm, Erich   1900–1980

German-American social psychologist, psychoanalyst, sociologist, humanistic philosopher, and democratic socialist; author of *The Art of Loving*.

"If I truly love one person I love all persons, I love the world, I love life. If I can say to somebody else, 'I love you,' I must be able to say, 'I love in you everybody, I love through you the world, I love in you also myself.'"

"Love is an active power in man; a power which breaks through the walls which separate man from his fellow men, which unites him with others; love makes him overcome the sense of isolation and separateness, yet it permits him to be himself, to retain his integrity. In love, the paradox occurs that two beings become one and yet remain two."

"Love is not primarily a relationship to a specific person; it is an attitude, an orientation of character which determines the relatedness of a person to the world as a whole, not toward one 'object' of love."

"To love somebody is not just a strong feeling—it is a decision, it is a judgment, it is a promise. If love were only a feeling, there would be no basis for the promise to love each other forever."

Fuller, R. Buckminster   1895–1983

American architect, systems theorist, writer, designer, inventor, philosopher, and futurist.

"Integrity is the essence of everything successful."

"Never forget that you are one of a kind. Never forget that if there weren't any need for you in all your uniqueness to be on this earth, you wouldn't be here in the first place. And never forget, no matter how overwhelming life's challenges and problems seem to be, that one person can make a difference in the world. In fact, it is always because of one person that all the changes that matter in the world come about. So be that one person."

Gandhi, Mahatma   1869–1948

Born Mohandas Karamchand Gandhi; Indian lawyer, anti-colonial nationalist and political ethicist; employed nonviolent resistance to lead the successful campaign for India's independence from British rule.

"Happiness is when what you think, what you say, and what you do are in harmony."

"It is wrong and immoral to seek to escape the consequences of one's acts."

"Truth is by nature self-evident. As soon as you remove the cobwebs of ignorance that surround it, it shines clear."

Gates, Bill   1955–

American businessman, investor, philanthropist, and writer; cofounder of Microsoft, held positions of chairman, CEO, president, and chief software architect; pioneer of microcomputer revolution; one of the wealthiest people in the world in his time.

"Only through focus can you do world-class things, no matter how capable you are."

Gbowee, Leymah   1972–

Liberian peace activist; awarded 2011 Nobel Peace Prize.

"Don't wait for a Gandhi, don't wait for a King, don't wait for a Mandela. You are your own Mandela, you are your own Gandhi, you are your own King."

"Leadership is standing with your people. People say you have to live to fight another day, but sometimes you have to show you are a true leader."

Geisel, Theodor Seuss, "Dr. Seuss"   1904–1991

American children's author and cartoonist; wrote and illustrated more than sixty books, including many of the most popular children's books of all time.

"To the world, you may be one person, but to one person, you may be the world."

Gray, Albert E.N.   1902–1984

American author and speaker; author of the essay "The Common Denominator of Success."

"The secret of success lies in forming the habit of doing things that failures don't like to do."

Greenleaf, Robert K.   1904–1990

American writer and speaker; founder of Greenleaf Center for Servant Leadership.

"Since we are the product of our own history, we see current prophecy within the context of past wisdom. We listen to as wide a range of contemporary thought as we can attend to. Then we choose those we elect to heed as prophets—both old and new—and meld their advice with our own leadings. This we test in real-life experiences to establish our own position."

Gyatso, Tenzin, "Dalai Lama" 1935–

Spiritual name: Jetsun Jamphel Ngawang Lobsang Yeshe Tenzin Gyatso; fourteenth Dalai Lama; highest spiritual leader and head of Tibet; considered a living Bodhisattva; leader of Gelug school of Tibetan Buddhism.

"Every day, think as you wake up: 'Today I am fortunate to have woken up. I am alive. I have a precious human life. I am not going to waste it.'"

"If you want others to be happy, practice compassion. If you want to be happy, practice compassion."

"My religion is very simple. My religion is kindness."

"The roots of all goodness lie in the soil of appreciation for goodness."

Hemingway, Mary 1908–1986

American journalist and author; fourth wife and widow of Ernest Hemingway.

"Don't worry. Never worry. If it is something you can fix, fix it. If it is something impossible to fix, all your worrying won't help."

Horowitz, Vladimir 1903–1989

Russian-American pianist; one of the most renowned and influential pianists of the twentieth century; known for virtuoso technique and timbre; kept performing into his eighties.

"If I skip practice for a day, I notice. . . If I skip practice for two days, my wife notices. . . If I skip practice for three days, the world notices."

James, William 1842–1910

American philosopher and psychologist; considered one of the most influential philosophers from the US and the father of American psychology.

"Do every day or two something for no other reason than its difficulty, so that, when the hour of dire need draws nigh, it may find you not unnerved and untrained to stand the test."

"Every good that is worth possessing must be paid for in strokes of daily effort."

"It is our attitude at the beginning of a difficult task which, more than anything else, will affect its successful outcome."

"Believe that life is worth living, and your belief will help create the fact."

Jefferson, Thomas   1743–1826

American statesman, diplomat, lawyer, architect, philosopher, and founding father; third president of the US; primary author of the Declaration of Independence.

"He who permits himself to tell a lie once finds it much easier to do it a second and third time, till at length it becomes habitual; he tells lies without attending to it, and truths without the world's believing him. This falsehood of the tongue leads to that of the heart, and in time depraves all its good dispositions."

"Honesty is the first chapter of the book wisdom."

"Whenever you are to do a thing, though it can never be known but to yourself, ask yourself how you would act were all the world looking at you, and act accordingly."

Kahneman, Daniel   1934–

Israeli-American author, psychologist, and economist; awarded Nobel Prize in Economic Sciences; author of *Thinking, Fast and Slow*.

"If you were allowed one wish for your child, seriously consider wishing him or her optimism. Optimists are normally cheerful and happy, and therefore popular; they are resilient in adapting to failures and hardships, their chances of clinical depression are reduced, their immune system is stronger, they take better care of their health, they feel healthier than others and are in fact likely to live longer."

Kant, Immanuel   1724–1804

German philosopher; central Enlightenment thinker; one of the most influential figures in modern Western philosophy; often called the father of modern philosophy.

"By a lie a man throws away and, as it were, annihilates his dignity as a man."

"Two things fill the mind with ever new and increasing admiration and awe, the oftener and the more steadily we reflect on them: the starry heavens above and the moral law within."

"Science is organized knowledge. Wisdom is organized life."

Keller, Helen   1880–1968

American author, disability rights advocate, political activist, and lecturer; lost sight and hearing at nineteen months old; first deafblind person in the US to earn a Bachelor of Arts degree.

"Alone we can do so little; together we can do so much."

"Character cannot be developed in ease and quiet. Only through experience of trial and suffering can the soul be strengthened, vision cleared, ambition inspired, and success achieved."

"My optimism is grounded in two worlds, myself and what is about me. I demand that the world be good, and lo, it obeys. I proclaim the world good, and facts range themselves to prove my proclamation overwhelmingly true. . . . I am never discouraged by absence of good. I never can be argued into hopelessness. Doubt and mistrust are the mere panic of timid imagination, which the steadfast heart will conquer, and the large mind transcend."

"Optimism is the faith that leads to achievement."

Kierkegaard, Søren   1813–1855

Danish theologian, philosopher, poet, social critic, and religious author.

"The most common form of despair is not being who you are."

King, Martin Luther, Jr.   1929–1968

American Christian minister, activist, and political philosopher; one of the most prominent leaders in the American civil rights movement in the middle of the twentieth century.

"Agape is understanding, creative, redemptive goodwill for all men. It is an overflowing love which seeks nothing in return. Theologians would say that it's the love of God operating in the human heart."

"Hate is just as injurious to the hater as it is to the hated. Like an unchecked cancer, hate corrodes the personality . . . Hate is too great a burden to bear."

"I believe that unarmed truth and Unconditional Love will have the final word."

"I have . . . decided to stick with love, for I know that love is ultimately the only answer to mankind's problems. . . . I have seen too much hate. . . . and I say to myself that hate is too great a burden to bear."

"Love is the only force capable of transforming an enemy into a friend."

"Our lives begin to end the day we become silent about things that matter."

"The time is always right to do what is right."

"The ultimate measure of a man is not where he stands in moments of comfort and convenience, but where he stands at times of challenge and controversy."

Kingsley, Charles   1819–1875

Priest of Church of England, university professor, social reformer, historian, novelist and poet.

"Being forced to work, and forced to do your best, will breed in you temperance and self-control, diligence and strength of will, cheerfulness and content, and a hundred virtues which the idle will never know."

Kushner, Harold   1935–2023

American rabbi, author, and lecturer; author of many books, including *When Bad Things Happen to Good People* and *When All You've Ever Wanted Isn't Enough*.

"If you concentrate on finding whatever is good in every situation, you will discover that your life will suddenly be filled with gratitude, a feeling that nurtures the soul."

Lanier, Sidney   1842–1881

American musician, poet, and author.

"Virtues are acquired through endeavor, which rests wholly upon yourself."

Lencioni, Patrick   1965–

American writer; author of *The Five Dysfunctions of a Team*.

"Failing to hold someone accountable is ultimately an act of selfishness."

Lewis, C. S. 1898–1963

British writer, literary scholar, and Anglican lay theologian: author of many books, including *The Chronicles of Narnia*, *The Screwtape Letters*, *Mere Christianity*, and *The Problem of Pain*.

"Love is not affectionate feeling, but a steady wish for the loved person's ultimate good as far as it can be obtained."

Lincoln, Abraham 1809–1865

American lawyer, politician, and statesman; sixteenth president of the United States.

"My great concern is not whether you have failed, but whether you are content with your failure."

Luther, Martin 1483–1546

German priest, theologian, author, hymnwriter, professor, and Augustinian friar; seminal figure of the Protestant Reformation; theological beliefs formed the basis of Lutheranism.

"You are not only responsible for what you say, but also for what you do not say."

Lyubomirsky, Sonja 1966–

Russian-born American psychology professor; author of *The How of Happiness: A Scientific Approach to Getting the Life You Want*.

"Gratitude is an antidote to negative emotions, a neutralizer of envy, hostility, worry, and irritation. It is savoring; it is not taking things for granted; it is present-oriented."

MacDonald, George 1824–1905

Scottish author, poet, and Christian Congregational minister; pioneer in modern fantasy literature; mentor of Lewis Carroll; also wrote several works of Christian theology.

"Few delights can equal the mere presence of one whom we trust utterly."

"To be trusted is a greater compliment than being loved."

Maraboli, Steve   1975–

American writer and speaker; author of *Unapologetically You: Reflections on Life and the Human Experience* and other books.

"Wisdom stems from personal accountability. We all make mistakes; own them... learn from them. Don't throw away the lesson by blaming others."

Maxwell, John C.   1947–

American author, speaker, and pastor; author of *The 21 Irrefutable Laws of Leadership*, *The 21 Indispensable Qualities of a Leader*, and many other books.

"A man must be big enough to admit his mistakes, smart enough to profit from them, and strong enough to correct them."

"If you aren't making any mistakes, it's a sure sign you're playing it too safe."

"No leader can break trust with his people and expect to keep influencing them."

"Trust is the foundation of leadership."

"We cannot achieve our wildest dreams by remaining who we are."

"When people respect you as a person, they admire you. When they respect you as a friend, they love you. When they respect you as a leader, they follow you."

Merton, Thomas   1915–1968

American Trappist monk, writer, theologian, mystic, poet, social activist, and scholar of comparative religion.

"The beginning of love is the will to let those we love be perfectly themselves, the resolution not to twist them to fit our own image. If in loving them we do not love what they are, but only their potential likeness to ourselves, then we do not love them: we only love the reflection of ourselves we find in them."

Michelangelo   1475–1564

Also Michelangelo di Lodovico Buonarroti Simoni; Italian sculptor, painter, architect, and poet of the High Renaissance; widely regarded as the most accomplished artist of his era.

"If you knew how much work went into it, you wouldn't call it genius."

Milne, A. A.   1882–1956

English writer; author of Winnie-the-Pooh book series and children's poetry.

"Piglet noticed that even though he had a Very Small Heart, it could hold a rather large amount of Gratitude."

"The things that make me different are the things that make me."

Monson, Thomas S.   1927–2018

American religious leader, author, and sixteenth president of the Church of Jesus Christ of Latter-day Saints; often wrote and spoke about gratitude and positivity.

"Happiness comes when we stop complaining about the troubles we have and offer thanks for all the troubles we don't have."

Muhammad, Prophet   circa 570–632 AD

Arab religious, social, and political leader; founder of Islam; the Qur'an and his teachings and practices form the basis for Islamic religious belief.

"Actions are judged by their intentions, and everyone will be rewarded according to their intention."

"He is not a believer whose stomach is filled while the neighbor to his side goes hungry."

"He who cheats us is not of us."

"Take account of yourselves before you are taken to account."

"The best of people are those with the most excellent character."

"When you speak, speak the truth; perform when you promise; discharge your trust. . . . Guard your tongue against swearing falsely, for swearing falsely leads a man far away from faith."

Neill, Michael   1968–

American writer; author of *The Inside-Out Revolution*.

"My fondest hope for you is that you find yourself on the pages of this book. Not the self you think you are and not the self you fear you might be, but rather the selfless self whose face you had before you were born."

Nhất Hạnh, Thích   1926–2022

Born Nguyễn Xuân Bảo; Vietnamese Buddhist monk, peace activist, author, and teacher; founded Plum Village Tradition, inspiration for engaged Buddhism; known as father of mindfulness; major influence on Western practices of Buddhism.

"Compassion is a verb."

"Waking up this morning, I smile. Twenty-four brand new hours are before me. I vow to live fully in each moment and to look at all beings with eyes of compassion."

Niebuhr, Reinhold   1892–1971

American theologian, ethicist, commentator on politics and public affairs; author of *Moral Man and Immoral Society* and *The Nature and Destiny of Man*.

"All human sin seems so much worse in its consequences than in its intentions."

Niemöller, Martin   1892–1984

German Lutheran pastor; early Nazi supporter but emerged as an outspoken public foe of Adolf Hitler and the Nazi regime.

"First they came for the socialists, and I did not speak out—
    Because I was not a socialist.
Then they came for the trade unionists, and I did not speak out—
    Because I was not a trade unionist.
Then they came for the Jews, and I did not speak out—
    Because I was not a Jew.
Then they came for me—and there was no one left to speak for me."

Osgood, Charles   1933–2024

Born Charles Osgood Wood III; American radio and television commentator, writer, musician.

"Once upon a time, there were four people named Everybody, Somebody, Anybody, and Nobody. There was an important job to be done. Everybody was asked to do it. Everybody was sure Somebody would do it. Anybody could have done it, but Nobody did it. Somebody got angry because it was Everybody's job. Everybody thought Anybody could do it, but Nobody realized Everybody wouldn't do it. In the end, Everybody blamed Somebody when Nobody did what Anybody could have."

Pichai, Sundar   1972–

Indian-American businessman; CEO of Alphabet Inc. and its subsidiary Google.

"A diverse mix of voices leads to better discussions, decisions, and outcomes for everyone."

Purmal, Kate, Goldman, Lisa, and Janzer, Anne   Various dates

American authors of *The Moonshot Effect: Disrupting Business as Usual*; Purmal: executive at various technology and life sciences companies; Goldman: partner at a management consulting firm; Janzer: nonfiction book coach.

"We set our sights on the moon to elevate ourselves."

Robinson, Edwin Arlington   1869–1935

American poet and playwright; awarded Pulitzer Prize for Poetry three times; nominated for Nobel Prize in Literature four times.

"There are two kinds of gratitude: The sudden kind we feel for what we take; the larger kind we feel for what we give."

Rogers, Fred, "Mister Rogers"   1928–2003

American television host, author, producer, and minister; creator, show-runner, and host of preschool television series *Mister Rogers' Neighborhood*.

"It's not so much what we have in this life that matters. It's what we do with what we have."

"It's not the honors and the prizes and the fancy outsides of life which ultimately nourish our souls. It's the knowing that we can be trusted, that we never have to fear the truth, that the bedrock of our very being is good stuff."

"There are three ways to ultimate success: The first way is to be kind. The second way is to be kind. The third way is to be kind."

"When we love a person, we accept him or her exactly as is: the lovely with the unlovely, the strong with the fearful, the true mixed in with the façade, and of course, the only way we can do it is by accepting ourselves that way."

"Who you are inside is what helps you make and do everything in life."

"You can't really love someone else unless you really love yourself first."

"You are the only person who is exactly like you, so in a way you've already won in this world. Because you're the only one who can be you."

Rondon, Cândido Mariano da Silva   1865–1958

Brazilian military officer; known for telegraph commission, exploration of Mato Grosso and the Western Amazon Basin, and support for indigenous Brazilians.

"True happiness consists of precisely carrying out one's duty."

Roosevelt, Theodore   1858–1919

American politician, statesman, conservationist, naturalist, and writer; twenty-sixth president of the US.

"Do what you can where you are with what you've got."

"Far and away the best prize that life offers is the chance to work hard at work worth doing."

"It is no use to preach to [children] if you do not act decently yourself."

"It is the doer of deeds who actually counts in the battle for life, and not the man who looks on and says how the fight ought to be fought, without himself sharing the stress and the danger."

"Nothing in the world is worth having or worth doing unless it means effort, pain, difficulty. . . I have never in my life envied a human being who led an easy life. I have envied a great many people who led difficult lives and led them well."

"The one thing I want to leave my children is an honorable name."

Sartre, Jean-Paul   1905–1980

French philosopher, playwright, novelist, screenwriter, political activist, biographer, and literary critic; leading figure in twentieth-century French philosophy.

"Commitment is an act, not a word."

"Freedom is what you do with what's been done to you."

"I am my own existence, and I am made responsible for it entirely."

"Man is condemned to be free; because once thrown into the world, he is responsible for everything he does."

"We are our choices."

Schurz, Carl   1829–1906

German revolutionary and American statesman, journalist, and reformer; represented Missouri in US Senate; thirteenth US Secretary of the Interior.

"Ideals are like stars; you will not succeed in touching them with your hands, but like the seafaring man on the desert of waters, you choose them as your guides, and following them, you reach your destiny."

Seinfeld, Jerry   1954–

American standup comedian, actor, writer, and producer.

"This whole concept of the team—'Your team,' 'My team,'. . .'That's our team.' Really? Is it our team? Who are these guys? Where are they from? They're not from around here. They're just paid to wear those clothes. The uniform is the only constant in sports. The guys are moving around, different teams. . .teams are moving from different towns. We're really just rooting for our clothes to defeat the clothes of the team from the other city. That's what sports is. We're rooting for laundry, and nothing else. I always find it weird how upset we get when a guy leaves our team and then plays against our team: 'Different shirt! I hate this guy! I can't believe he's wearing that shirt!' In the meantime, everyone we see every day is wearing a different shirt. We don't get upset with them, for some reason."

Silverstein, Sam   1961–

American writer and speaker; founder of The Accountability Institute™; author of several books, including *The Accountability Advantage*.

"I believe that accountability is the basis of all meaningful human achievement."

Simpson, Homer   1987

Cartoon character; protagonist of American animated sitcom The Simpsons; created by Matt Groening and voiced by Dan Castellaneta; widely considered an American cultural icon.

"Weaseling out of things is important to learn. It's what separates us from the animals. . . except the weasel."

Sirleaf, Ellen Johnson   1938–

Liberian politician; twenty-fourth president of Liberia; first elected female head of state in Africa.

"The size of your dreams must always exceed your current capacity to achieve them. If your dreams do not scare you, they are not big enough."

Spencer, Herbert   1820–1903

English philosopher, psychologist, biologist, sociologist, and anthropologist; originated expression "survival of the fittest" in *Principles of Biology* (1864) after reading Charles Darwin's *On the Origin of Species*.

"Science is organized knowledge. Wisdom is organized life."

Stafford, William   1914–1993

American author of over sixty-five volumes of poetry and prose; won National Book Award for Poetry in 1963; US Poet Laureate in 1970; known for reflections on nature, humanity, morality.

"Wisdom is having things right in your life and knowing why."

Stamp, Sir Josiah   1880–1941

English industrialist, economist, civil servant, statistician, writer, and banker; director of the Bank of England; chairman of the London, Midland, and Scottish Railway.

"It is easy to dodge our responsibilities, but we cannot dodge the consequences of dodging our responsibilities."

Steindl-Rast, David   1926–

Austrian-American Catholic Benedictine monk, author, and lecturer.

"It is not joy that makes us grateful; it is gratitude that makes us joyful."

Summitt, Pat   1952–2016

American women's college basketball head coach; widely regarded as one of the best basketball coaches in history.

"Responsibility equals accountability equals ownership. And a sense of ownership is the most powerful weapon a team or organization can have."

Swift, Jonathan   1667–1745

Anglo-Irish satirist, author, essayist, political pamphleteer, poet, and Anglican cleric.

"Vision is the art of seeing things invisible to others."

Syrus, Publilius   85–43 BC

Latin writer; known for sententiae, brief moral sayings, such as proverbs, adages, aphorisms, maxims, or apothegms taken from ancient or popular or other sources.

"Do not despise the bottom rungs in the ascent to greatness."

"Practice is the best of all instructors."

"You should not live one way in private and another in public."

Talbert, Bob   1931–1999

American journalist and columnist; writer at Detroit Free Press.

"Teaching kids to count is fine, but teaching them what counts is best."

Thoreau, Henry David   1817–1862

American naturalist, essayist, poet, and philosopher; leading transcendentalist; author of *Walden* and essay "Civil Disobedience."

"I know of no more encouraging fact than the unquestionable ability of man to elevate his life by conscious endeavor."

"If a man does not keep pace with his companions, perhaps it is because he hears a different drummer. Let him step to the music which he hears, however measured or far away."

"The greatest compliment that was ever paid me was when one asked me what I thought, and attended to my answer."

Tomlin, Lily   1939–

American actress, comedian, writer, singer, and producer; winner of seven Emmy Awards, a Grammy Award, and two Tony Awards.

"Man invented language to satisfy his deep need to complain."

Tzu, Lao   circa 6th century BC

Also Laozi; Chinese philosopher; author of the *Tao Te Ching*, the foundational text of Taoism.

"A journey of a thousand miles begins with a single step."

"Kindness in words creates confidence. Kindness in thinking creates profoundness. Kindness in giving creates love."

von Furstenberg, Diane   1946–

Born Diane Simone Michele Halfin; Belgian fashion designer; founder of fashion company DvF.

"Don't blame your parents, don't blame your boyfriend, don't blame the weather. Accept the reality, embrace the challenge, and deal with it. Be in charge of your own life."

"Never, ever, blame others for what befalls you, no matter how horrible it might be. Trust you, and only you, to be responsible for your own life."

Ward, William Arthur   1921–1994

American writer; author of many articles, poems, meditations, and column "Pertinent Proverbs" in the Fort Worth Star-Telegram.

"Feeling gratitude and not expressing it is like wrapping a present and not giving it."

"The mediocre teacher tells. The good teacher explains. The superior teacher demonstrates. The great teacher inspires."

Watson, Thomas J., Jr.   1914–1993

American businessman, diplomat, Army Air Force pilot, and philanthropist; second IBM president; eleventh president of the Boy Scouts of America; sixteenth US Ambassador to the Soviet Union.

"Would you like me to give you a formula for success? It's quite simple. Double your rate of failure. You are thinking of failure as the enemy of success. But it isn't at all. You can be discouraged by failure or you can learn from it, so go ahead and make mistakes. Make all you can. . . . That's where you will find success."

Willink, Jocko and Babin, Leif   Willink: 1971– , Babin: 1976–

John Gretton Willink, Jr.: American author, podcaster, and US Navy officer; commanded SEAL Team 3; coauthor of *Extreme Ownership* and *The Dichotomy of Leadership*; cofounder of Echelon Front, LLC.

Leif Babin: American author, podcaster, and US Navy officer; platoon commander in SEAL Team 3; coauthor of *Extreme Ownership* and *The Dichotomy of Leadership*; cofounder of Echelon Front, LLC.

"Admitting mistakes, taking ownership, and developing a plan to overcome challenges are integral to any successful team."

"In any organization, all responsibility for success and failure rests with the leader. The leader must own everything in his or her world. There is no one else to blame."

"When setting expectations, no matter what has been said or written, if substandard performance is accepted and no one is held accountable—if there are no consequences—that poor performance becomes the new standard."

"When things go wrong, look in the mirror and ask yourself: 'What can I do to make things better?'"

Wojtyła, Karol Józef (Pope John Paul II)   1920–2005

Head of Catholic Church and sovereign of Vatican City 1978–2005; one of youngest popes in history, first non-Italian pope since the sixteenth century, and third-longest-serving pope.

"We are all one family in the world. Building a community that empowers everyone to attain their full potential through each of us respecting each other's dignity, rights, and responsibilities makes the world a better place to live."

Wooden, John   1910–2010

American basketball coach and player; widely regarded as one the greatest coaches in modern sports history.

"Be more concerned with your character than your reputation, because your character is what you really are, while your reputation is merely what others think you are."

"'Did I win? Did I lose?' Those are the wrong questions. The correct question is: 'Did I make my best effort?' If so. . . you may be outscored, but you will never lose."

"Success is. . .knowing you made the effort to become the best you are capable of becoming."

"The true test of a man's character is what he does when no one is watching."

Bible

1 Corinthians 13:1–3 (New International Version): "If I speak in the tongues of men or of angels, but do not have love, I am only a resounding gong or a clanging cymbal. If I have the gift of prophecy and can fathom all mysteries and all knowledge, and if I have a faith that can move mountains, but do not have love, I am nothing. If I give all I possess to the poor and give over my body to hardship that I may boast, but do not have love, I gain nothing."

1 Thessalonians 5:18 (NIV): "Give thanks in all circumstances; for this is God's will for you in Christ Jesus."

Ephesians 5:20 (NIV): "Always giving thanks to God the Father for everything, in the name of our Lord Jesus Christ."

James 1:17 (NIV): "Every good and perfect gift is from above, coming down from the Father of the heavenly lights, who does not change like shifting shadows."

John 8:32 (NIV): "And you will know the truth, and the truth will set you free."

Matthew 5:6 (NIV): "Blessed are those who hunger and thirst for righteousness, for they will be filled."

Philippians 2:14 (New Living Translation): "Do everything without complaining."

Proverbs 13:4 (Common English Version): "The lazy have strong desires but receive nothing; the appetite of the diligent is satisfied."

Proverbs 14:23 (CEV): "There is profit in hard work, but mere talk leads to poverty."

Psalm 107:1 (NIV): "Give thanks to the Lord, for he is good; his love endures forever."

Psalm 118:24 (NIV): "This is the day the Lord has made; let us rejoice and be glad in it."

Pirkei Avot

1:14: "If I am not for myself, who will be for me? And if I am only for myself, what am I? And if not now, when?"

4:2: "The reward of a good deed is the deed itself."

Qur'an

53:39: "Man will not get anything unless he works hard."

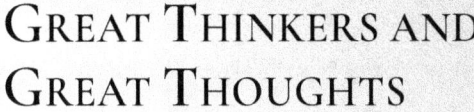

GREAT THINKERS AND
GREAT THOUGHTS

Referenced in *The Unconditionals*

Achor, Shawn, *The Happiness Advantage: The Seven Principles of Positive Psychology That Fuel Success and Performance at Work*. New York: Crown Currency Publishing, 2010.

Ariely, Dan, *The (Honest) Truth About Dishonesty: How We Lie to Everyone—Especially Ourselves*. New York: HarperCollins, 2012.

Augustine, Saint, *Confessions*, translated by Maria Boulding, New York: Vintage Books, 1998.

Bowen, Will, *A Complaint Free World: How to Stop Complaining and Start Enjoying the Life You Always Wanted*. New York: Doubleday, 2007.

Clear, James, *Atomic Habits: An Easy & Proven Way to Build Good Habits & Break Bad Ones*, New York: Avery Publishing, 2018.

Covey, Stephen R., *The 7 Habits of Highly Effective People: Restoring the Character Ethic*, New York: Free Press, 1990.

Covey, Stephen R., *Primary Greatness: The 12 Levers of Success*, New York: Simon & Schuster, 2015.

Csikszentmihalyi, Mihaly, *Creativity: Flow and the Psychology of Discovery and Invention*, New York: Harper Perennial, 1996.

Csikszentmihalyi, Mihaly, *Flow: The Psychology of Optimal Experience*, New York: HarperCollins, 1990.

Dweck, Carol, *Mindset: The New Psychology of Success*, New York: Ballantine Books, 2007.

Fromm, Erich, *The Art of Loving*, New York, NY: Harper, 1956.

Gladwell, Malcolm, *Outliers: The Story of Success*, New York, NY: Back Bay Books, 2011.

Golden, Bernard, *Overcoming Destructive Anger: Strategies That Work*, Baltimore: John Hopkins University Press, 2016.

Gostick, Adrian and Elton, Chester, *Leading with Gratitude: Eight Leadership Practices for Extraordinary Business Results*, New York: Harper Business, 2020.

Green, Bryan, *Make the Leap: Think Better, Train Better, Run Faster*, Independently published, 2020.

Greenleaf, Robert K., *Servant Leadership [25th Anniversary Edition]: A Journey into the Nature of Legitimate Power and Greatness*, Mahwah, NJ: Paulist Press, 2012.

Kralik, John, *Simple Act of Gratitude: How Learning to Say Thank You Changed My Life*, New York: Hachette Books, 2011.

Lewis, C. S., *The Four Loves*, London: Geoffrey Bles, 1960.

Massimino, Mike, *Spaceman: An Astronaut's Unlikely Journey to Unlock the Secrets of the Universe*, New York: Three Rivers Press, 2016.

Maxwell, John C., *The 21 Irrefutable Laws of Leadership*, Nashville, TN: HarperCollins Leadership, 2022.

Maxwell, John C., *The 360-degree Leader: Developing Your Influence From Anywhere in the Organization*, Nashville, TN: Nelson Business, 2005.

Morin, Amy, *13 Things Mentally Strong People Don't Do*, New York, NY: HarperCollins Publishers, 2014.

Niebuhr, Reinhold, *The Nature and Destiny of Man: A Christian Interpretation*, First edition, Louisville, KY: Westminster John Knox Press, 1964.

Ostrom, Elinor, *Governing the Commons: The Evolution of Institutions for Collective Action*, Cambridge, England: Cambridge University Press, 1990.

von Furstenberg, Diane, *Own It: The Secret to Life*, New York: Phaidon Press, 2021.

Willink, Jocko and Babin, Leif, *Extreme Ownership: How U.S. Navy SEALs Lead and Win*, New York: St. Martin's Press, November 21, 2017.

Other Recommended Reading

Aquinas, Saint Thomas: https://www.gutenberg.org/ebooks/author/7489

Aristotle: https://www.gutenberg.org/ebooks/author/2747

Arouet, François-Marie, "Voltaire": https://www.gutenberg.org/ebooks/author/913

Augustine, Saint: https://www.gutenberg.org/ebooks/author/1156

Aurelius, Marcus: https://www.gutenberg.org/ebooks/author/998

Chesterton, G. K.: https://www.gutenberg.org/ebooks/author/80

Churchill, Winston: https://www.gutenberg.org/ebooks/author/213

Cicero, Marcus Tullius: https://www.gutenberg.org/ebooks/author/128

Confucius: https://www.gutenberg.org/ebooks/author/1180

Covey, Stephen R.: https://www.franklincovey.com/the-7-habits/

Emerson, Ralph Waldo: https://www.gutenberg.org/ebooks/author/1071

Faulkner, William: https://faulkner.iath.virginia.edu/

Franklin, Benjamin: https://www.gutenberg.org/ebooks/author/92

Fromm, Erich: https://fromm-online.org/

Fuller, R. Buckminster: https://www.bfi.org/

Geisel, Theodor Seuss, "Dr. Seuss": https://www.seussville.com/

Gyatso, Tenzin, "Dalai Lama": https://dalailama.com/

James, William: https://www.gutenberg.org/ebooks/author/325

Jefferson, Thomas: https://www.gutenberg.org/ebooks/author/1638

Kahneman, Daniel: https://kahneman.scholar.princeton.edu/

Kant, Immanuel: https://www.gutenberg.org/ebooks/author/1426

Keller, Helen: https://www.gutenberg.org/ebooks/author/895

Kierkegaard, Søren: https://www.imdb.com/name/nm0452567/

King, Martin Luther, Jr.: https://thekingcenter.org/

Kingsley, Charles: https://www.gutenberg.org/ebooks/author/344

Lewis, C. S.: https://www.gutenberg.org/ebooks/author/782

Lincoln, Abraham: https://www.gutenberg.org/ebooks/author/3

Luther, Martin: https://www.gutenberg.org/ebooks/author/155

MacDonald, George: https://www.gutenberg.org/ebooks/author/127

Maxwell, John C.: http://www.johnmaxwell.com/

Milne, A. A.: https://www.gutenberg.org/ebooks/author/730

Niebuhr, Reinhold: https://niebuhrsociety.typepad.com/

Robinson, Edwin Arlington: https://www.gutenberg.org/ebooks/author/175

Roosevelt, Theodore: https://www.gutenberg.org/ebooks/author/729

Sartre, Jean-Paul: https://curlie.org/Society/Philosophy/Philosophers/S/
Sartre%2C_Jean-Paul/

Spencer, Herbert: https://www.gutenberg.org/ebooks/author/1887

Swift, Jonathan: https://www.gutenberg.org/ebooks/author/326

Syrus, Publilius: http://www.quotationspage.com/quotes/Publilius_Syrus

Thoreau, Henry David: https://www.gutenberg.org/ebooks/author/54

Tzu, Lao (Laozi): https://www.gutenberg.org/ebooks/author/2427

Wooden, John: https://www.coachwooden.com/

NOTES

Preface

1.   Kate Purmal, Lisa Goldman, and Anne Janzer, *The Moonshot Effect: Disrupting Business as Usual* (San Carlos, CA: Wynnefield Business Press, 2016), Kindle.

2.   Stephen R. Covey, *Primary Greatness: The 12 Levers of Success* (New York: Simon & Schuster, 2015). Kindle.

Introduction

1.   Robert K. Greenleaf, *Servant Leadership [25th Anniversary Edition]: A Journey into the Nature of Legitimate Power and Greatness* (Mahwah, NJ: Paulist Press, 2012), Kindle.

Chapter 1 – Unconditional Love

1.   "The Four Loves," Wikipedia, last modified March 24, 2023, https://en.wikipedia.org/wiki/The_Four_Loves.

2.   "The Four Loves," Wikipedia.

3.   "The Four Loves," Wikipedia.

4.   "The Four Loves," Wikipedia.

5.   Steven D. Hales, "The Impossibility of Unconditional Love," *Public Affairs Quarterly* 9, no. 4 (1995): 317-20, http://departments.bloomu.edu/philosophy/pages/content/hales /articlepdf/love.pdf.

6.   Mario Beauregard et al., "The Neural Basis of Unconditional Love," *Psychiatry Research: Neuroimaging* 172 (2009): 93–8, https://institutpsychoneuro.com/wp-content/uploads/2015 /08/Beauregard2009-Unconditional-love.pdf.

7.   Joanna Maselko et al., "Mother's Affection at 8 Months Predicts Emotional Distress in Adulthood," *Journal of Epidemiology and Community Health* 65, no. 7

(2011): 621-25, https://www.researchgate.net/publication/45366547_Mother's_affection_at_8_months_predicts_emotional_distress_in_adulthood.

8. Judith E. Carroll et al., "Childhood Abuse, Parental Warmth, and Adult Multisystem Biological Risk in the Coronary Artery Risk Development in Young Adults Study," *Proceedings of the National Academy of the Sciences*, 110, no. 42 (2013), 17149-53, https://www.pnas.org/doi/abs/10.1073/pnas.1315458110.

9. ChatGPT (GPT-4) (GPT-4), Response to "What are benefits of Unconditional Love?" OpenAI, September 7, 2023.

10. Crystal Raypole, "What's (Unconditional) Love Got to Do with It?" *Healthline*, September 15, 2020, https://www.healthline.com/health/relationships/unconditional-love#what-it-isnt.

11. Thomas Merton, *No Man Is an Island* (New York: Mariner Books, 2002). Kindle.

12. "Switching from Love to Hate in Just One Single Moment," *Reddit*, accessed November 12, 2023, https://www.reddit.com/r/love/comments/18896ko/switching_from_love_to_hate_in_just_one_single/.

13. Allison Abrams, "The Psychology of Hate," *Psychology Today*, March 9, 2017, https://www.psychologytoday.com/gb/blog/nurturing-self-compassion/201703/the-psychology-hate.

14. Abrams, "The Psychology of Hate."

15. *Frontline*, "A Class Divided," episode 9, produced by William Peters, on PBS, March 26, 1985, https://www.pbs.org/wgbh/frontline/documentary/class-divided/.

16. Abrams, "The Psychology of Hate."

17. Abrams, "The Psychology of Hate."

18. Abrams, "The Psychology of Hate."

19. Abrams, "The Psychology of Hate."

20. *Jerry Before Seinfeld*, directed by Michael Bonfiglio (2017; Columbus 81 Productions), Netflix, 40:64, https://www.netflix.com/title/80163156.

21. Katharine Lang, "Are Humans 'Wired' to Hate, and If So, Why?" *Medical News Today*, May 30, 2022, https://www.medicalnewstoday.com/articles/are-humans-wired-to-hate-and-if-so-why.

22. Lang, "Are Humans 'Wired' to Hate?"

23. Semir Zeki and John Paul Romaya, "Neural Correlates of Hate," *PLoS ONE* 3, no. 10 (2008), https://doi.org/10.1371/journal.pone.0003556.

24. Martin Luther King Jr., "Where Do We Go From Here?" speech delivered at the 11th Annual Southern Christian Leadership Conference Convention, Atlanta, Georgia, August 16, 1967, *The Singju Post*, https://singjupost.com/full-transcript-where-do-we-go-from-here-martin-luther-king-jr/?singlepage=1.

25. Rick Hanson, "Let It R.A.I.N.," *Psychology Today*, May 20, 2014, https://www.psychologytoday.com/us/blog/your-wise-brain/201405/let-it-rain.

26. Brad Stulberg, "How to Create Space Between Stimulus and Response," *The Growth Equation*, August 4, 2018, https://thegrowtheq.com/how-to-create-space-between/.

27. ChatGPT (GPT-4), Response to "Who are the most influential thinkers on Unconditional Love?" OpenAI, September 17, 2023.

28. ChatGPT (GPT-4), "Who are the most influential thinkers on Unconditional Love?"

29. ChatGPT (GPT-4), "Who are the most influential thinkers on Unconditional Love?"

30. ChatGPT (GPT-4), Response to "What are the main aspects of Unconditional Love?" OpenAI, September 17, 2023.

31. ChatGPT (GPT-4), Response to "Who are the most influential thinkers on respect?" OpenAI, September 17, 2023.

32. "Mister Rogers' Neighborhood," Wikipedia, last modified June 11, 2024, https://en.wikipedia.org/wiki/Mister_Rogers%27_Neighborhood.

33. "Walking the Beat in Mr. Rogers' Neighborhood, Where a New Day Began Together," produced by Jasmyn Belcher Morris, *Morning Edition*, NPR, March 11, 2016, https://www.npr.org/2016/03/11/469846519/walking-the-beat-in-mr-rogers-neighborhood-where-a-new-day-began-together.

34. Nicholas Cannariato, "Officer Clemmons, Mister Rogers' Neighborhood Policeman Pal, Tells His Story," NPR, April 30, 2020, https://www.npr.org/2020/04/30/847315345/officer-clemmons-mister-rogers-neighborhood-policeman-pal-tells-his-story.

35. Chris Azzopardi, "François Clemmons on What Has—And Hasn't—Changed Since Making History on Mister Rogers," *Oprah Daily*, August 5, 2020, https://www.oprahdaily.com/entertainment/a33473086/mr-rogers-cop-francois-clemmons-interview.

36. Sara Kettler, "In 1969, When Black Americans Were Still Prevented from Swimming Alongside White People, an Episode of 'Mister Rogers' Neighborhood'

Broke the Color Barrier," *Biography*, June 24, 2020, https://www.biography.com/actors/mister-rogers-officer-clemmons-pool.

37. "Walking the Beat in Mr. Rogers' Neighborhood," *Morning Edition*.

38. Azzopardi, "François Clemmons."

39. "Walking the Beat in Mr. Rogers' Neighborhood," *Morning Edition*.

40. Cannariato, "Officer Clemmons."

41. Azzopardi, "François Clemmons."

42. Kettler, "In 1969."

43. Luke 6:31 (New International Version).

44. ChatGPT (GPT-4), Response to "What does the Qur'an say about kindness?" OpenAI, September 17, 2023.

45. ChatGPT (GPT-4), Response to "What does Buddhism say about kindness?" OpenAI, September 17, 2023.

46. ChatGPT (GPT-4), Response to "What does Lao Tzu say about kindness?" OpenAI, September 17, 2023.

47. Deana Landers, "The Power of Compassion," *Morning Coffee Beans*, accessed September 23, 2023, http://morningcoffeebeans.com/the-power-of-compassion.

48. Clara Strauss et al., "What Is Compassion and How Can We Measure It? A Review of Definitions and Measures," *Clinical Psychology Review* 47 (2016): 15-27, https://doi.org/10.1016/j.cpr.2016.05.004.

49. Dalai Lama, *The Power of Compassion* (New Delhi: HarperCollins, 1995).

50. ChatGPT (GPT-4), Response to "What are famous Buddhist quotes about compassion?" OpenAI, September 17, 2023.

51. "Nicholas Winton and the Rescue of Children from Czechoslovakia, 1938–1939," *Holocaust Encyclopedia*, United States Holocaust Memorial Museum, last modified September 8, 2023, https://encyclopedia.ushmm.org/content/en/article/nicholas-winton-and-the-rescue-of-children-from-czechoslovakia-1938-1939.

52. "Nicholas Winton," Wikipedia, last modified June 11, 2024, https://en.wikipedia.org/wiki/Nicholas_Winton.

53. "Nicholas Winton," Wikipedia.

54. Laura E. Brade and Rose Holmes, "Troublesome Sainthood: Nicholas Winton and the Contested History of Child Rescue in Prague, 1938–1940," *History & Memory* 29, no. 1 (2017): 3-40, https://doi.org/10.2979/histmemo.29.1.0003.

55. "Nicholas Winton and the Rescue," *Holocaust Encyclopedia.*

56. "Nicholas Winton," Wikipedia.

57. Brade and Holmes, "Troublesome Sainthood."

58. Vanessa Abrahams and Christine Mason, "Unarmed Truth and Unconditional Love," *Center for Educational Home Improvement*, January 19, 2015, https://www.edimprovement.org/post/unarmed-truth-and-unconditional-love.

59. Martin Luther King Jr., "Dr. Martin Luther King, Jr. Speech at Illinois Wesleyan University, 1966," *Illinois Wesleyan University*, accessed September 23, 2023, https://www.iwu.edu/mlk/page-5.html.

60. Fran Singh, "How an Oklahoma Bombing Victim's Dad Made Friends with Timothy McVeigh's Father," *The Guardian*, April 18, 2015, https://www.theguardian.com/us-news/2015/apr/18/oklahoma-bombing-victim-father-friends-tim-mcveigh-dad.

61. Singh, "How an Oklahoma Bombing Victim's Dad Made Friends."

62. Dmitrij Agroskin, Johannes Klackl, and Eva Jonas, "The Self-Liking Brain: A VBM Study on the Structural Substrate of Self-Esteem," *PubMed Central* 9, no. 1 (2014), January 29, 2014, https://www.ncbi.nlm.nih.gov/pmc/articles/PMC3906048.

63. Sharon Martin, "What is Self-Love and Why Is It So Important?" *Psych Central*, accessed September 18, 2023, https://psychcentral.com/blog/imperfect/2019/05/what-is-self-love-and-why-is-it-so-important.

64. Martin, "What is Self-Love and Why Is It So Important?"

65. Martin, "What is Self-Love and Why Is It So Important?"

66. ChatGPT (GPT-4), Response to "What are the benefits of self-love?" September 18, 2023, https://chat.openai.com.

67. Arlin Cuncic, "What is Unconditional Love?" *Very Well Mind*, November 16, 2022, https://www.verywellmind.com/does-unconditional-love-make-for-healthy-relationships-4165457.

68. "Romanian Orphans," Wikipedia, last modified April 7, 2024, https://en.wikipedia.org/wiki/Romanian_orphans.

69. "Unconditional Love," produced by Alix Spiegel, *This American Life*, NPR, September 15, 2006, 35:30, https://www.thisamericanlife.org/317/unconditional-love.

70. Kendra Cherry, "Compassion vs. Empathy: What's the Difference?" *Very Well Mind*, June 5, 2023, https://www.verywellmind.com/compassion-vs-empathy-what-s-the-difference-7494906.

71. Cherry, "Compassion vs. Empathy."

72. Cherry, "Compassion vs. Empathy."

73. Cherry, "Compassion vs. Empathy."

74. Sigal Barsade, "All You Need is Love…At Work?" *Freedom at Work Talks*, YouTube, November 3, 2015, 20:11, https://www.youtube.com/watch?v=sKNTyGW3o7E.

75. Caroline Njogu, "Leadership and Love: How to Best Influence Those You Lead," *Leaderonomics*, February 25, 2021, https://www.leaderonomics.com/articles/personal/influence-those-you-lead-with-love.

76. Tamiko Cuellar, "Leading with Love: An Unconventional Approach to Leadership," *Forbes*, June 29, 2018, https://www.forbes.com/sites/forbescoachescouncil/2018/06/29/leading-with-love-an-unconventional-approach-to-leadership.

77. Barsade, "All You Need is Love."

Chapter 2 – Unconditional Gratitude

1. R.A. Emmons and M.E. McCullough, "Counting Blessings Versus Burdens: An Experimental Investigation of Gratitude and Subjective Well-being in Daily Life," *Journal of Personality and Social Psychology* 84, no. 2 (2003): 377–389, https://doi.org/10.1037/0022-3514.84.2.377.

2. Dawn Elizabeth, "7 Ways to Practice Unconditional Gratitude in Your Life," *Wild Simple Joy*, February 27, 2023, https://wildsimplejoy.com/what-is-unconditional-gratitude/.

3. Summer Allen, "The Science of Gratitude: A White Paper Prepared for the John Templeton Foundation by the Greater Good Science Center at UC Berkeley," *Greater Good Science Center at UC Berkeley*, accessed September 29, 2023, https://ggsc.berkeley.edu/images/uploads/GGSC-JTF_White_Paper-Gratitude-FINAL.pdf, 3.

4. ChatGPT (GPT-4), Response to "What are the main aspects of Unconditional Gratitude?" OpenAI, September 12, 2023.

5. John Kralik, *Simple Act of Gratitude: How Learning to Say Thank You Changed My Life* (New York: Hachette Books, 2011), Kindle.

6. Kralik, *Simple Act of Gratitude.*

7. "The Mental Health Benefits of Gratitude and How to Cultivate It in Your Life," *Radias Health*, August 28, 2023, https://radiashealth.org/the-mental-health-benefits-of-gratitude-and-how-to-cultivate-it-in-your-life/.

8. Emmons and McCullough, "Counting Blessings Versus Burdens."

9. C.N. Harbaugh and M.W. Vasey, "When Do People Benefit Gratitude Practice?" *The Journal of Positive Psychology* 9, no. 6 (2014): 535–546, https://doi.org/10.1080/17439760.2014.927905.

10. Alex M. Wood, Stephen Joseph, and John Maltby, "Gratitude Uniquely Predicts Satisfaction with Life: Incremental Validity Above the Domains and Facets of the Five-factor Model," *Personality and Individual Differences* 45, no. 1 (2008): 49–54, https://www.sciencedirect.com/science/article/abs/pii/S0191886908000767.

11. J.A. Rash et al., "Gratitude and Well-being: Who Benefits the Most a Gratitude Intervention?" *Applied Psychology: Health and Well-Being* 3, no. 3 (2011): 350–369, https://doi.org/10.1111/j.1758-0854.2011.01058.

12. Kristin J. Homan, Brittany L. Sedlak, and Elizabeth A. Boyd, "Gratitude Buffers the Adverse Effect of Viewing the Thin Ideal on Body Dissatisfaction," *Body Image* 11, no. 3 (2014): 245–250, https://doi.org/10.1016/j.bodyim.2014.03.005.

13. Emmons and McCullough, "Counting Blessings Versus Burdens."

14. Roland Zahn et al., "The Neural Basis of Human Social Values: Evidence from Functional MRI," *Cerebral Cortex* 19, no. 2 (2009): 276–283, https://doi.org/10.1093/cercor/bhn080.

15. P.J. Mills et al., "The Role of Gratitude in Spiritual Well-Being in Asymptomatic Heart Failure Patients," *Spirituality in Clinical Practice* 2, no. 1 (2015): 5--17, https://doi.org/10.1037/scp0000050.

16. Mei-Yee Ng and Wing-Sze Wong, "The Differential Effects of Gratitude and Sleep on Psychological Distress in Patients with Chronic Pain," *Journal of Health Psychology* 18, no. 2 (2013): 263--71, http://dx.doi.org/10.1177/1359105312439733.

17. F.M. Sirois and A.M. Wood, "Gratitude Uniquely Predicts Lower Depression in Chronic Illness Populations," *Health Psychology* 36, no. 2 (2016): 122--32, https://doi.org/10.1037/hea0000436.

18. ChatGPT (GPT-4), Response to "What are the major benefits of gratitude?" OpenAI, September 12, 2023.

19. Shawn Achor, *The Happiness Advantage: The Seven Principles of Positive Psychology That Fuel Success and Performance at Work* (New York: Crown Currency, 2010), Kindle.

20. Nathaniel M. Lambert et al., "More Gratitude, Less Materialism: The Mediating Role of Life Satisfaction," *The Journal of Positive Psychology* 4, no. 1 (2009): 32--42, https://doi.org/10.1080/17439760802216311.

21. ChatGPT (GPT-4), "What are the major benefits of gratitude?"

22. ChatGPT (GPT-4), "What are the major benefits of gratitude?"

23. ChatGPT (GPT-4), Response to "What are the major benefits of gratitude?" OpenAI, September 12, 2023.

24. "Giving Thanks Can Make You Happier," *Harvard Health Publishing*, August 14, 2021, https://www.health.harvard.edu/healthbeat/giving-thanks-can-make-you-happier.

25. Christina N. Armenta, Megan M. Fritz, and Sonja Lyubomirsky, "Functions of Positive Emotions: Gratitude as a Motivator of Self-Improvement and Positive Change," *Emotion Review* 9, no. 3 (2017): 183-190, https://doi.org/10.1177/1754073916669596.

26. Lea Waters, "Predicting Job Satisfaction: Contributions of Individual Gratitude and Institutionalized Gratitude," *Psychology* 3, no. 12 (2012): 1174-1176, https://doi.org/10.4236/psych.2012.312A173.

27. A.M. Grant and A. Wrzesniewski, "I Won't Let You Down... Or Will I? Core Self-evaluations, Other-orientation, Anticipated Guilt and Gratitude, and Job Performance," *Journal of Applied Psychology* 95, no. 1 (2010): 108-121, https://doi.org/10.1037/a0017974.

28. Lynne M. Andersson, Robert A. Giacalone, and Carole L. Jurkiewicz, "On the Relationship of Hope and Gratitude to Corporate Social Responsibility," *Journal of Business Ethics* 70, no. 4 (2007): 401-9, https://doi.org/10.1007/s10551-006-9118-1.

29. Jeffrey R. Spence et al., "Helpful Today, But Not Tomorrow? Feeling Grateful as a Predictor of Daily Organizational Citizenship Behaviors," *Personnel Psychology* 66, no. 3 (2013): 705-38, https://doi.org/10.1111/peps.12051.

30. "Giving Thanks Can Make You Happier," *Harvard Health Publishing*.

31. M.T. Ford et al., "Chronic and Episodic Anger and Gratitude Toward the Organization: Relationships With Organizational and Supervisor Supportiveness and Extrarole Behavior," *Journal of Occupational Health Psychology* 23, no. 2 (2017): 175-87, https://doi.org/10.1037/ocp0000075.

32. Michael Schneider, "Employees Say This 1 Thing Would Make Them Work Harder (And 6 Reasons Why Managers Won't Do It)," *Inc.*, December 28, 2017,

https://www.inc.com/michael-schneider/employees-say-this-1-thing-would-make-them-work-harder-and-6-reasons-why-managers-wont-do-it.html.

33. "Gratitude Survey—Conducted for the John Templeton Foundation," overseen by Janice Kaplan, June-October 2012, https://www.templeton.org/discoveries/science-of-gratitude.

34. ChatGPT (GPT-4), "What are the major benefits of gratitude?"

35. Allen, "The Science of Gratitude," 30.

36. ChatGPT (GPT-4), Response to "Why do we fail to say thank you?" OpenAI, October 3, 2023.

37. Mary Welsh Hemingway, *How It Was* (New York: Knopf, 1976).

38. ChatGPT (GPT-4), Response to "What's wrong with worrying about first-world problems?" OpenAI, September 15, 2023.

39. ChatGPT (GPT-4), "What's wrong with worrying about first-world problems?"

40. Robin M. Kowalski, "Complaints and Complaining: Functions, Antecedents, and Consequences," *Psychological Bulletin* 119, no. 2 (1996): 179-96, https://doi.org/10.1037/0033-2909.119.2.179.

41. Brad J. Bushman, "Does Venting Anger Feed or Extinguish the Flame? Catharsis, Rumination, Distraction, Anger, and Aggressive Responding," *Personality and Social Psychology Bulletin* 28, no. 6 (2002): 724--31, https://doi.org/10.1177/0146167202289002.

42. Steven Parton, "The Science of Happiness: Why Complaining is Literally Killing You," *PsychPedia*, accessed June 26, 2024, https://psychpedia.blogspot.com/2015/11/the-science-of-happiness-why.html.

43. Susan T. Fiske, "Attention and Weight in Person Perception: The Impact of Negative and Extreme Behavior," *Journal of Personality and Social Psychology* 38, no. 6 (1980): 889--906, https://doi.org/10.1037/0022-3514.38.6.889.

44. Will Bowen, *A Complaint Free World: How to Stop Complaining and Start Enjoying the Life You Always Wanted* (New York: Doubleday, 2007), Kindle.

45. Bowen, *A Complaint Free World*.

46. Bowen, *A Complaint Free World*.

47. Bowen, *A Complaint Free World*.

48. Bowen, *A Complaint Free World*.

49. Bowen, *A Complaint Free World*.

50. Bowen, *A Complaint Free World*.

51. Bowen, *A Complaint Free World*.

52. Adrian Gostick and Chester Elton, *Leading with Gratitude: Eight Leadership Practices for Extraordinary Business Results* (New York: Harper Business, 2020), Kindle.

53. 1 Thess. 5:18 (NIV).

54. Eph. 5:20 (NIV).

55. Ps. 107:1 (NIV).

56. Ps. 118:24 (NIV).

57. Jas. 1:17 (NIV).

58. ChatGPT (GPT-4), Response to "What does Islam say about gratitude?" OpenAI, September 17, 2023.

59. ChatGPT (GPT-4), Response to "What does Buddhism say about gratitude?" OpenAI, September 17, 2023.

60. ChatGPT (GPT-4), Response to "What does Confucianism say about gratitude?" OpenAI, September 17, 2023.

61. Georgian Benta, "Losing Sight & Hearing But Not Losing Gratitude: Interview with Aaron Hale," *The Gratitude Podcast*, episode 846, July 3, 2023, 47:49, https://omny.fm/shows/the-gratitude-podcast/losing-sight-hearing-but-not-losing-gratitude-aaro.

62. ChatGPT (GPT-4), Response to "What forms does gratitude take?" OpenAI, September 17, 2023.

63. Adrian Gostick and Chester Elton, "Want a Happier Personal Life? Try Leading with Gratitude," *NBC News*, March 3, 2020, https://www.nbcnews.com/better/lifestyle/want-happier-personal-life-try-leading-gratitude-ncna1147371.

64. ChatGPT (GPT-4), "What forms does gratitude take?"

65. ChatGPT (GPT-4), Response to "What should we be grateful for?" OpenAI, September 17, 2023.

66. ChatGPT (GPT-4), "What forms does gratitude take?"

67. ChatGPT (GPT-4), "What forms does gratitude take?"

68. Gostick and Elton, *Leading with Gratitude*.

69. Ryan Fehr et al., "The Grateful Workplace: A Multilevel Model of Gratitude in Organizations," *Academy of Management Review* 42, no. 2 (2017): 361-381, https://doi.org/10.5465/amr.2014.0374.

70. Fehr et al., "The Grateful Workplace."

71. Jack Zenger and Joseph Folkman, "Why Do So Many Managers Avoid Giving Praise?" *Harvard Business Review*, May 2, 2017, https://hbr.org/2017/05/why-do-so-many-managers-avoid-giving-praise.

72. Gostick and Elton, *Leading with Gratitude*.

73. Anh Dao Pham, *Glue: How Project Leaders Create Cohesive, Engaged, High-Performing Teams* (New York: G&D Media, 2022), Kindle.

74. Gostick and Elton, *Leading with Gratitude*.

75. Shawn Achor, *The Happiness Advantage: The Seven Principles of Positive Psychology That Fuel Success and Performance at Work* (New York: Crown Currency Publishing, 2010), Kindle.

76. Gostick and Elton, *Leading with Gratitude*.

Chapter 3 – Unconditional Integrity

1. Terry Gross, "Pediatrician Who Exposed Flint Water Crisis Shares Her Story Of Resistance," *Fresh Air*, NPR, June 25, 2018, https://www.npr.org/sections/health-shots/2018/06/25/623126968/pediatrician-who-exposed-flint-water-crisis-shares-her-story-of-resistance.

2. Gross, "Pediatrician Who Exposed Flint Water Crisis."

3. Gross, "Pediatrician Who Exposed Flint Water Crisis."

4. Gross, "Pediatrician Who Exposed Flint Water Crisis."

5. Bob Day, "'Easy Eddie' and Butch O'Hare: Two Stories; One Lesson," *The Daily Declaration*, October 26, 2021, https://dailydeclaration.org.au/2021/10/26/easy-eddie-and-butch-ohare-two-stories-one-lesson/.

6. Day, "'Easy Eddie' and Butch O'Hare."

7. Day, "'Easy Eddie' and Butch O'Hare."

8. Craig Kaiser, "The Crucial Role of Empathy in Crisis Management," *Phillips Kaiser*, accessed September 7, 2024, https://phillipskaiser.com/crucial-role-of-empathy-in-crisis-management/.

9. Kaiser, "The Crucial Role of Empathy."

10. Kaiser, "The Crucial Role of Empathy."

11. *Meditations in Wall Street* (New York : W. Morrow & company, 1940).

12. Jean Decety and Jason M. Cowell, "Our Brains are Wired for Morality: Evolution, Development, and Neuroscience," *Frontiers for Young Minds*, March 9, 2016, https://kids.frontiersin.org/articles/10.3389/frym.2016.00003.

13. Meg Selig, "9 Surprising Superpowers of Knowing Your Core Values," *Psychology Today*, November 27, 2018, https://www.psychologytoday.com/us/blog/changepower/201811/9-surprising-superpowers-knowing-your-core-values.

14. Kat Boogaard, "What Is Personal Integrity and Why Is It Important?" *Fingerprint for Success*, accessed October 15, 2023, https://www.fingerprintforsuccess.com/blog/personal-integrity#toc-section-1.

15. Craig Neff, "Scorecard," *Sports Illustrated*, July 10, 1989, https://vault.si.com/vault/1989 /07/10/scorecard.

16. Travis Bradberry, "10 Ways Ridiculously Successful People Think Differently," *Talent Smart EQ*, December 13, 2017, https://www.talentsmarteq.com/articles/10-ways-ridiculously-successful-people-think-differently/.

17. Martin Niemöller, "First they came for the Socialists...," *Holocaust Encyclopedia*, accessed September 1, 2024, https://encyclopedia.ushmm.org/content/en/photo/quotation-from-martin-niemoeller.

18. Dan Ariely, *The (Honest) Truth About Dishonesty: How We Lie to Everyone—Especially Ourselves* (New York: HarperCollins, 2012), Kindle.

19. Ariely, *The (Honest) Truth About Dishonesty*.

20. "Facts and Statistics," *International Center for Academic Integrity*, accessed July 7, 2024, https://academicintegrity.org/resources/facts-and-statistics.

21. Aarti Maharaj, "What the Data Shows: A Global View of Workplace Integrity," *Ethisphere*, June 9, 2016, https://magazine.ethisphere.com/what-the-data-shows-a-global-view-of-workplace-integrity/.

22. Theresa Agovino, "How to Cultivate Ethical Leaders," *Society for Human Resource Management*, November/December 2018, https://www.shrm.org/hr-today/news/hr-magazine/1118/pages/how-to-cultivate-ethical-leaders.aspx.

23. Steven D. Olson, "Shaping an Ethical Workplace Culture," *Society for Human Resource Management's Effective Practice Guidelines Series*, 2013, https://www.shrm.org/hr-today/trends-and-forecasting/special-reports-and-expert-views/Documents/Ethical-Workplace-Culture.pdf.

24. Ariely, *The (Honest) Truth About Dishonesty*.

25. Ariely, *The (Honest) Truth About Dishonesty*.

26. Ariely, *The (Honest) Truth About Dishonesty*.

27. Ariely, *The (Honest) Truth About Dishonesty*.

28. Ariely, *The (Honest) Truth About Dishonesty*.

29. "The Hand of God," Wikipedia, last modified June 24, 2024, https://en.wikipedia. org/wiki/The_hand_of_God.

30. "The Hand of God," Wikipedia.

31. "The Hand of God," Wikipedia.

32. "The Hand of God," Wikipedia.

33. "The Hand of God," Wikipedia.

34. "The Hand of God," Wikipedia.

35. Steven G. Hertz and Tobias Krettenauer, "Does Moral Identity Effectively Predict Moral Behavior?: A Meta-Analysis," *Review of General Psychology* 20, no. 2 (2016): 129-140, https://doi.org/10.1037/gpr0000062.

36. ChatGPT (GPT-4), Response to "Who Are the Most Influential Thinkers on Integrity?" OpenAI, September 17, 2023.

37. ChatGPT (GPT-4), "Who Are the Most Influential Thinkers on Integrity?"

38. Noriko Takigami, "Essence of Confucius and Confucianism: Yi, Zhi, and Xin," *Research Institute for Creating New Paradigms based on Eastern and Western Wisdom*, November 19, 2019, https://inst-east-and-west.org/en/learning/2019/002725. html.

39. Daniel Shek, Lu Yu, and Xiao Fu, "Confucian Virtues and Chinese Adolescent Development: A Conceptual Review," *International Journal on Adolescent Medical Health* 25, no. 4 (2013): 335--344, https://doi.org/10.1515/ijamh-2013-0031.

40. ChatGPT (GPT-4), "Who Are the Most Influential Thinkers on Integrity?"

41. ChatGPT (GPT-4), "Who Are the Most Influential Thinkers on Integrity?"

42. ChatGPT (GPT-4), "Who Are the Most Influential Thinkers on Integrity?"

43. Linda Bloom and Charlie Bloom, "Self-trust and How to Build It," *Psychology Today*, September 12, 2019, https://www.psychologytoday.com/us/blog/stronger-the-broken-places/201909/self-trust-and-how-build-it.

44. ChatGPT (GPT-4), "Who Are the Most Influential Thinkers on Integrity?"

45. ChatGPT (GPT-4), "Who Are the Most Influential Thinkers on Integrity?"

46. ChatGPT (GPT-4), "Who Are the Most Influential Thinkers on Integrity?"

47. ChatGPT (GPT-4), "Who Are the Most Influential Thinkers on Integrity?"

48. Alexandre Sokolowski, "The Day Andy Roddick's Sportsmanship Cost Him a Win," *Tennis Majors*, May 5, 2024, https://www.tennismajors.com/our-features/on-this-day/may-5-2005-the-day-andy-roddicks-sportsmanship-cost-him-victory-210307.html.

49. Sokolowski, "The Day Andy Roddick's Sportsmanship Cost Him a Win."

50. Sokolowski, "The Day Andy Roddick's Sportsmanship Cost Him a Win."

51. Sokolowski, "The Day Andy Roddick's Sportsmanship Cost Him a Win."

52. Sokolowski, "The Day Andy Roddick's Sportsmanship Cost Him a Win."

53. Frank Deford, "In Praise of Roddick and Old-Fashioned Sportsmanship," *NPR*, May 11, 2015, https://www.npr.org/2005/05/11/4647602/in-praise-of-roddick-and-old-fashioned-sportsmanship.

54. Stuart Fensterheim, "Doing the Right Thing: Maintaining Integrity in Your Relationship," *Good Therapy*, January 8, 2018, https://www.goodtherapy.org/blog/doing-the-right-thing-maintaining-integrity-in-your-relationship-0108184.

55. Fensterheim, "Doing the Right Thing."

56. Fensterheim, "Doing the Right Thing."

57. Sokolowski, "The Day Andy Roddick's Sportsmanship Cost Him a Win."

58. Sokolowski, "The Day Andy Roddick's Sportsmanship Cost Him a Win."

59. Deford, "In Praise of Roddick."

60. Theresa Agovino, "How to Cultivate Ethical Leaders," *Society for Human Resource Management*, October 30, 2018, https://www.shrm.org/topics-tools/news/hr-magazine/how-to-cultivate-ethical-leaders.

61. "Integrity in the Workplace: Definition and Examples," *Indeed*, July 31, 2023, https://www.indeed.com/career-advice/career-development/integrity-at-work.

62. Boogaard, "What Is Personal Integrity and Why Is It Important?"

63. John C. Maxwell, *The 21 Irrefutable Laws of Leadership* (Nashville, TN: HarperCollins Leadership, 2022), Kindle. Originally published in 1998 by Thomas Nelson.

64. "Nelson Mandela," Wikipedia, last modified November 30, 2023, https://en.wikipedia.org/wiki/Nelson_Mandela.

65. "Nelson Mandela," Wikipedia.

66. "Nelson Mandela," Wikipedia.

Chapter 4 – Unconditional Accountability

1. For millennia, there have been philosophical and theological debates about whether or not humans have free will. I don't present other sides of those debates because (1) the majority of mainstream thinking—religious and secular—supports the notion of free will and (2) arguments against free will are, by definition, outside the bounds of this book, which is focused on how we can pursue values and virtues that matter.

2. Vanessa Jakubowski, "Do You Live The Accountability Cycle?" *LinkedIn*, March 24, 2016, https://www.linkedin.com/pulse/do-you-live-accountability-cycle-vanessa-jakubowski-llb-hons-/.

3. Jakubowski, "Do You Live The Accountability Cycle?"

4. Singh, "How an Oklahoma Bombing Victim's Dad Made Friends."

5. Kaiser, "The Crucial Role of Empathy."

6. Jonathan Eig, *King: A Life* (New York: Farrar, Straus and Giroux, 2023), Kindle.

7. Mahatma K. Gandhi, *Autobiography: The Story of My Experiments with Truth* (New York: Dover Publications, 1948).

8. ChatGPT (GPT-4), Response to "Why Does Accountability Matter?" OpenAI, October 17, 2023.

9. ChatGPT (GPT-4), "Why Does Accountability Matter?"

10. Amanda, "How Accountability Can Improve Your Life."

11. Apoorva Mandavilli, "The World's Worst Industrial Disaster is Still Unfolding," *The Atlantic*, July 10, 2018, https://www.theatlantic.com/science/archive/2018/07/the-worlds-worst-industrial-disaster-is-still-unfolding/560726/.

12. Mandavilli, "The World's Worst Industrial Disaster."

13. Mandavilli, "The World's Worst Industrial Disaster."

14. Mandavilli, "The World's Worst Industrial Disaster."

15. Anita Jackson, "The 3 D's of Avoiding Accountability: Deny, Deflect, Diffuse," *LinkedIn*, January 10, 2021, https://www.linkedin.com/pulse/3-ds-avoiding-accountability-deny-deflect-diffuse-anita-jackson/.

16. ChatGPT (GPT-4), Response to "What Are Ways We Can Fall Short on Accountability?" OpenAI, November 4, 2023.

17. Mandavilli, "The World's Worst Industrial Disaster."

18. Mandavilli, "The World's Worst Industrial Disaster."

19. Mandavilli, "The World's Worst Industrial Disaster."

20. Mandavilli, "The World's Worst Industrial Disaster."

21. Mandavilli, "The World's Worst Industrial Disaster."

22. Mandavilli, "The World's Worst Industrial Disaster."

23. Mandavilli, "The World's Worst Industrial Disaster."

24. ChatGPT (GPT-4), "What Are Ways We Can Fall Short on Accountability?"

25. Cara Amores, "Power Tool: Entitlement vs, Accountability," *International Coach Academy*, November 30, 2020, https://coachcampus.com/coach-portfolios/power-tools/cara-amores-entitlement-vs-accountability/.

26. Amores, "Power Tool."

27. Karen Deerwster, *The Entitlement-Free Child* (Naperville, IL: Sourcebooks, 2009), 5.

28. E. Ng, L. Schweitzer, and S. Lyons, "New Generation, Great Expectations: A Field Study of the Millennial Generation," *Journal of Business and Psychology* 25 (2010): 281-92, https://doi.org/10.1007/s10869-010-9159-4.

29. Amores, "Power Tool."

30. ChatGPT (GPT-4), Response to "Explain the Tragedy of the Commons," OpenAI, November 4, 2023.

31. "Prize in Economic Sciences 2009: Elinor Ostrom," *Nobel Prize*, accessed November 8, 2023, https://www.nobelprize.org/prizes/economic-sciences/2009/ostrom/facts/.

32. ChatGPT (GPT-4), Response to "How Does the Tragedy of the Commons Apply to Personal Accountability?" OpenAI, November 4, 2023.

33. ChatGPT (GPT-4), "How Does the Tragedy of the Commons Apply to Personal Accountability?"

34. ChatGPT (GPT-4), "How Does the Tragedy of the Commons Apply to Personal Accountability?"

35. Tim Russell and Drew Gysi, "The Parable of the Talents (Matthew 25)," *The Stewardology Podcast*, episode 48, produced by Tyler Rutherford, August 23, 2021, 41:14, https://stewardologypodcast.com/048-the-parable-of-the-talents/.

36. Russell and Gysi, "The Parable of the Talents."

37. Russell and Gysi, "The Parable of the Talents."

38. Russell and Gysi, "The Parable of the Talents."

39. ChatGPT (GPT-4), Response to "What Does Islam Say about Accountability?" OpenAI, November 4, 2023.

40. ChatGPT (GPT-4), Response to "What are Quotes by Prophet Muhammad about Accountability?" OpenAI, November 4, 2023.

41. ChatGPT (GPT-4), Response to "What are Quotes from Judaism about Accountability?" November 4, 2023, https://chat.openai.com.

42. ChatGPT (GPT-4), Response to "What are Quotes by Sartre about Moral Responsibility?" OpenAI, November 4, 2023.

43. ChatGPT (GPT-4), "What are Quotes by Sartre about Moral Responsibility?"

44. "Nicholas Winton and the Rescue," *Holocaust Encyclopedia*.

45. ChatGPT (GPT-4), Response to "Who Are the Greatest Writers on Personal Accountability?" OpenAI, November 4, 2023.

46. Amy Morin, "13 Things Mentally Strong People Don't Do," *Amy Morin LCSW*, accessed November 17, 2023, https://amymorinlcsw.com/mentally-strong-people.

47. ChatGPT (GPT-4), "Who Are the Greatest Writers on Personal Accountability?"

48. ChatGPT (GPT-4), "Who Are the Greatest Writers on Personal Accountability?"

49. Gross, "Pediatrician Who Exposed Flint Water Crisis."

50. ChatGPT (GPT-4), Response to "What Are Quotes by John Maxwell on Accountability?" OpenAI, November 4, 2023.

51. Amores, "Power Tool."

52. Amores, "Power Tool."

53. Day, "'Easy Eddie' and Butch O'Hare."

54. ChatGPT (GPT-4), Response to "What Are Ways to Provide Personal Added Value?" OpenAI, November 17, 2023.

55. Benta, "Losing Sight & Hearing But Not Losing Gratitude."

56. Maureen Corrigan, "The Incredible Story Of Chilean Miners Rescued From The 'Deep Down Dark,'" *Fresh Air*, NPR, October 29, 2014, https://www.npr.org/2014/10/29/359839104/the-incredible-story-of-chilean-miners-rescued-from-the-deep-down-dark.

57. Bryan Green, "The Five Stages of Responsibility (aka the Path to Accountability)," *Make The Leap Book*, February 19, 2022, https://maketheleapbook.com/blogs/news/five-stages-of-responsibility-aka-path-to-accountability.

58. Corrigan, "The Incredible Story Of Chilean Miners Rescued."

59. Corrigan, "The Incredible Story Of Chilean Miners Rescued."

60. Rachael Pace, "15 Easy Ways to Take More Accountability in Relationships," *Marriage*, December 9, 2022, https://www.marriage.com/advice/relationship/accountability-in-elationships/.

61. Pace, "15 Easy Ways to Take More Accountability in Relationships."

62. "Leadership and Unconditional Accountability," *Executive Forum*, accessed November 17, 2023, https://executiveforum.com/leadership-accountability/.

63. Pace, "15 Easy Ways to Take More Accountability in Relationships."

64. Matt James, "React vs. Respond: What's the Difference?" *Psychology Today*, September 1, 2016, https://www.psychologytoday.com/us/blog/focus-forgiveness/201609/react-vs-respond.

65. Corrigan, "The Incredible Story Of Chilean Miners Rescued."

66. Pace, "15 Easy Ways to Take More Accountability in Relationships."

67. Sanjana Gupta, "How Compromise Helps Your Relationship," *Very Well Mind*, July 18, 2023, https://www.verywellmind.com/compromise-in-relationships-7559559.

68. "Leadership and Unconditional Accountability," ExecutiveForum.com.

69. Larry Rohter, *Into the Amazon: The Life of Cândido Rondon, Trailblazing Explorer, Scientist, Statesman, and Conservationist* (New York: W.W. Norton & Company, 2023). Kindle.

70. Joe Mastey, "On 'Owning It,'" *Medium*, October 19, 2014, https://medium.com/@jmmastey/on-owning-it-d02006ec958c.

71. Kaiser, "The Crucial Role of Empathy."

72. Flora Richards-Gustafson, "Importance of Accountability & Integrity in Workplace," *BizFluent*, September 26, 2017, https://bizfluent.com/info-8211344-organizational-culture-negative-effects.html.

73. Amores, "Power Tool."

74. "Top Barriers to a More Accountable Culture at Work," *LSA Global*, November 19, 2023, https://lsaglobal.com/top-barriers-to-a-more-accountable-culture/.

75. Jocko Willink and Leif Babin, *Extreme Ownership: How U.S. Navy SEALs Lead and Win* (New York: St. Martin's Press, 2017), Kindle.

76. Willink and Babin, *Extreme Ownership*.

77. Willink and Babin, *Extreme Ownership*.

78. Bob Helbig, "Leadership Accountability: What It Looks Like, Why It Matters," *Washington Post*, August 22, 2023, https://jobs.washingtonpost.com/article/leadership-accountability-what-it-looks-like-why-it-matters/.

79. "Top Barriers to a More Accountable Culture at Work," *LSA Global*.

80. Helbig, "Leadership Accountability."

81. Willink and Babin, *Extreme Ownership*.

82. Willink and Babin, *Extreme Ownership*.

83. Willink and Babin, *Extreme Ownership*.

84. "Top Barriers to a More Accountable Culture at Work," *LSA Global*.

85. Helbig, "Leadership Accountability."

86. Willink and Babin, *Extreme Ownership*.

87. Willink and Babin, *Extreme Ownership*.

Chapter 5 – Unconditional Endeavor

1. Stephen, "The Power of Determination," *Academic Tips*, August 29, 2012, https://academictips.org/blogs/the-power-of-determination-true-story/.

2. Stephen, "The Power of Determination."

3. Stephen, "The Power of Determination."

4. Stephen, "The Power of Determination."

5. Stephen, "The Power of Determination."

6. "Glenn Cunningham (Athlete)," Wikipedia, last modified October 30, 2023, https://en.wikipedia.org/wiki/Glenn_Cunningham_(athlete).

7. "Glenn Cunningham," Wikipedia.

8. Stephen, "The Power of Determination."

9. "Walt Disney," Wikipedia, last modified January 7, 2024, https://en.wikipedia.org/wiki/Walt_Disney.

10. "Walt Disney," Wikipedia.

11. Sanju Pradeepa, "Why Attitude Is Important: 14 Ways to Develop and Maintain," *Believe In Mind*, February 23, 2023, https://www.believeinmind.com/self-growth/why-is-attitude-important.

12. Dulin, "How to Always Try Your Best."

13. Sanju Pradeepa, "18 Characteristics of Positive Attitudes," *Believe In Mind*, February 18, 2023, https://www.believeinmind.com/self-growth/characteristics-of-positive-attitudes.

14. Pradeepa, "Why Attitude Is Important."

15. Ece Elif Öcal et al., "Relationship between Mental Disorders and Optimism in a Community-Based Sample of Adults," *Behavioral Sciences* 12, no. 2 (2022), https://doi.org/10.3390/bs12020052.

16. Scott Lear, "How Optimism Benefits Your Health," *Heart and Stroke*, March 5, 2020, https://www.heartandstroke.ca/articles/how-optimism-benefits-your-health.

17. Dulin, "How to Always Try Your Best."

18. "Helen Keller," Wikipedia, last modified January 28, 2024, https://en.wikipedia.org/wiki/Helen_Keller.

19. Helen Keller, "Optimism: An Essay," *Project Gutenberg*, March 13, 2010, https://www.gutenberg.org/ebooks/31622.

20. "The Power of Preparation," *Kaizen Workforce Solutions*, May 3, 2022, https://www.kaizenworkforcesolutions.com/2022/05/the-power-of-preparation/.

21. Michael Preston, "Preparation is the Key to Facing Whatever May Come Your Way," *University of Central Florida News*, October 26, 2016, https://www.ucf.edu/news/preparation-key-helping-face-whatever-may-come-way.

22. Charles Murray and Catherine Bly Cox, *Apollo: The Race to the Moon* (New York, Simon & Schuster, 1989).

23. Christopher Klein, "Inside Theodore Roosevelt's Gilded Age Upbringing," *History*, May 3, 2022, https://www.history.com/news/theodore-roosevelt-childhood-new-york.

24. Klein, "Inside Theodore Roosevelt's Gilded Age Upbringing."

25. Klein, "Inside Theodore Roosevelt's Gilded Age Upbringing."

26. "Theodore Roosevelt," Wikipedia, last modified February 4, 2024, https://en.wikipedia.org/wiki/Theodore_Roosevelt.

27. Rainer Zitelmann, "What Focus Really Means: Learning From Bill Gates, Warren Buffett And Steve Jobs," *Forbes*, October 28, 2019, https://www.forbes.com/sites/rainerzitelmann/2019/10/28/what-focus-really-means-learning-from-bill-gates-warren-buffett-and-steve-jobs.

28. Jon Dulin, "How To Always Try Your Best," *Unfinished Success*, June 17, 2021, https://unfinishedsuccess.com/how-to-always-try-your-best/.

29. Stephen, "The Power of Determination."

30. John Crimmins, "Embracing Your Individuality: The Power of Uniqueness," *Health News*, December 13, 2023, https://healthnews.com/mental-health/self-care-and-therapy/individuality-the-power-of-uniqueness/.

31. John A. Wagner III et al., "Individualism—Collectivism and Team Member Performance: Another Look," *Journal of Organizational Behavior* 33 (2012): 946-963, https://doi.org/10.1002/job.783.

32. Tong Li and Ningyu Tang, "Inclusive Leadership and Innovative Performance: A Multi-Level Mediation Model of Psychological Safety," *Frontiers in Psychology* 13 (2022), https://doi.org/10.3389/fpsyg.2022.934831.

33. Maxwell King, *The Good Neighbor: The Life and Work of Fred Rogers* (New York: Abrams Press, 2018).

34. Maxwell King, "Mr. Rogers Had a Simple Set of Rules for Talking to Children," *The Atlantic*, June 8, 2018, https://www.theatlantic.com/family/archive/2018/06/mr-rogers-neighborhood-talking-to-kids/562352/.

35. N.H. Zainal and M.G. Newman, "Relation Between Cognitive and Behavioral Strategies and Future Change in Common Mental Health Problems Across 18 Years," *Journal of Abnormal Psychology* 128, no. 4 (2019): 295-304, https://doi.org/10.1037/abn0000428.

36. Sanju Pradeepa, "Benefits of Perseverance: 8 Reasons Why Perseverance Matters," *Believe In Mind*, September 3, 2023, https://www.believeinmind.com/self-growth/benefits-of-perseverance.

37. "All About Tom," *Thomas Alva Edison Foundations*, accessed February 24, 2024, https://www.thomasedison.org/all-about-tom.

38. "All About Tom," *Thomas Alva Edison Foundations*.

39. Srinivas Rao, "Why Practice Matters Just As Much If Not More Than Performance," *Medium*, August 25, 2016, https://medium.com/the-mission/why-practice-matters-just-as-much-if-not-more-than-performance-545bc6250d45.

40. Kuldeep Meena, "5 Reasons Practice Is Important," *Medium*, October 13, 2019, https://medium.com/speedlabs/5-reasons-practice-is-important-48667e15870c.

41. Erica Hendry, "7 Epic Fails Brought to You By the Genius Mind of Thomas Edison," *Smithsonian Magazine*, November 20, 2013, https://www.smithsonianmag.com/innovation/7-epic-fails-brought-to-you-by-the-genius-mind-of-thomas-edison-180947786/.

42. Hendry, "7 Epic Fails Brought to You By the Genius Mind of Thomas Edison."

43. "Thomas Edison National Historical Park New Jersey," *National Park Service*, accessed February 28, 2025, https://home.nps.gov/edis/learn/education/index.htm.

44. Richard Feloni, "Thomas Edison's Reaction To His Factory Burning Down Shows Why He Was So Successful," *Business Insider*, May 9, 2014, https://www.businessinsider.com/thomas-edison-in-the-obstacle-is-the-way-2014-5.

45. Diane Vaughan, *The Challenger Launch Decision: Risky Technology, Culture, and Deviance at NASA* (Chicago: University of Chicago Press, 1996).

46. Vibhu Kher, "How Following Someone Else's Path Can Lead to Depression," *Tiny Buddha*, accessed January 14, 2024, https://tinybuddha.com/blog/how-following-someone-elses-path-can-lead-to-depression.

47. Dulin, "How To Always Try Your Best."

48. John T. Cacioppo, Stephanie Cacioppo, and Jackie K. Gollan, "The Negativity Bias: Conceptualization, Quantification, and Individual Differences," *Behavioral and Brain Sciences* 37, no. 3 (2014): 309-310, https://doi.org/10.1017/s0140525x13002537.

49. T.A. Ito et al., "Negative Information Weighs More Heavily on the Brain: The Negativity Bias in Evaluative Categorizations," *Journal of Personality and Social Psychology* 75, no. 4 (1998): 887--900, https://doi.org/10.1037/0022-3514.75.4.887.

50. Daniel Kahneman, *Thinking, Fast and Slow* (New York: Farrar, Straus and Giroux, 2011), Kindle.

51. Elizabeth Scott, "Signs of Pessimism and How to Respond," *Very Well Mind*, September 12, 2022, https://www.verywellmind.com/is-it-safer-to-be-a-pessimist-3144874.

52. ChatGPT (GPT-4), Response to "How Do People Fall Short on Attitude?" OpenAI, January 6, 2024.

53. ChatGPT (GPT-4), "How Do People Fall Short on Attitude?"

54. ChatGPT (GPT-4), "How Do People Fall Short on Attitude?"

55. ChatGPT (GPT-4), "How Do People Fall Short on Attitude?"

56. Dorothy Herrmann, *Helen Keller: A Life* (New York: Knopf, 1999).

57. Courtney G. Brooks, et al., *Chariots for Apollo: The NASA History of Manned Lunar Spacecraft to 1969* (Garden City, NY, Dover Publications, 1979).

58. ChatGPT (GPT-4), Response to "How Can People Fall Short on Giving Effort?" OpenAI, January 6, 2024.

59. ChatGPT (GPT-4), "How Can People Fall Short on Giving Effort?"

60. Andrew Roberts, *Churchill: Walking with Destiny* (New York: Viking, 2018)

61. Sam Chia, "15 Ways to Improve Your Focus and Concentration," *Better Up*, April 7, 2023, https://www.betterup.com/blog/15-ways-to-improve-your-focus-and-concentration-skills.

62. Jill Jonnes, *Empires of Light: Edison, Tesla, Westinghouse, and the Race to Electrify the World* (New York: Random House, 2003).

63. Travis Bradberry, "9 Things Emotionally Intelligent People Won't Do," *Talent Smart EQ*, accessed January 19, 2024, https://www.talentsmarteq.com/9-things-emotionally-intelligent-people-wont-do/.

64. "Perfectionism," *Good Therapy*, last updated November 5, 2019, https://www.goodtherapy.org/learn-about-therapy/issues/perfectionism.

65. Remy Blumenfeld, "Why 'Doing Your Best' Is A Better Bet than 'Being The Best,'" *Forbes*, April 14, 2019, https://www.forbes.com/sites/remyblumenfeld/2019/04/14/why-doing-your-best-is-a-better-bet-than-being-the-best.

66. Xinjin Zhao, "Winning vs. Succeeding," *LinkedIn*, August 26, 2023, https://www.linkedin.com/pulse/winning-vs-succeeding-xinjin-zhao/.

67. Zhao, "Winning vs. Succeeding."

68. Diane Vaughan, *The Challenger Launch Decision: Risky Technology, Culture, and Deviance at NASA* (Chicago: University of Chicago Press, 1996).

69. "Walt Disney," Wikipedia.

70. Matthew Brzezinski, *Red Moon Rising: Sputnik and the Hidden Rivalries that Ignited the Space Age* (New York: Times Books, 2007).

71. Eliot Brown and Maureen Farrell, *The Cult of We: WeWork, Adam Neumann, and the Start-up Delusion* (New York: Crown Publishing, 2021).

72. Bob Casey, "Henry Ford: Case Study of an Innovator," *The Henry Ford*, July 21, 2021, https://www.thehenryford.org/explore/blog/henry-ford-case-study-of-an-innovator.

73. Casey, "Henry Ford."

74. Casey, "Henry Ford."

75. Casey, "Henry Ford."

76. Casey, "Henry Ford."

77. Travis Bradberry, "10 Ways Ridiculously Successful People Think Differently," *Talent Smart EQ*, December 13, 2017, https://www.talentsmarteq.com/articles/10-ways-ridiculously-successful-people-think-differently.

78. Stephen R. Covey, *The 7 Habits of Highly Effective People* (New York: Simon & Schuster, 1989), 99.

79. Keller, "Optimism."

80. ChatGPT (GPT-4), Response to "The Most Influential Thinkers on Attitude," OpenAI, January 6, 2024.

81. William James, "Is Life Worth Living?" *International Journal of Ethics* 6, no. 1 (1895): 1–24. http://www.jstor.org/stable/2375619.

82. Amy Morin, "18 Habits of Mentally Strong People," *Amy Morin LCSW*, accessed November 17, 2023, https://amymorinlcsw.com/mentally-strong-people.

83. Winston S. Churchill, *The Gathering Storm* (Delhi, India: Neha Publishers & Distributors, 2022).

84. Andrew Roberts, *Churchill: Walking with Destiny* (New York: Viking, 2018)

85. Scott H. Young, "What Does It Mean to Work Hard?" *Scott H Young*, November 16, 2015, https://www.scotthyoung.com/blog/2015/11/16/hard-work.

86. ChatGPT (GPT-4), Response to "What Did William James Say About Effort?" OpenAI, December 10, 2023.

87. Mihaly Csikszentmihalyi, *Flow: The Psychology of Optimal Experience* (New York: HarperCollins, 1990), Kindle.

88. Mike Oppland, "8 Traits of Flow According to Mihaly Csikszentmihalyi," *Positive Psychology*, May 16, 2022, https://positivepsychology.com/mihaly-csikszentmihalyi-father-of-flow/.

89. Chia, "15 Ways to Improve Your Focus and Concentration."

90. Chia, "15 Ways to Improve Your Focus and Concentration."

91. Chia, "15 Ways to Improve Your Focus and Concentration."

92. Stephen R. Covey, *Primary Greatness: The 12 Levers of Success* (New York: Simon & Schuster, 2015). Kindle.

93. Chia, "15 Ways to Improve Your Focus and Concentration."

94. David Erichsen, "Always Do Your Best & Watch Your Best Get Better," *Life Hack*, April 18, 2016, https://www.lifehack.org/379207/always-your-best-watch-your-best-get-better.

95. Erichsen, "Always Do Your Best & Watch Your Best Get Better."

96. "Unlocking Your Potential: Doing Your Best," *Farnam Street*, accessed November 27, 2023, https://fs.blog/doing-your-best.

97. William E. Wallace, *Michelangelo: The Artist, the Man and his Times* (Cambridge, England: Cambridge University Press, 2009).

98. ChatGPT (GPT-4), Response to "What's the Japanese concept that means success isn't required but doing your best is? Please explain the concept," OpenAI, December 15, 2024.

99. "Unlocking Your Potential: Doing Your Best," *Farnam Street*.

100. Erichsen, "Always Do Your Best & Watch Your Best Get Better."

101. Mihaly Csikszentmihalyi, *Creativity: Flow and the Psychology of Discovery and Invention* (New York: Harper Perennial, 1996), Kindle.

102. "10 Reasons Why Creativity Is Important," *Yonobi*, January 1, 2023, https://yonobi.com/blogs/news/being-creative-and-why-its-important-for-our-well-being.

103. Alec Nevala Lee, *Inventor of the Future: The Visionary Life of Buckminster Fuller* (New York: Dey Street Books, 2022).

104. Morin, "18 Habits of Mentally Strong People."

105. ChatGPT (GPT-4), Response to "What Did the Stoics Say About Perseverance?" OpenAI, February 16, 2024.

106. James Clear, *Atomic Habits: An Easy & Proven Way to Build Good Habits & Break Bad Ones* (New York: Avery Publishing, 2018), Kindle.

107. Bradberry, "10 Ways Ridiculously Successful People Think Differently."

108. Clear, *Atomic Habits*.

109. ChatGPT (GPT-4), Response to "What has basketball player Michael Jordan said about motivation from the fear of failure?" OpenAI, December 15, 2024.

110. ChatGPT (GPT-4), Response to "Tell me about other famous people who have used fear of failure as motivation," OpenAI, December 15, 2024.

111. Amy Morin, "13 Things Mentally Strong People Don't Do," *Amy Morin LCSW*, accessed November 17, 2023, https://amymorinlcsw.com/mentally-strong-people.

112. Bradberry, "10 Ways Ridiculously Successful People Think Differently."

113. "Abraham Lincoln," Wikipedia, last modified January 26, 2025, https://en.wikipedia.org /wiki/Abraham_Lincoln.

114. Malcolm Gladwell, *Outliers: The Story of Success* (New York, NY: Back Bay Books, 2011), Kindle.

115. K. Anders Ericsson and A. C. Lehmann, "Expert and Exceptional Performance: Evidence of Maximal Adaptation to Task Constraints," *Annual Review of Psychology* 47 (1996): 273--305, https://doi.org/10.1146/annurev.psych.47.1.273.

116. K. Anders Ericsson, "Deliberate Practice and Acquisition of Expert Performance: A General Overview," *Academic Emergency Medicine* 15, no. 11 (2008): 988-94, https://doi.org/10.1111/j.1553-2712.2008.00227.x.

117. Walter Isaacson, *Benjamin Franklin: An American Life* (New York: Simon & Schuster, 2003).

118. Mara S. Bloom, et al., "Motor Learning and Physical Exercise in Adaptive Myelination and Remyelination," *ASN Neuro* 14 (2022), https://doi.org/10.1177/17590914221097510.

119. Geoff Colvin, *Talent Is Overrated: What Really Separates World-Class Performers from Everybody Else* (New York: Portfolio Hardcover, 2008), Kindle.

120. Carol Dweck, *Mindset: The New Psychology of Success* (New York: Ballantine Books, 2007).

121. Dweck, *Mindset*.

122. Kelsey McDaniel, "Doing Your Best: What Does It Really Mean?" *Wooditch Enterprises*, March 8, 2017, https://billwooditch.com/best-really-mean.

123. Dweck, *Mindset*.

124. Mahatma K. Gandhi, *Autobiography: The Story of My Experiments with Truth* (New York: Dover Publications, 1948).

125. Mike Massimino, *Spaceman: An Astronaut's Unlikely Journey to Unlock the Secrets of the Universe* (New York: Three Rivers Press, 2016).

126. Massimino, *Spaceman*.

127. Steve Hogarty, "Nine Characteristics of Great Teamwork," *WeWork*, August 5, 2022, https://www.wework.com/ideas/professional-development/management-leadership/nine-characteristics-of-great-teamwork.

128. Foundation for a Better Life, "Jacqueline Nyetipei Kiplimo Demonstrates What Really Matters In Life and In Sports," *Denver Gazette*, May 23, 2023, https://gazette.com/life/jacqueline-nyetipei-kiplimo-demonstrates-what-really-matters-in-life-and-in-sports/article_71211a4e-e864-11ed-9997-2bff5f55ddf5.html.

129. Foundation for a Better Life, "Jacqueline Nyetipei Kiplimo."

130. Foundation for a Better Life, "Jacqueline Nyetipei Kiplimo."

131. Foundation for a Better Life, "Jacqueline Nyetipei Kiplimo."

132. Foundation for a Better Life, "Jacqueline Nyetipei Kiplimo."

133. Foundation for a Better Life, "Jacqueline Nyetipei Kiplimo."

134. Klein, "Inside Theodore Roosevelt's Gilded Age Upbringing."

135. "Helen Keller," Wikipedia.

136. Winston S. Churchill, *My Early Life: 1874-1904* (New York: Simon & Schuster, 1930).

137. Martin Gilbert, *Churchill: A Life* (New York: Henry Holt and Company, 1991).

138. "Famous Quotes by Thomas Edison," Thomas Alva Edison Foundations, accessed February 24, 2024, https://www.thomasedison.org/edison-quotes.

139. Hogarty, "Nine Characteristics of Great Teamwork."

140. James Lovell and Jeffrey Kluger, *Lost Moon: The Perilous Voyage of Apollo 13* (Boston: Houghton Mifflin, 1994).

141. Steven Watts, *The People's Tycoon: Henry Ford and the American Century* (New York: Alfred A. Knopf, 2005).

142. Paul Israel, *Edison: A Life of Invention* (New York: John Wiley & Sons, 1998).

143. "Leymah Gbowee," Wikipedia, last modified February 13, 2024, https://en.wiki pedia.org /wiki/Leymah_Gbowee.

144. "Leymah Gbowee," Wikipedia.

145. "Leymah Gbowee," Wikipedia.

146. "Leymah Gbowee," Wikipedia.

147. "The Nobel Peace Prize 2011 Press Release," *Nobel Prize*, October 7, 2011, https:// www.nobelprize.org/prizes/peace/2011/press-release.

148. ChatGPT (GPT-4), Response to "Give details on how Leymah Gbowee demon-strated love, gratitude, integrity, and accountability," OpenAI, March 8, 2024.

149. Matt Tenney, "The 7 Leadership Traits," *Business Leadership Today*, accessed on March 4, 2024, https://businessleadershiptoday.com/what-are-the-7-leadership-traits/.

150. Andy Frisella, "7 Qualities All Effective Leaders Have," *Andy Frisella*, May 6, 2022, https://andyfrisella.com/blogs/articles/7-qualities-all-effective-leaders-have.

151. "Leymah Gbowee," Wikipedia.

152. Frisella, "7 Qualities All Effective Leaders Have."

153. "15 Great Leadership Qualities and Characteristics," *Vistage*, July 25, 2023, https://www.vistage.com/research-center/personal-development/leadership-competencies/20230725-what-makes-a-great-leader/.

154. "Leymah Gbowee," Wikipedia.

155. Frisella, "7 Qualities All Effective Leaders Have."

156. Tenney, "The 7 Leadership Traits."

157. "Leymah Gbowee," Wikipedia.

158. Frisella, "7 Qualities All Effective Leaders Have."

159. Tenney, "The 7 Leadership Traits."

160. "Leymah Gbowee," Wikipedia.

161. ChatGPT (GPT-4), Response to "Give details on how Leymah Gbowee demonstrated purpose, attitude, preparation, effort, focus, excellence, individuality, perseverance, practice, and growth," OpenAI, March 8, 2024.

162. ChatGPT (GPT-4), "Give details on how Leymah Gbowee demonstrated purpose...."

INDEX

www.ingramcontent.com/pod-product-compliance
Lightning Source LLC
Chambersburg PA
CBHW061549120626
46550CB00004B/1422